ATLANTIC CANADA

Pictorial Research by E. Boyde Beck, Paul Kenney, Peter Larocque, and L.J. Payzant

"Partners in Progress" by Dorothy Dearborn, Marjorie Doyle, Brent King, and Bob Wall

*Produced in co-operation with
the Atlantic Provinces Chamber of Commerce*

*Windsor Publications, Ltd.
Burlington, Ontario*

ATLANTIC CANADA

AT THE DAWN OF A NEW NATION

An Illustrated History by E. Boyde Beck, Greg Marquis,
Joan M. Payzant, and Shannon Ryan

Windsor Publications, Ltd.—History Books Division
Managing Editor: Karen Story
Design Director: Alexander D'Anca
Photo Director: Susan L. Wells
Executive Editor: Pamela Schroeder

Staff for *Atlantic Canada: At the Dawn of A New Nation*
Senior Manuscript Editor: Jerry Mosher
Photo Editor: Robin Sterling
Senior Editor, Corporate Biographies: Judith L. Hunter
Production Editor, Corporate Biographies: Doreen Nakakihara
Co-ordinator, Corporate Biographies: Gladys McKnight
Editorial Assistants: Phyllis Feldman-Schroeder, Kim Kievman, Kathy B. Peyser,
Susan Schlanger, Theresa J. Solis
Publisher's Representatives, Corporate Biographies: Richard Bean, Lois Noonan,
Bill Pickard, Eric Sinclair
Layout Artist, Corporate Biographies: C.L. Murray
Production Assistant: Deena Tucker
Designer: Ellen Ifrah

Windsor Publications, Ltd.
Elliot Martin, Chairman of the Board
James L. Fish III, Chief Operating Officer
Michele Sylvestro, Vice President/Sales-Marketing
Mac Buhler, Vice President/Acquisitions

ISBN: 0-89781-328-6

The beautiful Bras d'Or Lakes of Cape Breton, where Alexander Graham Bell had his summer home, "Beinn Breagh," have long been noted for pleasure boating. In this 1873 artist's sketch a side-paddle steamer passes the mouth of Long Island Passage. A schooner and a small dinghy exemplify the more traditional vessels of that time. Courtesy, National Library of Canada

FRONTISPIECE: The Halifax Harbour lighthouse shines its solitary light, guiding the way for all seafaring vessels. Photo by Ron Watts/First Light

CONTENTS

CHAPTER ONE

NEWFOUNDLAND

FISHERY TO CANADIAN PROVINCE

By Shannon Ryan

The province of Newfoundland (sometimes referred to as the province of Newfoundland and Labrador) consists of the island of Newfoundland and part of the North American mainland—Labrador. The island has a total area of just over 111,000 square kilometers (43,000 square miles) while Labrador has an area of over 294,000 square kilometers (113,000 square miles) for a total land mass of about 405,000 square kilometers (156,000 square miles).

There are two major land regions: Labrador is part of the Canadian Shield and is cut by valleys containing rivers that flow into the Atlantic Ocean, and the island is part of the Appalachian Region. The entire coastline is dented by fjords, bays, and harbours, and dotted by thousands of small islands. The climate varies from the sub-arctic continental climate of central Labrador to the maritime climate of the coastal areas of both Labrador and the island. However, the arctic current keeps the island and the coastal areas of Labrador much cooler than comparable latitudes in the eastern North Atlantic or the Pacific Coast of North America, and these same arctic currents help create the fogs that hover over the province's coasts and coastal waters.

FIRST INHABITANTS

People identified as belonging to the Maritime Archaic culture populated parts of Labrador as early as 7000 B.C. and gradually spread southward to the island. Their presence on the island seems to have lasted from about 3000 B.C. to 1200 B.C. and one of their burial sites has been discovered at Port au Choix on the west coast. From about 600 B.C. to 100 B.C. the island was occupied by Paleo-Eskimo people sometimes known as the Groswater people, who were succeeded by another Paleo-Eskimo people—the Dorset Eskimos (A.D. 100 to A.D. 500). From that time to the beginning of European expansion in North America most of the island was home to a branch of the Algonquian language family—the Beothuks—while the coast of Labrador was occupied by Inuit (originally called Eskimos by the Europeans). At the same time, Labrador's interior and parts of its southern coast were populated by other branches of the Algonquian family known, by the Europeans, as Naskapi and Montagnais, but now known as Innu.

This drawing of early St. John's, Newfoundland, was rendered by William Eager in 1831. As viewed from Signal Hill overlooking the harbour entrance known as the "Narrows," the developing city is seen here during the time of majestic sailing ships and burgeoning society. Note the battery in the foreground which was manned to secure the harbour. Courtesy, Provincial Archives of Newfoundland and Labrador

Pictorial Research by Paul Kenney

ABOVE: Shanawdithit was the last woman of the native Beothuk Indian tribe of Newfoundland. She died from tuberculosis in St. John's in 1829. Courtesy, Provincial Archives of Newfoundland and Labrador

RIGHT: The ancient Viking site of L'Anse aux Meadows is located on the northern tip of Newfoundland. Courtesy, Parks Canada

EARLIEST EUROPEAN CONTACTS

Although a semi-legendary Irish monk, St. Brendan, and a group of his companions are reputed to have reached North America—travelling in a curragh (a boat made from hides stretched over a wooden frame)—in the eighth century A.D., the first documented contact between Europeans and Newfoundland occurred around the year A.D. 1000. Beginning in the seventh century many Norsemen (Vikings) left their homelands in Scandinavia and for the next several hundred years played a major role in the history of Europe: They explored and traded south into Russia; established major settlements in Western Europe; entered the Mediterranean Sea to trade and explored as far east as the Black Sea; colonized Iceland and then Greenland; and toward the close of this era reached Newfoundland.

According to the evidence available, the Norsemen, while sailing and rowing their longships between their main centre in Iceland and their satellite settle-

ments in Greenland, discovered the coast of Labrador and the island of Newfoundland (and probably much more of eastern North America). They found the area particularly attractive for its timber and berries, both of which were unavailable in Greenland. They named the northern part of their discovery Markland and the southern part Vinland, and many historians today conclude that these are present-day Labrador and the island of Newfoundland, respectively.

While the extent of the Viking discoveries in North America cannot be determined with any certainty, at present a Viking site, dating from about A.D. 1000, has been excavated at L'Anse aux Meadows on the northern tip of the island of Newfoundland. This site was occupied as the Viking expansion was beginning to wane. Within a few years of their peak expansion their kings had become powerful enough to impose travel and trade restrictions on the Vikings at home. At the same time climatic changes—and possibly intermarriage with the local Eskimo population—turned the Greenland settlers from agriculturalists and traders into food gatherers. Records and memories of Markland and Vinland were retained only in the sagas.

THE AGE OF DISCOVERY

In the fifteenth century, when other western Europeans also interested in trade and plunder embarked on a period of overseas expansion that dwarfed even that of the Vikings, the second discovery of the New World began.

In the early fifteenth century Portugal began to send explorers and traders southward along the coast of Africa in search of, among other things, a sea route to the Far East. In 1487 they sailed around the Cape of Good Hope and into the Indian Ocean and opened up direct trade between Asia and Europe. Spain, not to be left behind, gambled that the Far East could be reached by sailing westward and in 1492 sent Christopher Columbus on a voyage of exploration. He reached the Caribbean and within a few years the Spanish discovered that they had stumbled on an area of tremendous wealth. England, unable to challenge the Portuguese on their routes and in their conquests, but wanting, nevertheless, to find wealth on the new continent or a northern route to Asia, sent John Cabot westward in 1497.

Newfoundland was first discovered by the Europeans as early as A.D. 1000, and many explorers followed, including the French explorer Jacques Cartier, who sailed the St. Lawrence River in 1534 in search of a route to Asia. From Cirker, Dictionary of American Portraits, *Dover, 1967*

Cabot (a Venetian navigator and captain) left Bristol on May 2 with a crew of 16 (maybe 18) on board a small vessel of 50 tons named the *Matthew*. The location of Cabot's actual landfall is uncertain, but the most convincing evidence indicates that on June 24 he landed in the vicinity of present-day Bonavista in Newfoundland. Upon his return to Bristol, apparently, Cabot was greeted with considerable joy by the local population because he brought reports that the sea around the "new-found-land" was filled with fish "which are taken not only with the net but with a basket . . . " In December Henry VII granted a pension of £20 (sterling) to Cabot; on February 3, 1498, he issued a warrant authorizing a second voyage. However, information about this second voyage and, indeed, any subsequent information about Cabot is scarce and adds nothing to our knowledge of his initial discovery.

Although some historians, including D.W. Prowse, maintain that Bristol fishermen were visiting Newfoundland before Cabot's first voyage, hard evidence is lacking, and most use 1497 to date the rediscovery of Newfoundland by Europeans. Meanwhile, the Portuguese quickly followed the English to this area and in 1501 explored the region—at least one early map referred to the island of Newfoundland as "Terra Nova de Cortereal." In 1534 Jacques Cartier, sailing from France, explored the St. Lawrence River for a considerable distance into present-day Canada and began the first of several attempts to find a route through the continent to Asia. However, it was because of its rich fishing grounds that Newfoundland became known, and it was to this island part of the New World that the English applied the name "Newfoundland"; this became "Terre Neuve" to the French, and "Terra Nova" to the Portuguese.

THE ENGLISH COD FISHERY

Meanwhile English fishermen from the "West Country," but particularly from Bristol, developed a limited cod fishery in Icelandic waters. Although England did import some stockfish, kippered herring, and pickled herring, the country

Caplin was and is the major source of bait for cod fishing. Photo by Stephen Homer/First Light

had rich coastal fisheries and its own small Icelandic fishery and therefore it was nearly self-sufficient in fish. It was continental Europe that provided most of the national and international markets for preserved fish. Therefore, while the news that there were vast quantities of cod fish in Newfoundland waters was received in Bristol with a certain amount of rejoicing, it seemed at the time that there was very little scope in this trade for English fishermen.

AN EARLY INTERNATIONAL FISHERY

If the English were not in a position to take full advantage of the stocks of cod fish in Newfoundland waters, fishermen from other nations were. By 1500 the Portuguese had a cod fishery organized and by 1520 were reported to have 100 ships in Newfoundland waters. Similarly, about 100 French fishing ships from Brittany and Normandy were crossing the Atlantic annually by 1517. Spanish fishing interests did not begin to prosecute this industry until 1540, but from that point on its fleet expanded and in 1553 about 200 Spanish ships carrying about 6,000 men were engaged in the cod and whale fisheries in Newfoundland. The English-Newfoundland fishery developed much more slowly and by 1570 only 30 English ships were engaged in this enterprise.

In Newfoundland these early fishermen learned to prosecute two distinct cod fisheries. On what quickly became known as the Grand Banks of Newfoundland, which was shallow water extending over 300 kilometers (200 miles) offshore, they could catch cod at any time; although, because of the autumn winds, rather harsh winters, and spring ice floes, it was usually a summer activity. In addition to this "bank fishery" the fishermen discovered that in Newfoundland some cod migrated into coastal waters. Therefore, every spring these fishermen anchored their vessels in the harbours, built temporary covered wharves ("stages"), drying platforms ("flakes"), wooden vats to hold the cod livers for the production of oil, and living and cooking accommodations, and lived ashore for the whole season. They caught fish from small boats during the daylight hours and split and salted it at night in their stages.

A few French ships fished inshore but most fished on the banks. Spain and Portugal supported both inshore and bank fisheries. In addition to their cod fishery the Spanish developed an extensive whale fishery and built, for this purpose, major processing facilities at Red Bay on the southern coast of Labrador. The smaller English fleet engaged exclusively in the inshore cod fishery.

The shore fishery in Newfoundland very quickly became an international industry and developed its own rules. The ships from Europe would arrive in the various harbours on the island's east coast, especially around the Avalon Peninsula, in the spring. The first captain to enter a harbour would choose the best site to build his "fishing room" (landing stages, sheds, and drying flakes). Furthermore, he was looked upon by later arrivals as the unofficial "admiral" of that harbour for the season and was called upon to settle disputes. Each ship would carry a fishing crew, fishing boats, and supplies, and would build its fishing room for the season's use. Around the end of August the ships would load their catches and return to their individual ports in Europe. This international fishery proceeded informally without direction or even much attention from the European governments until the middle of the sixteenth century.

THE WEST OF ENGLAND COD FISHERY

By the mid-1500s, however, relations between some of the governments involved were changing, as were certain perceptions about the fishery. The English fishermen from the West Country—particularly from the counties of Devon and Dorset—were gradually accumulating expertise as sailors and navigators; it was becoming increasingly clear to their government that other advantages might lie in this direction. A larger fishery would result in a stronger navy, but a larger fishery could only be possible if foreign markets for saltfish could be found. The obvious markets were those of France, Spain, and Portugal; if markets in the latter two could be opened up to English-Newfoundland saltfish, then England would share, indirectly, in the wealth that these nations were obtaining from their overseas empires. However, in spite of one far-sighted if unrealistic suggestion that England attack the fisheries of the others, nothing changed until 1562.

In that year civil war broke out in France and that nation's fishery was interrupted. France began to import saltfish from England and this gave the latter's industry a much-needed boost. Meanwhile England was becoming more self-confident at sea and was boldly siding with those Dutch provinces in the Spanish Netherlands that had begun their war of independence from Spain in 1568. As relations between England and Spain continued to deteriorate, Portugal came under the Spanish crown. Now the Portuguese also became enemies of the Dutch.

In 1585 hostilities broke out into the open. In that year Bernard Drake led a small English fleet to Newfoundland, ostensibly to warn English ships that it was unsafe for them to sail to Spain with any fish because conditions with that nation had deteriorated. However, he had been given a secret commission by Queen Elizabeth ordering him to destroy the Portuguese and Spanish fishing fleets. He carried out his instructions successfully and crippled these fisheries. During the following two years all Portuguese and Spanish ships, including fishing and whaling ships, were ordered by King Philip to remain in port while preparations were made for the invasion of England. The Spanish Armada's failure to conquer England in 1588, and indeed the loss of so many of Spain's finest ships and men, ended the cod fisheries of both Spain and Portugal in Newfoundland waters.

The English fishery prospered as events unfolded. The demand for saltfish in both Spain and Portugal was such that supplies were welcomed from almost anywhere. From the 1580s on England's product was reaching these markets via France, and even Dutch ships sailing under other flags entered this carrying trade while they were still at war with Spain. In 1595, despite urgent demands for manpower in the war with Spain, as many as 100 English ships engaged in the Newfoundland fishery. As the war wound down this figure rose to about 200 ships by 1600,

Sir Humphrey Gilbert (1537-1583) sailed to St. John's and claimed Newfoundland as a British possession in 1583. He was lost at sea that same year and his plans for colonization collapsed. Courtesy, Provincial Archives of Newfoundland and Labrador

and to a peak of about 300 ships by 1620. The English fishery was now secure, and instead of an international fishery shared by four nations the Newfoundland fishery was now dominated exclusively by England and France.

ENGLISH COLONIZATION

Meanwhile, certain interest groups in England had concluded that it was time for the English to follow the example of the Portuguese and Spanish and establish colonies in the New World. In 1583 Sir Humphrey Gilbert sailed his small fleet into St. John's harbour and claimed Newfoundland as part of the grant awarded to him by Queen Elizabeth. However, he was lost at sea and his colonization project collapsed. Then, having observed the Devon and Dorset merchants prospering from the burgeoning Newfoundland fishery, a number of merchants in Bristol and London invested in a new company for the purpose of establishing a

colony on the island. In 1610 they sent John Guy to Newfoundland with settlers and supplies and instructions to found a colony, which he did at the small harbour of Cupids, Conception Bay. This colonization attempt was strictly a business venture; it was followed by other attempts, some for business purposes, others for personal reasons: "Bristol's Hope" in Harbour Grace; Sir William Vaughan's, and later Lord Falkland's, philanthropic efforts in Renews; Sir George Calvert's (Lord Baltimore) family refuge in Ferryland; and finally Sir David Kirke's business investment, in 1637, also in Ferryland.

The colonists were almost completely dependent on the shore fishery, and because the summers were too short to grow grain, they were forced to rely on imports of most of their supplies—in contrast to other English colonies (indeed European colonies) on the mainland. They adapted to the seamen's diet of salt pork, peas, ship's biscuit (hardbread), and flour, all of which was brought out from England, and later Ireland. The difficulty in trying to support permanent settlement in Newfoundland with such a short fishing season, the lack of any worthwhile winter employment, and the necessity to import most supplies of food as well as nearly all equipment, resulted in the resident population remaining very small—only 1,500 people in 1650.

The migratory fishery experienced problems after 1625. Wars with France and Spain, a decline in attention to the English navy, an increase in piracy, civil war, and the Anglo-Dutch wars all combined to reduce the fishing fleet. By 1640 ship owner/operators who had gone bankrupt became small boat operators (bye boat keepers). These individual bye boat keepers invested in a fishing boat (or two), hired four or five (or eight or ten) men, and came to Newfoundland annually as passengers on board those fishing ships still operating. However, wars continued to play havoc with the migratory fishery (both the bye boat and ship fisheries), because not only were fishermen in danger of being captured by enemy ships, but they also ran the risk of being pressed into service in the English navy—where they were valued as among the best experienced sailors available.

THE ENGLISH AND FRENCH AT WAR

England and France went to war in 1689, and by the time peace was restored in 1697 nearly all English-Newfoundland dwellings and other buildings on the island had been destroyed by French soldiers and their Indian allies from New France. During the War of the Spanish Succession which followed in 1702-1713 these devastating attacks were repeated, so that between Trepassey and Bonavista (the extent of traditional English-Newfoundland) not an original building remained. The English navy, on the other hand, destroyed French fishing premises on the island's south coast during summer campaigns, but did not attack the French colony of Placentia from which the winter raids were launched. Nevertheless, France had not been so successful in Europe, and therefore in the Treaty of Utrecht, signed by these two antagonists, France surrendered its small colony of Placentia (established in 1662) and gave up all ownership rights to the island. However, as part of this treaty France was granted the right to carry on a seasonal shore fishery on that part of Newfoundland's coast from Bonavista northward to Point Riche on the west coast (the "French Shore").

THE SPREAD OF SETTLEMENT

If settlement had not been growing it had been spreading. In 1677 there were 28 harbours permanently occupied and containing 162 home owners ("planters") and 167 dwelling houses. There were 94 wives, 137 sons, 130 daughters, 1,327 men servants, and 13 women servants for a total population of 1,863 residents. The men servants would normally move on to New England at the end of their contract with the planters, and it is very likely that women servants married single planters. In any event, the true permanent population of Newfoundland consisted of planters and their families. Twenty years later, in 1697, Newfoundland's population occupied 38 harbours, but the total number of men (planters and men servants) was still only 1,581.

This settlement expansion into all the harbours along the coast was closely related to developments in the migratory fishery, rather than to the extension of the colonization efforts, which had originally concerned only four harbours. The

OPPOSITE: The annual caplin spawn along Newfoundland beaches brought an abundance of cod into the coastal waters. Besides serving as a lure for the profitable cod, caplin was also gathered for its own value in the marketplace. Courtesy, B.J. Kenny's Photos

migratory fishery had been very environmentally destructive. Each spring trees were cut for building purposes and other trees were "rinded" to acquire sheets of rind (bark) for roof coverings and for coverings for fish piles. In the autumn the stages, flakes, and shacks were torn apart as fishermen took the best of this dry timber back to their home ports. Each harbour became a tinder box of old wooden structures, dead brush, and forests of rinded dead trees. In 1583, when Sir Humphrey Gilbert was in St. John's, the forests of mature trees were too thick for his crew members to walk ashore with any degree of satisfaction. By 1611 John Guy, the governor of Cupids, had discovered that old fishing structures were being intentionally destroyed and that the forests were being set on fire. He also noted that the harbours and beaches were being gradually littered and clogged with numerous stones carried as ballast on board the ships arriving for cargoes of fish. Guy was moved to publish a set of laws prohibiting such destructive practices, and a list of heavy fines to be imposed on those who broke these laws.

Therefore, building new structures every spring became increasingly expensive because crews were forced to go farther and farther inland to acquire the necessary timber and rinds. In order to save their fishing premises from being destroyed, or taken by early arrivals the following year, fishing ship captains began to hire caretakers in the autumn. This created a thin line of English settlements which by 1719 stretched from Placentia Bay in the south to Bonavista in the north, and which numbered as follows: 264 planters, 172 wives, 466 children, 1,346 men servants, and 81 women servants, for a total of 2,329 people. The slow growth of population in Newfoundland is better appreciated when compared to that of other English colonies on the Atlantic Coast: In 1700 Massachusetts alone had a population of 80,000; Virginia had a population of 55,000; and the total English population between New Hampshire and South Carolina amounted to almost 300,000 people.

Although permanent settlement in Newfoundland was insignificant in comparison with English settlement in the rest of North America, it had become a thorny problem for the home government. Until the 1650s, when the government began to formulate trade and plantation policies for its North American possessions, colonization was permitted in Newfoundland. After the middle of the century, however, the government tried to discourage it because of fears, largely unfounded, that a resident fishery might supplant the migratory one and thus eliminate this industry as a recruitment pool for the navy. At first the fishing ship captains were also opposed to colonization attempts and the threat of settlement, but by the time the government was beginning to oppose the establishment of a resident population the migratory fishery was becoming dependent on the Newfoundland planters. The government tried to develop policies to resolve this increasingly complex situation.

THE WESTERN CHARTER

John Guy's laws were the first ever published in Newfoundland and these were incorporated into the Western Charter, which the government issued in 1633-1634. One of the major clauses in the charter appointed the captain of the first ship to arrive in each harbour as the admiral of that harbour, thereby making official what had become the custom. The second captain became the vice-admiral, and the third became the rear-admiral. The admiral, assisted by the two others, became the official law enforcement officer charged with upholding the clauses of the charter (which included bringing back to England those charged with capital offenses) and settling disputes.

In the 1660s the charter was revised in an effort to keep the bye boat keepers out of the fishery because they travelled as passengers and therefore received no training as sailors capable of manning navy ships. The attempt was unsuccessful because it was difficult to distinguish between bye boat keepers and planters spending part of the year in England, and in addition some ship owners were making money from passengers. So the government revised the charter once more to close all loopholes and prevent any people who were not members of the fishing ship crews from travelling to Newfoundland—this also failed to have the desired effect and soon the prohibitory clauses were repealed.

FORTIFICATION AND LEGISLATION

Since the 1650s a naval convoy had been sent annually to the Newfoundland fishery for the protection of the fishing fleet, and the commander of this fleet was fast becoming the government's chief representative and most trusted source of information. Having seen the complete destruction of all fishing property in Newfoundland and having received numerous complaints from the West Country, New England, and other colonies about a lack of proper protection, the English government was finally forced to act. In 1697 a military garrison was established in St. John's and fortifications were built around the harbour. Two years later Parliament passed an act which incorporated many of the clauses of Guy's laws and those of the charters, as well as new ones.

The new clauses were in two important areas. First, settlement was permitted—resident planters could build fishing rooms on the shore in places not used by fishing ships since 1685, and any fishing rooms occupied by planters since before 1685 could be legally retained. Second, a party dissatisfied with the decision of a fishing admiral could now appeal his decision to the convoy commander.

The government realized that its concerns about settlement growth could not be resolved because settlement could not be controlled without a governmental presence in Newfoundland—and a governmental presence would only introduce a further infrastructure and make settlement more attractive to some fishermen. The Act of 1699 illustrates the problem. Instead of confining and limiting settlement, and protecting and encouraging the expansion of the ship fishery, it had the opposite effect, which was soon discovered when the French withdrew from Placentia in 1713. Upon the French withdrawal the government found out that, because the ship fishery had not used Placentia since 1685, planters could not be prevented from occupying the newly vacated fishing rooms. A similar development occurred in the 1720s when some planters moved north beyond Cape Bonavista to fish for salmon and hunt seals and created a resident fishery.

By the beginning of the eighteenth century, English fishermen had been visiting Newfoundland for over 200 years. In spite of this, only 200-plus householders temporarily employing 1,000-plus single men during any given winter lived permanently on the island.

TRIANGULAR TRADE

In late autumn, when the hurricane season was over, ships arrived from Boston to trade supplies in exchange for fish of poorer quality, not acceptable in the European markets, which was destined for the West Indies. New England ships were becoming an integral part of the English-Newfoundland saltfish trade. The ships brought livestock, vegetables, apples, tobacco, rum, molasses, and sugar. These products were exchanged for the West India fish, which would then be carried to the Caribbean and exchanged for molasses and sugar. It was becoming a very important trade. The ships also welcomed aboard fishermen who could pay their passage to New England, and sometimes hired an additional seaman or two.

The British government was well aware of the continuous drain of manpower to America via Newfoundland but was helpless to act. In order to control the situation customs officials would need to be stationed in many of the harbours; this kind of governmental presence was the very thing the government was trying to avoid because it would only encourage population growth. Thus Newfoundland continued to be the conduit to Boston for English (and by now, Irish) fishermen.

DEPRESSION AND DIVERSIFICATION

The end of the war in 1713 also marked the beginning of a depression that would affect the planter and migratory fisheries. Production of saltfish, which had briefly exceeded 300,000 quintals (one quintal equals approximately 50.8 kilograms or 112 pounds) in 1699 and 1700, had declined drastically during the war and did not immediately recover. However, production gradually improved from a low point of 80,000 quintals in 1720 to 300,000 quintals annually in the 1730s.

As a reaction to the depression, migratory fishermen developed a bank fishery. Fishing ships carrying 10 to 15 men would come to Newfoundland in early summer, procure bait, and proceed to the fishing banks offshore. When they had spent several weeks fishing they returned to a Newfoundland port and placed the fish in the care of a planter for curing. Throughout the eighteenth century this new fishery was another component of the total fishery. It operated in conjunction with the traditional ship fishery, the century-old planter fishery, and the slightly more recent bye boat fishery.

Planters reacted somewhat differently to the depression, trying to diversify and thus make themselves a little less dependent on the saltfish industry. It was a minor adjustment that could only be carried out in certain ways in certain places. In the areas around St. John's and Conception Bay subsistence farming increased. Some planters moved to the south coast where some salmon fishing could be carried on; others moved to the north, beyond Cape Bonavista, where they could engage in both salmon fishing and sealing.

These latter planters came into contact with the native Beothuks, who were dependent on the coast in this area for part of their livelihood. This livelihood was threatened when planters began netting salmon at the mouths of the rivers. The Beothuks retaliated by carrying out sporadic attacks on the planters; in addition, they tried to procure the European goods they needed by stealing. Conflicts between the two were to continue throughout the century.

MORE QUINTALS OF FISH, MORE MEN

The Newfoundland fishery increased steadily after 1730, and in 1749 production reached 500,000 quintals. At the same time planters were increasing their share of the catch and in that same year their production amounted to about 293,000 quintals, compared with 111,000 quintals by the fishing ships (including bankers), and 95,000 quintals by the bye boat keepers. This growth in the planter fishery resulted largely from the increase in settlement. In 1749, for example, there were 690 masters, 540 mistresses, 920 children, 3,727 men servants, and 202 women servants who spent the winter in Newfoundland.

One reason for the increase in the number of planters during this period was the increased security available to those who stayed in Newfoundland. In 1729, after many complaints from planters, fishing ships, and convoy commanders about the destruction of property, drunkenness, and general lawlessness in the winter months, the convoy commander's position was upgraded to that of naval governor. In addition, he was given the authority to appoint constables and magistrates and to build jails. The magistrates were supposed to deal with criminal cases in the wintertime and leave all winter civil cases, as well as all civil and criminal cases arising during the fishing season, for the admirals. In practice, however, the magistrates, supported by the naval governors, began to hear all cases brought before them winter and summer. In addition, the governor had the authority to hear cases and to appoint his lieutenants as surrogate justices capable of deciding cases brought to their attention while patrolling the harbours during the fishing season. In 1750 magistrates in St. John's were given the additional authority to preside over cases involving capital offenses and to sentence those convicted. Thus life and property in Newfoundland became somewhat more secure after 1729.

THE SEVEN YEARS' WAR

The Seven Years' War broke out in 1756; it was not only a turning point in North American history but brought changes to Newfoundland as well. Bye boat keepers avoided the annual hazardous trans-Atlantic voyage by settling on their fishing rooms, and men servants followed suit. Thus the resident population grew, assisted by the introduction in 1750 of the potato, which provided an important staple and eradicated scurvy. In 1764 it was reported that, during the previous winter, the following numbers resided in Newfoundland: 1,250 masters; 753 mistresses; 4,226 children; 8,976 men servants; and 776 women servants, for a grand total of 15,981. The number of children is significant when compared with 1749 because it shows that in the 15-year period not only had the number of families grown, but the average size of each family grew as well. This burst of growth did not sustain itself and during the postwar depression population declined again; but even at its lowest, in 1769, permanent population never again fell below 11,000. The resident population remained fairly constant, increasing sharply during the American Revolution, and totalled about 18,000 in the 1790s. The residents' year of peak production occurred in 1788, when they alone produced over 450,000 quintals of saltfish.

Meanwhile, the Seven Years' War had caused the migratory fishery to fall off and the resident fishery to increase—both temporarily—and in 1762 the French occupied St. John's for several months until expelled by the British. The war had two long-term effects. First, the French lost all their mainland North American possessions but received in return the islands of St. Pierre and Miquelon off the south coast of Newfoundland as a shelter for their bank fishing fleet. These islands developed their own resident fishery and an extensive trade, usually illicit, with Newfoundland's south coast inhabitants. In addition, the coast of Labrador was placed under the jurisdiction of Newfoundland's naval governor—whose

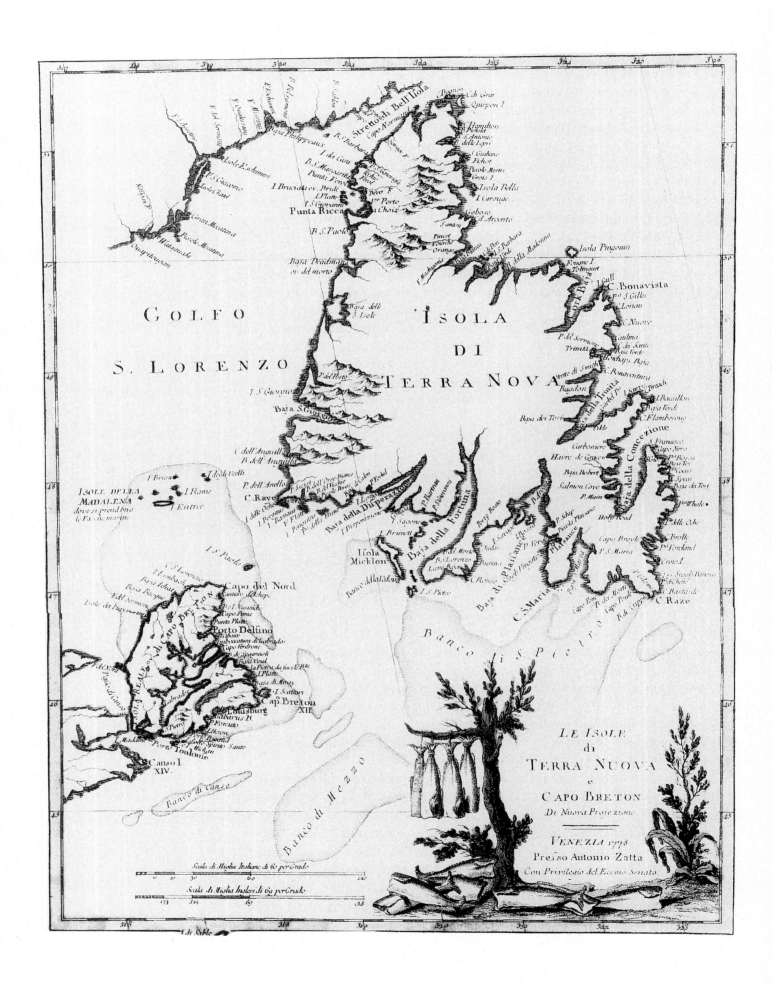

duties included the establishment there of a British migratory fishery. The governor also acted to protect the Inuit on the northern part of this coast from unscrupulous traders; this included encouraging the development of Moravian mission stations in the area. Second, the new trade links between Britain and Quebec (instead of France and Quebec) significantly increased British shipping in the area. Many of the ships going to and from Quebec stopped in Newfoundland with partial cargoes of supplies, or to take on partial cargoes of saltfish and cod oil. These developments added to the island's stability and attractiveness.

THE AMERICAN REVOLUTION

The American Revolution was a significant milestone in Newfoundland's history. It coincided with the passage of a major piece of parliamentary legislation in 1775—commonly referred to as Palliser's Act—as Britain made one last attempt to discourage and restrict settlement of the island. While some of the clauses, including one requiring that servants be paid in full only after their return to England, and one giving servants of bankrupt employers first claim to their former employers' fish and oil, had ramifications for settlement, all developments were overshadowed by the war.

The break in relations between Britain and its colonies resulted in a trade embargo imposed upon the Newfoundland fishery by the 13 Colonies. The fisheries had become dependent on flour, livestock, vegetables, molasses, rum, and other supplies from the colonies, and when trade ceased, shortages and even starvation were the result. In addition, some coastal settlements on the island and Labrador were raided by American privateers. However, the British navy soon regained the upper hand at sea and, as the trade adjusted, flour was obtained from other sources, especially Quebec.

The major long-term effect of the war was the development of direct trade between Newfoundland and the British Caribbean. A local Newfoundland mercantile community grew up around this trade—especially in what was becoming the major commercial and administrative centre, St. John's. Unlike all previous British-Newfoundland trade involving the fishery, the ships which became involved in the Caribbean trade did not cross the Atlantic. In fact, for a ship owner to engage in this trade and continue to live in Britain was a distinct disadvantage.

Ship owners in St. John's began to send cargoes of inferior fish to the British Caribbean and to import on the return voyage molasses, sugar, and rum. In addition, since ships could no longer be purchased from the American colonies, a local ship building industry sprang up. Tradesmen were brought out from England, Scotland, and Ireland, and carpenters, masons, coopers, and other tradesmen were also in demand. A final result of the war was the change, agreed upon by both countries, in the boundary of the French Shore. The Bonavista boundary was moved north to Cape St. John, giving Newfoundland residents more coast to the north, while the Point Riche boundary was moved south to Cape Ray as compensation to the French.

The war did not shift the fishery from the migratory men to the residents. In fact, the bank fishery expanded in the 1780s to a level never before reached, although this expansion did not last. The market glut created by the enormous production of 1788—949,000 quintals—caused bankruptcies, and the end of the bye boat fishery meant the loss, to the fishing ships, of a regular group of paying passengers.

OPPOSITE: Produced by Antonio Zatta of Venice in 1778, this early map of Newfoundland illustrates the degree of exploration and settlement around the time of the American Revolution. Courtesy, Provincial Archives of Newfoundland and Labrador

OPPOSITE: With its strategic location overlooking the city and the harbour, Signal Hill played a major defensive role in the early development of St. John's. Courtesy, B.J. Kenny's Photos

LEGAL REFORMS

By the late 1780s events forced Britain's hand again. A jumble of conflicting and competing judicial bodies had grown up in Newfoundland since 1633-1634. Because most local lawlessness and civil matters did not lend themselves to appeals to higher courts, and because lawsuits between merchants had always been settled in Britain, no one had questioned the legality of decisions reached by fishing admirals, magistrates, naval governors, and their surrogates. However, with the growth of a local mercantile community it was only a matter of time before a local decision would be appealed to a higher court. When this finally happened in the 1780s the higher court declared the Newfoundland court in question to lack legal authority. To resolve the matter, especially in light of the 1788 bankruptcies, Britain was forced in 1791-1792 to create on the island a proper civil and criminal legal system with a chief justice and other officials.

By the time the French Revolution broke out in 1793 Newfoundland had a substantial resident fishery and trade, as well as a still vigorous migratory fishery. Whether both could continue to co-exist was fast becoming questionable.

MOVING INTO THE NINETEENTH CENTURY

In 1793 Newfoundland had served for three centuries as the "Grand Cod Fishery of the Universe." However, the island itself was still viewed by the British government as a "fishing ship moored on the Grand Banks," and the government could not reconcile itself to its settlement.

The majority of Newfoundland residents still clung to the same eastern harbours that had been frequented since the sixteenth century. Roman Catholics from Ireland made up about half the population, and although many had become planters in harbours south of St. John's, others had found employment as labourers in the larger ports like Carbonear, Harbour Grace, and particularly St. John's. Emigration to the new United States had become much more difficult now that trade with that nation was by permit only. Restrictions on Roman Catholics—which had cost them large fines, their houses and property, and often expulsion from the island—had eased as penal laws in general were being relaxed. Roman Catholics, members of the Church of England, and the followers of John Wesley were all being served by their respective clergy. Nevertheless, there were few other indicators that Newfoundland was a colony—and the fact was not officially admitted.

THE BEOTHUKS

The Beothuk Indians had suffered enormously during the eighteenth century. They deserted the south and west coasts, probably because of pressure from the Micmac Indians, who had moved in from the nearby mainland. As well, they were hindered from access to the north coast by the growing number of resident fishermen. Because of the abundance of European objects left behind by the migratory fishermen, the Beothuks had fallen into a pattern of pilfering from seasonally abandoned fishing premises. As a result, fishermen, and later furriers, retaliated against the Beothuks for what was perceived by the Europeans as wanton theft. No missionaries or traders ventured among them and, as far as it can be ascertained, no Europeans learned their language. Various governors attempted to open communications with them, but their attempts failed. A number of Beothuks were captured by fishermen and brought to St. John's, where the last woman of the tribe, Shanawdithit, died in 1829. While it is true that some Beothuks were shot—and because they never acquired guns they were very vulnerable—it is most likely that malnutrition and European diseases were the major factors contributing to their extinction. Given the climate and limited resource base, their existence was marginal during the best of times. When the scales tipped even slightly against them, the Beothuks could no longer survive. The Micmacs, especially those operating from their settlement on the island's south coast, were meanwhile becoming recognized as the native hunters, explorers, and guides of the interior.

W A R

Although major changes occurred in Newfoundland during the eighteenth century, the period of greatest change was to occur during the prolonged wars between Britain and France—the French Revolutionary War (1793-1802) and the

Napoleonic War (1803-1815).

The French Revolutionary War created the same pattern of events as that of the two previous wars in 1756-1763 and 1776-1783. The migratory fishery, which by now meant almost exclusively the bank fishery, declined sharply. However, the resident fishery held firm until Spain entered the war in 1796 on the side of France and closed its markets to Newfoundland. The fishery became exceptionally depressed. At the same time, Newfoundland was subjected to an attack by a substantial French fleet under Admiral Richery. When the fleet approached St. John's, the naval governor, Sir Richard Wallace, proclaimed martial law and strengthened the harbour's defences, especially on Signal Hill overlooking the entrance. Richery withdrew and contented himself with raids on smaller outports where the residents were defenceless. During this period, the British navy had occupied St. Pierre and Miquelon, thereby removing France's settlement and fishery from the region.

Born in Scotland in 1770, William Carson immigrated to Newfoundland in 1808. A medical doctor by trade, Carson became a prolific pamphleteer and a leading force in the campaign to establish responsible government in Newfoundland. Courtesy, Provincial Archives of Newfoundland and Labrador

The local fishery recovered somewhat when Americans began to supply the Spanish markets both from their own fishery on the coast of Labrador, and also with fish purchased from Newfoundland residents. The brief period of peace in 1803—between the two wars—was to be only a short interruption in what was becoming a conflict of major proportion with considerable consequences.

In 1805 the Napoleonic War took a significant turn when the British destroyed the Franco-Spanish fleet at Trafalgar, thereby removing all serious threat to British shipping and to the Newfoundland fishery. However, this did not change the situation in Newfoundland because the Americans continued to monopolize the Spanish trade. Then, Napoleon, hoping to reduce Britain's trade, banned all British imports into Europe, and prohibited trade with third-party ships that entered continental ports from Britain. In retaliation, the British announced that all third-party ships trading with the continent must first enter a British port. This, of course, seriously affected American commerce; in 1807 the Americans placed an embargo on all foreign trade, hoping to force the two combattants to lift their restrictive policies. During the following year France invaded Spain and Portugal in an attempt to put an end, once and for all, to the importation of British goods into Europe through Portugal.

As a result, a Spanish junta established a government at Cadiz and asked Britain for assistance in driving out the French invaders and the French-appointed king. The British merchant marine began to supply the junta by sea and they were able to hold out against all attacks by the French. At the same time a British army landed on the Iberian peninsula. After some initial setbacks they drove the French out of Lisbon and launched a major campaign on Spanish soil which was to last six years.

These developments had a very significant impact on the marketing of Newfoundland saltfish. In fact, the residents of the island found themselves with an almost complete monopoly on the production and sale of the product. The British migratory fishery ceased because press gangs needed all the men they could lay their hands on, and West Country fishermen who managed to get to Newfoundland stayed. In addition, the French fishery had also ceased; the Norwegian and Icelandic fish trades had been stopped by the British blockade, and finally, the American fish trade had come to an end with that nation's own trade embargo.

The result in Newfoundland was a rise in fish prices and an increase in investment. In 1804 Newfoundland exported 559,442 quintals of saltfish, of which 425,446 went to Spain, Portugal, and Italy. In 1814 total exports had risen to 947,811 quintals, with Spain alone importing about 400,000 quintals. Newfoundland and its residents enjoyed an economic boom the likes of which had never been known before. Although the cost of some imports rose as well, there was a real rise in living standards and Newfoundland was, for several years, the most

prosperous community in the whole North Atlantic.

With a growing demand for saltfish, every planter and merchant in New-foundland wanted to expand operations. More men—in fact, more people in general—were needed. But, as stated previously, the war made it difficult to obtain men from the traditional West Country ports because press gangs were too active.

During the spring seal fishery season, groups of men were unloaded from their ships directly onto the ice. These sealers would usually remain on the ice, working from morning until the day's end. Courtesy, B.J. Kenny's Photos

IRISH IMMIGRATION

For over 100 years, Ireland had been supplying some servants to the Newfound-land fishery via sack ships calling at Irish ports—especially Waterford—for what was referred to as "wet" provisions (salt beef, salt pork, and dairy products). Many Irish people were anxious to leave their overpopulated, impoverished country, and Newfoundland became an attractive destination as they received news of the demand for labour in the fishery and related trades. Also, sack ship captains were not disinterested parties because they too profited from this passenger trade. The Irish were further attracted by the fact that, under the British Passenger Act of 1803, ships sailing to Newfoundland were not classified as emigrant ships. This act placed strict limits upon the number of passengers an emigrant ship from Britain could carry, and the amount of food and water that was to be supplied. The act protected emigrants, but it also raised the cost of travel to North America. Ships sailing to Newfoundland were permitted to carry as many passengers as the captain chose—with the passengers often providing their own food and drink, and sleeping wherever they could find space.

The increase in the number of Irish versus English passengers is obvious from the records. In 1803 there were 1,047 arrivals from England compared to 1,642 from Ireland; during 1811 through 1813, 676 passengers arrived from England while 5,153 arrived from Ireland; and during the three-year period 1814 through 1816 the total figures were 2,447 and 10,728, respectively. The total New-

foundland population increased from about 20,000 people in 1804 to about 40,000 in 1815, some 50 percent of whom were Irish Roman Catholics. St. John's, by 1815, contained about 10,000 people—one-quarter of the whole population—composed of approximately 2,500 English Protestants and 7,500 Irish Roman Catholics.

THE NEW NEWFOUNDLAND

The influx of such a large number of people unskilled in the fishery created a situation unique in the history of Newfoundland. Newcomers arrived in the ships' principal ports and there, by and large, they remained. They did not attempt to strike out to the north or to the south in search of vacant fishing rooms because they had no experience, no capital, and they needed employment immediately. Some men worked in the warehouses and on the docks of the established firms, and women found work as domestic servants. Many men were hired as fishermen because the industry was expanding. However, there was a limit to the amount of expansion that the traditional fishing centres could accommodate. By building small schooners, and sending crews to the French Shore for the fishing season, the planters solved this problem. With the war in progress the French were no longer in Newfoundland and the residents' small ships could fish uninterrupted in the vacant harbours on the French Shore, either drying their fish on the deserted French fishing rooms or bringing it back in salt to their own harbours. The operation required an increased investment compared to the cost of outfitting a traditional fishing boat, but the price that fish was fetching at this time more than compensated for the extra investment. The northern part of the French Shore was referred to by the British as the "North Shore," and the number of ships on the North Shore increased every summer: from 47 carrying 435 men in 1803, to 129 carrying 1,101 men in 1814. St. John's and the Conception Bay ports, especially Harbour Grace, dominated this fishery.

The development of the North Shore fishery occurred simultaneously with the development of another entirely new fishery—the seal fishery.

OPPOSITE: This late 1800s photograph shows a group of sealers waiting on the wharf in St. John's in preparation for their departure to the ice fields. Courtesy, The Literary Executors, Cater Andrews Collection, Memorial University of Newfoundland

THE SPRING SEAL FISHERY

Seals had been netted and shot by resident fishermen in the northern harbours since the beginning of the 1700s. In the 1790s fishermen from Conception Bay began the practice of sailing north in search of the seal herds in March and April.

This spring seal fishery became the island's native industry because only residents were in a position to take advantage of the resource; in the summer, when the migratory fishing ships and the bye boat keepers were present, the seals were in the Arctic. Sea mammals and fish supplied much of the industrial world's demand for oil, and there was a growing demand for seal oil and for seal skins in the British markets. In 1813 exports of seal products consisted of 133,847 seal skins and 1,583.5 tuns of seal oil (one tun equals 1,125 liters) valued at £50,161 (sterling)—compared to cod oil exports of 4,054.25 tuns of cod oil valued at £121,628.

One of the most significant features of the North Shore cod fishery and the spring seal fishery was that at the same port, ships and men became involved in both. For the first time since the European discovery of North America, Newfoundland fishermen had acquired a second resource—one that they could exploit during late winter and early spring, well before the summer cod fishery. Thus the seal and cod fisheries complemented each other and led not only to economic growth but increased economic and social stability.

A SENSE OF PERMANENCY

Patterns of settlement changed and the very shape of society changed. Servants (i.e., hired fishermen), no longer restricted to three or four months work, were not forced to leave the island in the autumn. Now they could find adequate employment as cod fishermen and sealers and, consequently, they could afford to marry and raise families in Newfoundland. At the same time it was not necessary for them to be dependent on a piece of waterfront property on which to live and make their living. Since the North Shore and seal fisheries were both prosecuted at considerable distances from the harbours in Conception Bay and St. John's in which they dwelt, these newcomers moved back from the shoreline, cleared land, and engaged in considerable subsistence agriculture. Thus restraints on population growth of Conception Bay ports and St. John's were removed. Finally, the general prosperity allowed many of the newcomers to acquire their own schooners and engage in the two fisheries as employers as well as employees.

The British government could not prevent the growth of population in Newfoundland and by now no longer tried. As a result, signs of permanent settlement began to appear throughout the island: In 1795 the first Royal Newfoundland Regiment was created; in 1796 a Roman Catholic bishop for Newfoundland was consecrated; in 1803 the St. John's Charity School Society was instituted, and Sunday Schools in 1804; also in 1804 the Phoenix Insurance Company, London, donated the first fire engine to St. John's; in 1805 a post office was opened; in 1806 the Benevolent Irish Society was founded to aid impoverished Irish; in 1807 the first newspaper, the *Royal Gazette and Newfoundland Advertiser,* was published with John Ryan, a United Empire Loyalist, as editor and publisher; in 1811 the St. John's waterfront was cleared of fishing ships' rooms and leased to commercial firms, and permission was granted for the erection of permanent houses irrespective of their uses for the fishery or their locations; in 1813 the cornerstone was laid for a hospital in St. John's, and the first grants of land—110—were issued; and, in 1811, probably the most significant development occurred when the first pamphlet attacking the system of government in Newfoundland was published. Dr. William Carson, a medical doctor who came to Newfoundland from Scotland in 1808, wrote in part:

A naval commander accustomed to receive obedience, whether his orders are dictated by justice or injustice, by reason or false prejudice, cannot be expected to brook with temper any opposition to his will. The man whose duty calls upon him to defend his rights, and the just interest of his family, in opposition to the opinions and passions of such a Governor, will have but a small chance of success. An act of independence would be arraigned as an act of mutiny. All the influence of his office, all the arts of his satellites would be marshalled to effect his overthrow. Accustomed to use force to knock down opposition—force being the power he knows best how to direct—the toils of investigation, deliberation, and judgement, are seldom had recourse to by a Naval Governor.

Indian Harbour, Labrador, settled on a seasonal basis only, was used by stationers and floaters engaged in the summer Labrador fishery. Sir Wilfred Grenfell opened a hospital here in 1894 to serve the health care needs of the summer residents. Courtesy, Provincial Archives of Newfoundland and Labrador

Two years later, in 1813, Dr. Carson wrote in another pamphlet:

The only remedy against the evils flowing from the present system, will be found in giving to the people, what they most ardently wish, and what is unquestionably their right, a civil Government, consisting of a resident Governor, a Senate House and House of Assembly.

This was the beginning of agitation for political reform—agitation which was to yield results during the succeeding decades.

The wars, which ended in 1815, completed the transformation of Newfoundland. For 300 years it had been a fishery dependent upon an island; by 1815 it had become a colony dependent upon the fishery. Furthermore, St. John's had become the capital. As Governor Richard Godwin Keats wrote in 1813:

St. John's, with a population of nearly 10,000, seems to have grown out of its original situation, and to be changing its character from a fishery to a large commercial town.

The British migratory cod fishery never recovered because by 1815 Newfoundland residents were numerous enough (and with the development of the seal fishery, secure enough—although barely) to dominate completely what had been one of Britain's oldest foreign trades.

These sealing steamers are pictured in the ice at Harbour Grace, Conception Bay, in the late 1800s. The SS Vanguard (foreground) was owned by John Munn & Company of Harbour Grace and later by Bained Johnson & Co. Ltd. of St. John's. The ship was used in the annual spring seal fishery from 1873 until it sank in 1909. Courtesy, B.J. Kenny's Photos

The SS Iceland, *seen here docked at Harbour Grace, Conception Bay, was part of the sealing fleet that sailed from Harbour Grace until the early 1870s, when St. John's became the pre-eminent port for the sealing industry. Courtesy, The Literary Executors, Cater Andrews Collection, Memorial University of Newfoundland*

FAMINE, FROST, AND FIRE

With the end of the war in 1815 prosperity quickly faded and Newfoundland experienced a depression unequalled in its history. World fish prices, in general, declined and other producers entered the trade. According to historian D.W. Prowse, "In the winter of 1815 the capital and all the outports were in a state of actual starvation." Unaware of this reversal in the economy, immigrants continued to flock in from Ireland—5,838 in 1815, followed by 2,636 in 1816. In 1816 the economic situation deteriorated even more, and the following year, 1817-1818, is recorded in Newfoundland history as the "Winter of the Rals" (Rowdies). Prowse wrote about this winter:

In the former season, starvation alone had to be contended with; now famine, frost, and fire combined, like three avenging furies, to scourge the unfortunate Island. A frost that sealed up the whole coast commenced early in November, and continued almost without intermission through the entire season, and on the nights of the 7th and 21st of November 1817, three hundred houses were burnt, rendering two thousand individuals, in depth of that cruel winter, homeless . . . To add to this misery, gangs of half-famished, lawless men everywhere threatened the destruction of life and property . . . The suffering that winter no pen can fully describe.

As Prowse concluded, "During these three unhappy years everything was against us; even the seal fishery failed in 1817."

In 1818, however, the seal fishery was successful and began to increase in importance in both relative and absolute terms. The worst of the crisis was over.

THE NINETEENTH-CENTURY SALTFISH TRADE

Newfoundland retained almost exclusively an export-oriented economy during the nineteenth century. Exports of saltfish, which averaged 935,450 quintals annually from 1811 to 1815, declined after the war—reaching an average low of 737,805 quintals during 1831-1835. Exports recovered after 1835 and reached an average of 1,236,868 quintals from 1856 through 1860. The years after 1860 brought a series of small depressions and recoveries until a major depression hit in the late 1880s, lasting until the start of the twentieth century. An average of 1,529,215 quintals of saltfish were being exported annually from 1906 through 1910.

After 1815 Portugal replaced Spain as Newfoundland's principal export market; other markets included Norway, Italy, Greece, the British Caribbean, and Brazil. Trade with Brazil developed slowly, but by 1914 Brazil was the largest consumer of Newfoundland saltfish.

The Newfoundland saltfish industry made certain readjustments during the nineteenth century. The most important of these was the development of a migratory fishery—for islanders—on the coast of Labrador.

Following the close of the Napoleonic War, French fishermen returned to the Newfoundland French Shore and resumed their traditional seasonal fishery. Newfoundland residents who had been fishing the area during the war were now excluded, and they decided to cross the Straits of Belle Isle and fish on the coast of Labrador.

The fishermen who utilized this Labrador fishery continued to live in St. John's and the Conception Bay ports, and they were gradually joined by fishermen from Trinity Bay, Bonavista Bay, and harbours farther north.

Although it was adversely affected by market problems and catch failures, the Labrador fishery increased steadily during the century. In the 1820s and 1830s about 250 ships, carrying an average of nine men each, participated in this fishery and the fleet had grown to over 400 registered vessels (not including boats of between 10 and 30 tons). Harbour Grace, with a fleet of 90 vessels in this fishery in 1867, was the leading port involved; but Brigus, Carbonear, and St. John's had considerable fleets as well. The investment was large and the season was short. Therefore, in order for the Labrador fishery to prosper, the men and ships involved needed other employment. So, as long as the seal fishery prospered it provided employment during the winter and spring, and the Labrador fishery flourished. During the latter part of the century the seal fishery declined. This development, combined with growing problems in the saltfish markets, caused depression and bankruptcies and led to the decline of the "outports." Most of the importing, exporting, and supplying business transferred to the capital, St. John's.

With the withdrawal of the British garrison in 1870 there was a need for a new law enforcement body. As a result, the Newfoundland Constabulary was formed a year later. Pictured here is the Constabulary's mounted force in 1890. Courtesy, Royal Newfoundland Constabulary

THE GROWING SEAL FISHERY

The development of the seal fishery was the major economic advance of the early nineteenth century. In 1818 a harvest of over 165,000 seals helped Newfoundland out of its depression, and the industry grew rapidly. Production rose to over 386,000 seals in 1822, over 600,000 in 1831, and to about 700,000 during the peak years of the 1840s. The exportation of seal oil increased from about 1,400 tuns in 1815 to over 7,500 tuns in the early 1830s. During the 1830s and 1840s over one-third of the value of all Newfoundland's exports was derived from seal oil and seal skins. In 1827 there were 290 ships and 5,418 men engaged in this industry. These figures increased—as did the size of the individual ships—and in 1857, 370 ships carrying 13,700 men "went to the ice." St. John's, Harbour Grace, Brigus, and Carbonear were the major ports involved, but most harbours on the northeast coast of the island participated.

The population of the colony grew from about 40,000 people in 1815 to 124,000 in 1857, largely because of the winter employment provided by this industry. While the launching of Newfoundland into colonial status was a direct result of the Napoleonic War, Newfoundland could not have retained its population and status without the lucrative seal fishery. Indeed, without the seal fishery the Labrador fishery would have quickly withered because of costs, and with it the island's jurisdiction over the Labrador coast.

In the second half of the century the seal fishery changed. The seal herds had been overexploited and the number of seals harvested gradually declined. At the same time the discovery and use of mineral oils reduced the value of seal oil from about $200 per tun in the 1860s to about $77 in the 1890s. During the 1860s St. John's and Harbour Grace merchants introduced steamers into this fishery and the sailing fleet was replaced very quickly—eliminating all the other ports from the seal fishery. The last major mercantile operation in Harbour Grace went bankrupt in 1894. At that time St. John's took over the entire—although by now much reduced—sealing fleet. By then the value of seal exports had declined to only 9 percent of the total value of all exports. As pointed out previously, the Labrador seal fishery was also considerably reduced, and much of its focus shifted to St. John's.

POLITICAL DEVELOPMENT

While its economic development during the nineteenth century was unique in the context of British North America, eventually Newfoundland's political development followed the same pattern as that of the other colonies, although initially at a much slower pace. During the "Winter of the Rals" the naval governor was ordered to remain on the island over the winter, and the British government finally recognized the island, and the Labrador coast, as a colony in 1824. Agitation by Roman Catholics, indigenous merchants, and reformers—such as Dr. William Carson and newspaper publisher R.J. Parsons—resulted in Newfoundland being granted representative government in 1832.

The new government consisted of the usual appointed governor, appointed legislative council, appointed executive council, and elected representative assembly. It was necessary for legislation to be passed by both the assembly and the legislative council before it could become law. Conflict between the two bodies quickly arose. During the first years the council was dominated by British officials who still opposed the very idea of an assembly and obstructed legislation. When

OPPOSITE: The railway station at St. John's, shown here circa 1910, was the eastern terminus of the trans-island railway. Courtesy, B.J. Kenny's Photos

this problem was resolved by appointing local merchants to the council, the assembly became dominated by Roman Catholic and anti-Church of England reformers. Religion became an issue because the Roman Catholic population, newly enfranchised since the Emancipation Act of 1829, demanded its share of the government patronage which had traditionally gone to the Church of England establishment. Deadlock resulted and in 1841 the British Colonial Office, as a temporary measure, ordered the assembly and the council to sit as one body. This eliminated the deadlock; but, given developments in the other colonies, the British government felt it could not make this unusual system permanent. In 1848 Newfoundland's government reverted to its pre-1841 model.

The next major political issue to arise was responsible government (whereby the executive council is chosen from the elected legislative assembly and responsible to it). In the election of 1855 Roman Catholics and Wesleyans (Methodists) campaigned together for responsible government and won.

The "Liberal" party, under a Roman Catholic prime minister, P.F. Little, took office in 1855 and governed quite successfully during the prosperous late 1850s. However, party leadership changed and under the new prime minister, John Kent, the Wesleyans became alienated. Then the Roman Catholic bishop and Kent publicly disagreed over certain social and economic policies. The former anti-responsible-government forces were able to reorganize to win the following election and install a "Conservative" administration. Religious sectarianism was a major issue during this period, and on one occasion British troops (stationed in

This view of St. John's was taken from the south side of the harbour in 1892, and shows the devastation created by the "Great Fire" of that year. The twin-spired Cathedral of St. John the Baptist is visible to the right on the horizon. Still in use today, the cathedral was elevated to a basilica in 1955. Courtesy, B.J. Kenny's Photos

St. John's since 1697) were called upon to maintain order and fired upon a threatening gathering of Roman Catholics outside the courthouse.

By the late 1860s religious sectarianism and party titles took second place to the issue of confederation with the other British North American colonies—which became Canada after 1867. The election of 1869 was fought on the question between "Confederates" and "Anti-Confederates," and it was a bitter campaign. Much was made of the fact that Newfoundland's exports were sent to Britain, Southern Europe, Brazil, and the Caribbean—and that there were few ties with Canada. Combined with warnings that Canada would increase taxation and force Newfoundlanders to join its army, the campaign resulted in the rejection of confederation and a victory for the Anti-Confederates.

ECONOMIC DECLINE AND POLITICAL RESPONSE

Beginning in the 1860s, as the seal and cod fisheries were increasingly unable to support the growing population—146,536 people in 1869—governments were forced to pay more attention to the deteriorating economy. Consequently, although religious sectarianism was used whenever any political advantage could be derived from it, political parties and governments tended more and more to become identified with economic strategies.

Confederation had been viewed as a solution to the economic problems of the 1860s; but the failure of the government of the day to be re-elected on that platform eliminated it as a practical alternative. From that point on parties and governments followed two basic policies.

The governments of F.B.T. Carter, William Whiteway, and their successors favoured diversification and industrialization—beginning with the construction of a railway across the island. It was assumed that a railway would open up the resources of the interior—agricultural lands, timber lands, and mines. A railway across the island to Port-aux-Basques was completed between 1883 and 1898, and several branch lines were built during this construction period and shortly afterward. In 1895 iron ore mines were opened on Bell Island, a paper mill was opened in Grand Falls in 1909, another at Corner Brook in 1925, and shortly thereafter a lead and zinc mine opened at Buchans. These operations, combined with their actual construction and maintenance, absorbed a fair number of fishermen who desperately needed to supplement their incomes from the fishery—especially after the mid-1880s.

The second approach to economic growth centred on the improvement of the existing fisheries and the expansion into other fisheries. Robert Thorburn's government of 1885-1889 is the best example of this approach (although elements of both approaches were carried on as governments changed). Efforts were undertaken to improve the quality of Newfoundland's saltfish; pressure was exerted on the British Foreign Office to convince the foreign markets to reduce their tariffs on the colony's fish; bait supplies to French fishermen were prohibited where possible; a bank fishery was encouraged, as was a new lobster fishery and a new whale fishery; and a superintendent of fisheries was appointed to help implement government policies.

However, neither approach was timely nor capable of staving off the disastrous 1890s. When the colony's two banks failed in December 1894, many firms also declared bankruptcy. The colony, with a population of over 200,000 people, barely survived the depression that followed.

Furthermore, throughout the latter decades of the nineteenth century, as successive governments cast around for solutions to their problems, they became somewhat obsessed with the "French Shore problem." The French Shore was viewed as a place of great wealth and opportunity, and governments and the St. John's merchants were convinced that if the French could be forced—or persuaded—to surrender their fishing rights on this coast then it could be fully developed for the benefit of Newfoundlanders. The French, meanwhile, after decades

Sir William V. Whiteway (1828-1908) was a native of England who came to Newfoundland in 1843. Entering politics in 1859, he held the office of prime minister for most of the last quarter of the nineteenth century. Courtesy, B.J. Kenny's Photos

Italian inventor Guglielmo Marconi (1874-1937) received the first transatlantic wireless signal (the letter "S," transmitted from Poldhu, England) in St. John's on Signal Hill in 1901. Courtesy, Provincial Archives of Newfoundland and Labrador

34   ATLANTIC CANADA

of intransigence, and concentrating more on their bank fishery, finally agreed in 1904 to surrender all rights to this coast as part of their new agreement with Britain. The solution to the French Shore problem did not produce the economic benefits that many had anticipated.

MIGRATION

Fishermen and their families coped with the economic problems in their own way. Many, particularly from among those of Irish descent on the Avalon Peninsula, revived the ancient practice of moving to New England when work could not be obtained on the island. Combined with this was the more recent Conception Bay tradition of spending from four to six weeks away from home in the seal fishery, and approximately four months away from home in the Labrador fishery. Men and women from this area turned naturally to Boston whenever the fishery failed to provide them with an adequate income. Although initially this migration involved their regular return to Newfoundland with their savings, many eventually settled and became American citizens. In fact, because of this migration, the population of Conception Bay actually declined after the mid-1880s.

The introduction of the cod trap (a square box-like arrangement made from netting and anchored in an area frequented by migrating fish) into the fishery around this time seems to have had important consequences for the employ-

ABOVE:
Activist and social reformer William Coaker helped to unionize Newfoundland's fishermen by establishing the Fishermen's Protective Union (F.P.U.) in 1913. After his death Coaker was buried at Port Union, a community which he and the union created. Courtesy, Provincial Archives of Newfoundland and Labrador

RIGHT: The west coast of Newfoundland, pictured here at Bay of Islands in the late 1800s, was connected by rail with the east coast by the end of the nineteenth century. The expense of building and maintaining the railway was a major factor in Newfoundland's economic decline of the 1930s. Courtesy, Provincial Archives of Newfoundland and Labrador

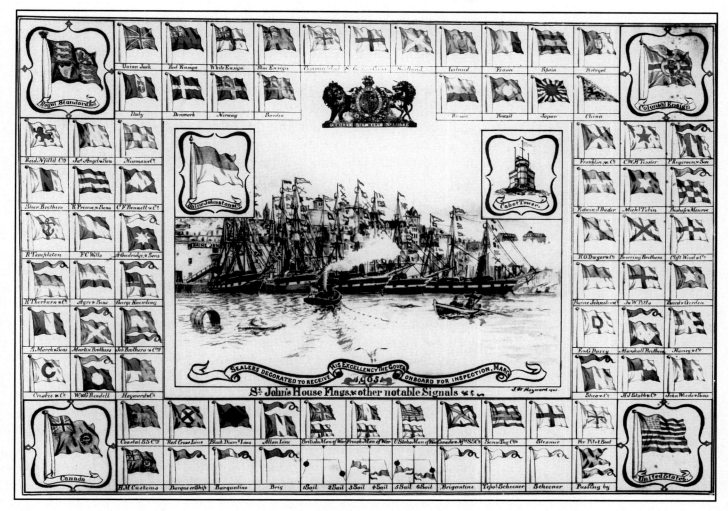

ment of women. Up to this point women were employed splitting and heading the catch in the fishing room stage, but the cod trap allowed the men to spend more time ashore processing the catch. However, stationary crews in the Labrador fishery continued to employ women as cooks, a practice that was also common on board floater schooners. Surplus women workers, certainly many from Conception Bay, joined the migration to Boston. With the completion of the trans-island railway, and up until the United States put an end to immigration during the Great Depression, many Newfoundlanders looked to Boston for regular employment and sometimes for a new home. Newfoundland, which had been one of the first places in the "New World" to welcome immigrants, had now become a part of the "Old World" and was seeking a haven for its emigrants.

THE UNION ALTERNATIVE

Fishermen (mostly Protestants) living to the north of the Avalon Peninsula had always coped with overcrowding and economic adversity by moving on to other harbours and islands in search of new and better places to build their fishing rooms. Emigrating or commuting to Boston was not an important part of their tradition. However, by the end of the century the problems confronting them were no longer so readily resolved because they related to saltfish marketing, rather than production, and also to the decline in the seal fishery. Therefore, when William Coaker, an educated activist who lived among them, promised that

The centre scene of this 1905 signal flag illustration by local artist John W. Hayward (1843-1913) depicts a fleet of sealing vessels awaiting the governor's inspection in St. John's Harbour. Both national emblems and the house flags of various local firms make up the surrounding elements of this detailed picture. Courtesy, Parks Canada

their own union would provide them with the power to improve their lives, they listened and followed him—thus creating the Fishermen's Protective Union. The F.P.U. entered politics and elected its first members of the House of Assembly in 1913, but before they could influence developments World War I broke out and the economic situation changed.

Meanwhile, on the south and west coasts of the island a certain amount of trade, usually illicit, was carried out with the French on the French Shore and at St. Pierre and Miquelon, and there was also a direct trade with Prince Edward Island and Nova Scotia. The latter colony/province was the usual destination for Newfoundland emigrants from these areas.

THE END OF THE NINETEENTH CENTURY
Newfoundland society during the nineteenth century had become much more complex than it had ever been. There had been many developments and much progress since its recognition as a colony. However, although the population had increased to over 220,000 by 1901, the fishery continued to be prosecuted under a credit system which had originated in Britain, and which had first been applied to Newfoundland by the early English fishing ships. Under this system fishermen were advanced supplies by the local merchant in the spring; in the fall they brought their fish and oil to the merchant, paid their accounts, and ideally had enough of a balance in their favour to purchase winter supplies. They saw very little cash as cod fishermen; however, when they engaged in the seal fishery most received cash for their shares. Generally, fishermen who failed to meet their obligations to the merchant were carried for a time—and many firms went bankrupt because of this. Some firms refused credit after a certain point, thus forcing fishermen to seek relief from the government or go to New England to work. The firms that survived the depression of the 1890s were those which had their headquarters in St. John's and engaged only in wholesale trade operations in the outports; thus small traders and local merchants were left to suffer the consequences dealing with individual fishermen.

The old planter fishery declined, and eventually disappeared, everywhere except on the Labrador coast. In its place all over the island a family fishery developed. Father and son(s) were responsible for catching, splitting, and salting the fish while the mother, young children, and elderly folk were responsible for drying it. In the 1870s the use of the cod trap became common and allowed men and boys to spend more time ashore because the trap needed to be checked and emptied only periodically. However, the trap, because of its greater efficiency, sometimes created a glut for individual fishermen who did not have the manpower to process a large catch, and quality control became a problem.

St. John's was the centre of government, higher education, most health services, and commerce. The opening of the railway across the island between 1883 and 1898 introduced a link between the capital and the principal bays, thereby making it possible for most outport fishermen and their families to acquire access to at least some of these services; thus the population became more integrated.

Meanwhile, Labrador remained a frontier region. Thousands of the island's fishermen commuted there annually, but the Naskapi and Montagnais (Innu) continued to have very little contact with the island's political and economic forces. Farther to the north the Eskimos (Inuit) continued to fish, hunt, and trap under the direction of the Moravian missionaries. On the southern Labrador

OPPOSITE: A vital centre of trade and commerce, St. John's provided a wealth of economic opportunity in the early 1900s. Here, an excited crowd gathers to greet incoming passengers at the city's bustling harbour. Courtesy, B.J. Kenny's Photos

coast "livyers" of British descent made a precarious living from fishing and sealing with only minimal services provided. It was in response to the lack of medical services among the fishermen on the Labrador coast that Wilfred Grenfell, an English medical doctor, established his now famous and internationally recognized medical missions. However, the Labrador coast was of primary importance to the colony because it was the location of the island's migratory cod fishery.

PROSPERITY AND POLITICS

The early years of the twentieth century were prosperous. The Liberal government of Robert Bond followed cautious policies combining encouragement of both industry and the fisheries; he was, of course, assisted by the fact that markets for saltfish were much improved. Edward Morris, one of his cabinet ministers, deserted him to create his own party, the Peoples' Party, which advocated greater industrial growth. Morris won the election of 1909 and the following one in 1913. While he was in office the Grand Falls paper mill was brought into operation. During World War I, Newfoundland, under Morris, created its own regiment for service overseas. In 1917 Prime Minister Morris resigned after being appointed to the House of Lords, and a National Government containing opposition members, including the F.P.U. leader, William Coaker, succeeded him. By and large,

Sir Robert Bond (1857-1927) was a prominent Liberal in Sir William Whiteway's administration. He succeeded Whiteway as the party leader and was Newfoundland's prime minister from 1900 until 1909. Courtesy, B.J. Kenny's Photos

the period up to the end of the war was one of prosperity, although also one of increasing public debt.

The postwar depression created market problems that were beyond Newfoundland's control. Saltfish markets collapsed, and although Coaker was minister of fisheries for awhile and introduced some far-sighted measures, the major problems were outside Newfoundland and beyond his area of influence. Nevertheless, a second paper mill was opened in Corner Brook and a lead and zinc mine opened in Buchans. Gradually the economy recovered and by the late 1920s there seemed every reason to be optimistic.

LOSS OF RESPONSIBLE GOVERNMENT

The Great Depression brought worldwide recovery to a halt. Exports declined, and fish prices and prices for exports in general declined. The government was forced to borrow to pay interest on the public debt accumulated since the 1880s. By now this amounted to $100 million and interest payments on it began to increase steeply. In 1929-1930, interest on the debt cost the government 35.9 percent of its current revenue; in 1930-1931 this rose to 44.8 percent; in 1931-1932 to 59.7 percent, and in 1932-1933 to 63.2 percent. Finally, forbidden by the British government to declare bankruptcy, Newfoundland was forced to surrender responsible government and accept government by a British-appointed council—the Commission of Government.

Newfoundland's political development after World War I was closely tied to its economic development. Richard Squires, in the tradition of Morris and others, tried to diversify the economy into the areas of mining and paper milling. His administrations (1919-1924 and 1928-1932) were extremely unlucky in that he was forced to deal with both the postwar depression and the onslaught of the Great Depression. Furthermore, he was entangled in major scandals and was accused of corruption on an exceptional scale. Prime Minister Walter Monroe's administration, 1924-1928 (between Squires' two administrations), has been described by political scientist S.J.R. Noel as a "merchant junta, zealously dedicated to their own financial self-interest." It soon lost the confidence of the population and indeed of many of its own elected members. Frederick Alderdice, whose party defeated Squires in 1932, remained in office briefly. In 1934 his government, and the House of Assembly, voted themselves out of

office and handed the administration over to the Commission of Government.

THE COMMISSION OF GOVERNMENT

The Commission of Government lasted until 1949 and its administration can be divided into two periods: the depressed 1930s and the prosperous 1940s. During the 1930s saltfish exports remained depressed and thousands of fishermen were unable to receive a living wage from their catch or to obtain credit. Mining and pulp and paper milling were also down and labourers, tradesmen, and others were unemployed or underemployed. With emigra-

tion to the United States no longer an option they were forced to apply for government relief. At that time the relief rate which prevailed was six cents per day per person; in 1938, 85,000 people, out of the total population of 290,000, were living on this meagre allowance.

The traditional fisheries continued to operate. Prices were low but some merchants still advanced credit, and the government advanced supplies to others. Every spring the few remaining sealing steamers went to the ice and those fortunate enough to obtain berths on these ships usually earned a well-appreciated share. Every summer the fishing boats continued to prosecute the shore fishery and the traditional saltfish was produced; thousands of Labrador fisher-

ABOVE: Pictured left, Captain Robert A. Bartlett (1875-1946) was born in Brigus, Conception Bay, and spent his career at sea. He became internationally famous as an Arctic explorer, commanding Robert Peary's ship on the successful polar expedition in 1909. Aside from his seagoing life, Bartlett wrote for National Geographic *and published his autobiography,* The Log of Bob Bartlett. *Courtesy, The Literary Executors, Cater Andrews Collection, Memorial University of Newfoundland*

LEFT: A rapidly developing city in the late 1800s, the southeast section of St. John's is shown here surrounding its well-protected harbour basin. Courtesy, B.J. Kenny's Photos

men were given subsidized passage to that coast on government-chartered steamers. People in most outports kept vegetable gardens and all had access to firewood. Nevertheless, life was harsh and opportunities almost nonexistent.

WORLD WAR II

After war broke out in Europe, the British government, desperate for American ships, signed an agreement allowing the United States to establish armed forces bases in Newfoundland. The demand for workers soared, and many fishermen deserted the fisheries to work on the construction of these bases. Historian Peter Neary writes:

At the height of the base building boom about 20,000 Newfoundlanders were employed in military construction, which in effect had suddenly, some would say providentially, given the country a major new industry. Amazingly, in 1942 the government did not have to pay out any able-bodied relief, and was able to confine itself to the support of the sick, aged, and infirm. From a figure of $1,382,000 in 1939-40, relief expenditure fell away by 1942-43 to a wartime low of $280,000. In short order, Newfoundland's most corrosive social and economic problem had been almost magically solved.

Meanwhile, the Commission of Government rationalized the saltfish trade with regulations governing quality standards and shipping, and—with wartime demand—this industry improved. At the end of World War II the American bases continued to operate and to require civilian labour; thus the type of postwar

The Commission of Government inauguration on February 16, 1934, heralded a new era of Newfoundland's government until the time of Canadian Confederation in 1948. Governor Murray Anderson (centre) is seen addressing the audience at the inauguration ceremonies. Courtesy, Provincial Archives of Newfoundland and Labrador

depression that had bedeviled Newfoundland in the past did not occur.

CONFEDERATION WITH CANADA

In 1946, following instructions from Britain, 45 representatives were elected to a National Convention which met in St. John's to discuss and make recommendations concerning Newfoundland's political future. The discussions centred on the continuation of the Commission of Government; the return to responsible government; or confederation with Canada. Two referenda were held to decide this matter. The first was inconclusive, although "Responsible Government" led the poll and "Commission of Government" was last. The second referendum, between "Responsible Government" and "Confederation," was narrowly won by the Confederates, led by Joseph R. Smallwood. The campaign was bitter and included religious sectarianism, anti-fish merchant propaganda, and anti-Canadian propaganda. However, responsible government had failed the people in 1934, and in 1948 they turned their backs on it to become Canadians in Canada's 10th province—the only province to use the referendum in making this decision.

Disaster struck the SS Viking in 1931 when the ship exploded and sank off the Newfoundland coast. Some 24 men were killed, including American filmmaker Varrick Frissell, who was on board shooting final footage for his film The Viking, which was posthumously released. The wooden ship had been in use since 1881, serving the whaling and sealing industries. Courtesy, The Literary Executors, Cater Andrews Collection, Memorial University of Newfoundland

POST-CONFEDERATION ECONOMICS

By becoming the 10th province Newfoundland brought to the Canadian Confederation about 405,000 square kilometers of territory; enormous mineral, hydro, forest, and fish resources; and improved security for Canada. Confederation changed the economic parameters of Newfoundland. Newfoundlanders immediately became eligible for family allowance payments, old age pensions, unemployment insurance payments, and transfer payments to health, education, and other services. In addition, Newfoundlanders were now permitted to work on the Canadian mainland without restrictions, and great numbers of young men and women left to take jobs in the mines, mills, and factories of southern Ontario. Many men commuted in order to raise their families in Newfoundland; others settled and made their homes on the mainland.

Back in Newfoundland the traditional saltfish industry was viewed by many as an anachronism and, worse still, one that had, like responsible government, failed the people in 1934. Ottawa was not interested in marketing the product, so this industry was allowed to decline. Instead, government and business turned to the production of fresh-frozen cod fish for the American market. The new provincial government attempted to introduce light industry into the province but without success. Next the government turned to industrial mega-projects including iron ore mining and hydro-electric power in Labrador and, most recently, offshore gas and oil development.

World War II produced a considerable amount of submarine activity off the shores of Newfoundland and Labrador. Pictured here in 1945 in St. John's Harbour is the German U-boat, U-190, which was picked up and then escorted to the harbour upon Germany's surrender. Courtesy, Provincial Archives of Newfoundland and Labrador

POST-CONFEDERATION POLITICS

In 1949 J.R. (Joey) Smallwood swept to power as the leader of the newly formed Liberal party and first premier of the new Canadian province. He, of course, received credit for the immediate benefits derived from confederation. Smallwood was able to win the following five elections and he made major attempts to develop light and heavy industry—including iron ore mining in Labrador—but he gradually began to lose touch with the younger electorate that did not remember the pre-1949 period. In the 1972 elections the Liberal party was defeated by the more positive campaign of the Progressive Conservative party, led by F.D. (Frank) Moores. It was at this time that the fishermen—led by Desmond McGrath and Richard Cashin—organized themselves into a new union and, with Canada extending its control over coastal waters to a distance of 200 miles, fishery development began to receive greater emphasis under the Moores administration. A vigorous bank fishery was developed to complement the shore fishery; the fishing operation was rationalized, working conditions improved, and quality controls tightened. Moores retired as premier in 1979 and was succeeded by A. Brian Peckford, who led a Progressive Conservative government until 1989. Under the Peckford administration the government sought control of the offshore gas and oil resources. Peckford resigned in early 1989, and was succeeded by Tom Rideout as premier. Rideout called an election, which he lost to the Liberal party, led by Clyde Wells. Development of the offshore gas and oil resources and management of the fishing stocks remain the principal concerns of the government.

CONTEMPORARY NEWFOUNDLAND

The free-trade agreement between Canada and the United States, which went into effect January 1, 1989, has been supported by the Newfoundland government. It can be viewed, as well, as a reinforcement of the connections between Newfoundland and the northeastern United States—connections that originated in the early seventeenth century.

The fishery, pulp and paper production, and mining continue to be the main industries. In the early 1980s about 500,000 metric tonnes of fish, with a landed value of $170 million and a processed value of $500 million, were taken annually by 32,000 fishermen and women. About 40 percent of this fish has been produced by the offshore fleet and is made up mainly of cod, plaice, grey sole, redfish, turbot, and herring; 60 percent is cod produced by the inshore fishermen. At the same time about 4,000 people were employed in the production of newsprint, valued at $300 million in 1981. And in 1982 approximately one billion dollars worth of ore was produced by 4,000 to 5,000 miners. Ship building and repair, lumber mills, canneries, and other smaller industries operate throughout the province. Offshore gas and oil exploration activities, although marred by the tragic sinking of one oil rig—the *Ocean Ranger*—is also providing employment for Newfoundland workers. Federal transfer payments to the province and directly to the unemployed, the old, and families with children make up an important part of the economy as well.

Newfoundland and Labrador continue to be affected by climate and geography. Most food and consumer goods are imported, which makes the cost of living higher than in the other provinces. Unemployment is the highest of any province and wages are generally the lowest. Therefore people who live in the province must be prepared to accept, on the whole, a somewhat lower standard of living. However, Newfoundland has the highest rate of home ownership of any province; the lowest crime rate, less pollution, less traffic, and easy access to large wilderness areas. These advantages produce a quality of life which is unique in Canada.

As leader of the Confederate forces in Newfoundland, former reporter, author, broadcaster, and farmer Joseph R. Smallwood became the first premier of the new Canadian province in 1949, a post he held until 1972. Courtesy, Provincial Archives of Newfoundland and Labrador

CHAPTER TWO

NOVA SCOTIA

H O M E O F T H E B L U E N O S E

By Joan M. Payzant

In a small museum in Bayeux, Normandy, a 230-foot length of embroidered cloth known as the Bayeux Tapestry chronicles the Norman invasion of England by William the Conqueror in 1066. Another invasion was recorded in the same manner in this century when Lord Dulverton commissioned the "Overlord Embroidery." It is even longer than the Bayeux Tapestry, its 34 large panels telling the story of the Allied war effort during the Second World War. The work took 20 girls of the Royal School of Needlework five years to complete.

What a tapestry could be created from a chronicle of Nova Scotia's history! Almost surrounded by water, with the island of Cape Breton pointing its lobster-claw shape off to the northeast, the story could be told through pictures of the varied vessels that have plied its waters.

Such a tapestry would begin with the native Micmac Indians paddling their birchbark canoes through Nova Scotia's inland waterways and along its shores. On the next panel the Viking longboats with their dragon prows, striped sails, and fierce warriors could appear. Then the ships of early European explorers—carracks and caravels, high-sided, with square sterns and sails—that briefly touched our coasts: Prince Henry Sinclair, a Scot, in 1398 (whom Frederick J. Pohl, American historian, believes to be the man behind the legend of Glooscap); John Cabot in his 50-ton *Matthew*, who planted the English flag of St. Mark for King Henry VII in 1497; Estevan Gomez, a Portuguese in the employ of the King of Spain in 1524 to 1525; and Giovanni da Verrazano, on the 100-ton *Dauphine* for the King of France in 1524.

A fresh panel in this embroidered work could duplicate one of Samuel de Champlain's maps, drawn when he cruised along the south shore of Acadia (now Nova Scotia) in 1604, with Pierre du Guast, Sieur de Monts, looking for the best site at which to found the first French colony in this new land. The sturdy, wooden "Habitation" they built at Port Royal was the site from which the history of Nova Scotia's Acadian people began.

For the next century and a half, France, Scotland, and England vied for ownership of this new colony, their flags raised over little communities that struggled for existence. There would be plenty of scope for embroidery in re-creating

With a handsome lead over its competitors, the swift yacht Wave *(centre) is shown here crossing the bow of the majestic* St. George *(left) to win the Prince of Wales Cup in Halifax Harbour, Nova Scotia, in 1861. This annual regatta has maintained its popularity over the years and is still held today. Courtesy, Photograph Collection, Public Archives of Nova Scotia*

Pictorial Research by L.J. Payzant

45

those early flags, and the dominant one would have to be Nova Scotia's flag flying proudly today, granted with a charter and coat-of-arms by King Charles I to Sir William Alexander in 1625.

Great fleets of men-of-war depicting battles for supremacy in Acadia or Nova Scotia would make up a large part of the tapestry: the fleet that conquered Port Royal; the little sailing ships that carried Acadians at the time of their expulsion from their beloved homeland, scattering them along the coast of the 13 Colonies to the south; the ill-fated stragglers of the Duc D'Anville flotilla from France that limped into Bedford Basin; and the enormous British fleets that assembled in Halifax Harbour to besiege Louisbourg and Quebec, finally defeating the French in Canada.

Of course, the tapestry of shipping in Nova Scotia's history should not be entirely dominated by warships and battles. Vessels which carried new settlers to the province are fondly remembered today: the *Sphinx*, which brought Governor Edward Cornwallis to Halifax; the *Alderney*, which brought 353 settlers to Dartmouth; the *Anne*, with 300 Germans who eventually settled Lunenburg; the *Hector*, with the first Scots for Pictou; and the 25 ships with Loyalists for Port Roseway. Some of these ships may have previously been used as transports for troops. Later, swift schooners and brigs, crowded, squalid, and once used as slavers, brought the Scots of the Highland Clearances across the Atlantic to their new homeland.

Nova Scotia's long, jagged coastline, with its many harbours, coves, and bays, has provided its people with opportunities to earn their living at fishing, boat building, transportation by sea, and various marine occupations. The Germans of Lunenburg, the Loyalists of Shelburne, and the Scots of Pictou quickly excelled in boat building skills, and in these areas shipyards are still turning out fishing boats, ferries, and small coastal vessels for various duties at sea.

Certain of the early shipbuilders gained renown for some of their vessels. At New Glasgow, Captain George McKenzie built and launched his huge 1,444-ton ship, the *Hamilton Campbell Kidston*, in 1851; Donald McKay of Shelburne County moved to Boston, where he specialized in clipper ships. One of these, the *Sovereign of the Seas*, won a world record when it sailed from New York to Liverpool, England, in 13 days, 22 hours.

In addition, Maitland, on Cobequid Bay, has had its share of shipbuilding fame. It was there in 1872 that William Dawson Lawrence launched the largest square-rigged ship ever built in Canada, the *W.D. Lawrence*, almost 250 feet in length.

An entire panel would be needed to celebrate Samuel Cunard's shipping accomplishments. Born in Halifax, he first ran a coastal shipping business from

ABOVE: *Thought to be a possible relic of a Viking landfall near Yarmouth, this stone is now exhibited in the Yarmouth County Historical Museum. At one time a scholar translated the stone's runic characters as "Leif to Erik raises this monument." More recent experts, however, have cast some doubt on the stone's validity, but many still cling to the original belief. Courtesy, L.B. Jenson. From* Nova Scotia Sketchbook, *1969*

RIGHT: *The graceful flag of Nova Scotia was first used on the high seas when it flew at the masthead of many merchant ships. The design derives from the Ancient Arms granted in 1625, with the cross of St. Andrew extended in a rectangle. Courtesy, Nova Scotia Information Service*

that port, which rapidly expanded when steam propulsion guaranteed speedier delivery. Cunard won a contract with the British government to carry mail across the Atlantic with his four steam paddle-wheelers—the *Britannia, Caledonia, Columbia,* and *Acadia*—forerunners of many famous Cunard ships like the *Queen Mary, Queen Elizabeth,* and *QE2.*

It was the Smith and Rhuland Shipyard in Lunenburg from which the *Bluenose,* a fishing schooner, was launched in 1921. Designed by William Roue of Halifax and Dartmouth, and captained by Angus Walters, the *Bluenose* raced against American schooners, winning every time. The original *Bluenose* sank on a reef off Haiti in 1946, but today a replica built in the same yard carries Nova Scotia's flag to festivities around the province and to ports on the eastern seaboard.

Although the Age of Sail was one of prosperity for Nova Scotia, steamships, too, have played a vital role in its history, and should be included in the panels of the tapestry. Before the Second World War, great liners called regularly at Halifax. During both world wars convoys assembled in Bedford Basin and, escorted by ships of the Royal Navy and then the Royal Canadian Navy, crossed the treacherous North Atlantic where German U-boats lay in wait. The lifelines were kept open and Halifax played its part.

Smaller ports such as Sydney, Pictou, Lunenburg, Digby, and Shelburne had their share of naval vessels as well. During Britain's darkest hours, when the Germans threatened invasion, tentative plans were made to move the entire Royal Navy to Country Harbour on Nova Scotia's eastern shore, where it could have been entirely and safely accommodated.

Shipping magnate Samuel Cunard, pictured here circa 1840, was born to a Loyalist Halifax family in 1787. He established a successful shipping business with his father, transporting a variety of goods in sailing ships, and eventually ventured into whaling, trade in the West Indies, and mail transport to Newfoundland and Bermuda. The British government later awarded Cunard the contract to carry mail across the Atlantic by steamship. The Cunard Steamship Line is still in operation today. Courtesy, Photograph Collection, Public Archives of Nova Scotia

Today, yacht clubs are scattered around the province's shoreline, where Nova Scotians sail for pleasure and in keen competition locally and in Olympic races. In 1987, young sailor John Hughes completed a single-handed, round-the-world trip in his small sailboat, the sloop *Joseph Young.* He was following in the wake of an earlier Nova Scotian, Captain Joshua Slocum. Born in Annapolis County in 1844, Slocum set forth in 1895 in his small yawl-rigged *Spray* to sail around the world single-handedly, the first person ever to accomplish this feat. The voyage took him three years. In 1900, his book, *Sailing Alone Around the World,* was published. It is a classic, still in print.

The Tall Ships paid a visit to Nova Scotia's shores in 1984, and the NATO fleet adds colour to Halifax when ships' crews from many nations throng its streets. Scientific research ships from the Bedford Institute of Oceanography,

The Britannia *was the first of Samuel Cunard's fleet of steamships to carry trans-Atlantic mail. It made its 1840 maiden voyage from Liverpool to Halifax in about 12 days. Its sister ships were the* Acadia, Columbia, *and the* Caledonia, *named for Nova Scotia, the United States, and Scotland. In more recent days the Cunard fleet has included the* Queen Mary, Queen Elizabeth, *and the* Queen Elizabeth II. *Courtesy, Photograph Collection, Public Archives of Nova Scotia*

great unwieldy container ships, and huge tankers come and go, proof that Nova Scotians' seafaring days are far from over.

So it can clearly be seen what tremendous opportunities exist for expert needlewomen of the province to create a "Tapestry of Nova Scotia Sea Adventures." Perhaps those ladies who produce exhibitions of exquisite patchwork quilts will pick this as a theme, and we will one day see an auditorium filled with Nova Scotia's history in needlework.

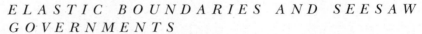

ELASTIC BOUNDARIES AND SEESAW GOVERNMENTS

No part of Canada had a more unstable beginning than the province we know today as Nova Scotia. From the time of its first governor in 1605, Pierre du Guast, Sieur de Monts, until Cape Breton was reclaimed by the mainland in 1820, Nova Scotia was governed at various times by the French, the Scots, and the English. Islands were added or subtracted, and so was the territory that today is the province of New Brunswick. Even the map makers of early days could not define the shape or name of this land called Acadia by the French, and Nova Scotia by the British.

Giovanni da Verrazano referred to the northeast coast of America as Arcadia. Variations of this have appeared on maps through the centuries—Arcadie, Acadie, and Acadia.

One of the earliest map makers, Bolognino Zaltieri of Venice, drew a very rough shape of North America in 1566, showing greatly distorted views of the St. Lawrence River and the Bay of Fundy. He labelled the land between the two waterways "Larcadia."

Three years later, in 1569, Dutchman Gerardus Mercator drew his version of North America. It gave a more realistic idea of the St. Lawrence, and for the first time Cape Breton appeared.

An Englishman, Luke Foxe, searching for the northwest passage to the Orient, produced his map in 1635, and although Nova Scotia and New Brunswick had begun to assume their familiar shapes, Cape Breton appears like a misplaced

piece of a jig-saw puzzle well to the south of the mainland.

Not surprisingly, Samuel de Champlain's 1612 map of Acadia, a result of his extensive explorations around its coasts during the days of the Habitation at Port Royal, more nearly resembles the present outline of the province than any of the previous maps. In addition he mentioned his landfalls with names still familiar today. By the time his 1632 map was published, Champlain had travelled widely in New France, and there were twice as many place names in Acadia—an indication of the growth of communities between 1612 and 1632.

The Habitation at Port Royal which began so successfully was destroyed in 1613 by Captain Samuel Argall from Virginia. This was the first of a series of struggles for possession of Acadia that went on for over a century. In 1629 a Scot, Sir William Alexander the Younger, sailed in company with Lord Ochiltree (Sir James Stewart) with the intention of setting up two Scottish colonies—one at Port Royal and the other at Baleine, Cape Breton. Neither colony was successful.

Alexander's ships went to Port Royal, which had been deserted by the French after Argall's attack. (The few French settlers who remained moved to Cape Sable.) The Scots' colony was short-lived because its benefactor, Charles I, in the 1632 Treaty of Saint Germain en Laye traded Port Royal back to France—much as small boys casually trade a pen knife for a few marbles. Shortly thereafter, Isaac de Razilly arrived at Port Royal with his new commission from the French king, and New Scotland came to an abrupt end.

Lord Ochiltree's settlement at Baleine in Cape Breton fared even worse, for it was attacked and destroyed by French Captain Charles Daniel just a few months after its founding in 1629. He took the Scots as prisoners to St. Ann's, and then across the Atlantic to Plymouth, where most of them were released. Lord Ochiltree, however, was imprisoned in France for two additional years.

De Razilly governed Acadia for three years until his death, when controversy

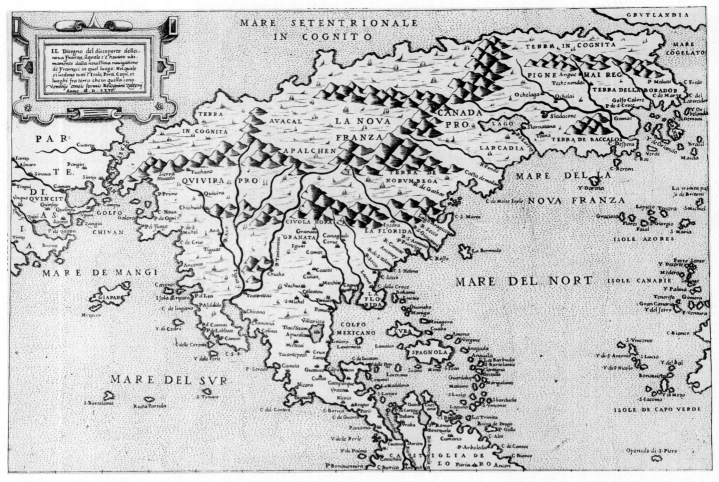

arose between two possible successors, each of whom had been granted charters by French kings at different times. These men were Charles La Tour, who had been in favour with the King in 1631, and D'Aulnay Charnisay, who inherited his rights directly from de Razilly.

A period of great instability followed, with struggles for power between French and French, and French and New Englanders, until the final capture of Port Royal by Colonel Francis Nicholson (governor of Virginia) in 1710. Then, by the Treaty of Utrecht in 1713, both the mainland and Newfoundland came under English rule. Prince Edward Island and Cape Breton Island were granted to the French. There was a great deal of doubt about the land beyond the Isthmus of Chignecto—in particular, just where the boundary of Acadia or Nova Scotia ended.

Port Royal was renamed Annapolis Royal in honour of Queen Anne. A few of the Acadians moved to French-owned Cape Breton, but most of them stayed

on their farms. In Cape Breton (known as Ile Royale by the French) plans were soon underway to build a large fortress at Louisbourg to guard both the island itself and French territory on the St. Lawrence River from further attacks by the British.

In 1737 a French priest, Abbé Jean-Louis Le Loutre, arrived in Nova Scotia as missionary to the Micmacs. However, he did not confine his activities to religious matters, and meddled in military affairs as well. From the French Fort Beauséjour, just inside what is now the New Brunswick border, he organized attacks on Annapolis Royal, incited Indian raids against the English, and dissuaded the Acadians from taking

the Oath of Allegiance to Queen Anne.

Fortress Louisbourg posed a tremendous threat to both Annapolis Royal and the colonies in New England; in 1745 New Englanders took matters in their own hands, attacking and capturing it to the surprise of the French. This enormous victory ended in a bitter blow for the colonies in 1748, however, when by the Treaty of Aix-la-Chapelle, England returned Cape Breton to France. Once again the French threat hung over Annapolis Royal and all English possessions along the Atlantic seaboard.

To counteract the menace of Fortress Louisbourg, Halifax was founded as the new capital of Nova Scotia in 1749. It was to be a military and naval stronghold as well. Initially the Acadians were helpful with its construction and in building a road to Minas. However, Abbé Le Loutre intervened and persuaded them not to be so co-operative, and once again urged them not to take the Oath of Allegiance. Further, he incited the Indians to make trouble, resulting in several bloody massacres. Finally, in desperation, Governor Charles Lawrence formulated a drastic plan: in 1755 he decided to expel the Acadians.

At the same time Governor William Shirley of Massachusetts had persuaded the secretary of state in England that Fort Beauséjour must be attacked and captured to rid the New England colonies of that threat—this was successfully accomplished in June 1755.

Meanwhile, Governor Charles Lawrence at Halifax chartered 17 transports from the firm of Apthorp and Hancock of Boston and sent them to Annapolis Royal, Minas, and Chignecto, where troops were stationed. The Acadians were given one last chance, but when they still refused to take the oath they were forced on board the vessels, and their homes were burned. Amid the confusion families were separated. The ships sailed south along the eastern seaboard, scattering the Acadian people at various ports in the 13 Colonies.

It was not until the end of the Seven Years' War in 1763 that some of the homesick Acadians made the long trek back to their homeland, where they dis-

This aerial photograph of the restored Fortress of Louisbourg shows the main entrance at the Dauphin Gate. To the upper right is the King's Bastion and barracks. The Spur Battery on the left guards the quay, behind which is the reconstructed village. Archaeological excavation, historical research, and concentration on accurate architectural detail have resulted in this impressive recreation of eighteenth-century Fortress Louisbourg. Courtesy, Canadian Parks Service, Fortress of Louisburg National Historic Park

C.W. Jefferys' artistic interpretation of the founding of Halifax in 1749 depicts a busy scene with a large fleet of sailing ships anchored in the harbour, and vigorous construction activity ashore. Notched logs are put to use for quick construction, and an armed guard keeps a wary eye out for possible enemies. Courtesy, Art Gallery of Ontario, Toronto

Although a peaceable people, the Acadians were expelled from Nova Scotia in 1755 in a desperate move by Governor Charles Lawrence. When they refused to take the Oath of Allegiance, swearing they would not take up arms against the English should another war with France occur, the Acadians were forced on board vessels and were shipped south along the eastern seaboard. This 1755 etching depicts a bedraggled group of Acadians being taken from their homes under the watchful eyes of British soldiers. Courtesy, National Archives of Canada

covered that their farmlands had been granted to the planters, or pre-Loyalists, who came to Nova Scotia from New England in 1760-1761. After finally agreeing to take the Oath of Allegiance, the Acadians were given new grants of land in the district of Clare in the southwest area of the province. The story of the expulsion of the Acadians has been romanticized in Henry Wadsworth Longfellow's long narrative poem, *Evangeline.*

At last, in 1758, came the final capture of Louisbourg by the British, followed a year later by the downfall of Quebec. The 1763 Treaty of Paris between France and England defined Nova Scotia to be what is today's province, with the addition of New Brunswick and Prince Edward Island. Six years later, Prince Edward Island was given its own separate government, and was no longer part of Nova Scotia.

While the latter half of the eighteenth century in Nova Scotia was anything but peaceful, more upheavals were yet to come, due to the American Revolution and the subsequent formation of the United States of America.

American colonists who kept their loyalty to the British monarchy emigrated northward. One group that went to Cape Breton founded Sydney in 1783, and a year later, that island (like Prince Edward Island) was given an independent government, with Sydney as its capital and Joseph Frederick Wallet Des Barres as lieutenant governor. A former army officer at the capture of Quebec, Des Barres perhaps is best known for *The Atlantic Neptune,* an artistically engraved survey of Nova Scotia's coastal waters used by British seamen for many years.

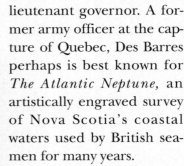

In 1820 Cape Breton was once again reclaimed as part of the province of Nova Scotia. A ferry service between Mulgrave and Point Tupper connected the island to the mainland

until 1955, when construction was completed on the Canso Causeway.

New Brunswick, too, had an influx of Loyalists at a time when boatloads of Europeans were also arriving on its shores. Like Cape Breton, in 1784 it was made a separate province, with the Isthmus of Chignecto making a convenient dividing line between it and Nova Scotia.

The first government at the new capital city of Halifax consisted of a governor and his appointed council. The early governors—Edward Cornwallis, Peregrine Thomas Hopson, and Charles Lawrence—were so involved with the settlement of Halifax and skirmishes with the French and Indians that they procrastinated about holding elections for a representative Assembly. However, in 1758, the year that Lawrence put on his brigadier's hat and sailed with Admiral Edward Boscawen to Louisbourg for its final capture, an election was held, and 22 men were chosen by ballot as the people's representatives in the Assembly—four from Halifax, two from Lunenburg, and 16 members at large. The tall stone Memorial Tower in Flemming Park on the Northwest Arm of Halifax commemorates this representative government, the first in Canada.

Many of the Loyalists who came to Nova Scotia were well-educated men who had formerly held positions of importance in the 13 Colonies. One was John Wentworth, previously governor of New Hampshire and surveyor general of the King's Woods. Wentworth was able to keep the latter position upon arrival in Nova Scotia, and in 1792 he was appointed lieutenant governor of the province. It was a colourful term of office; during those years Halifax played host to Prince William (later King William IV) and Edward, Duke of Kent, who later became

The architect for Nova Scotia's impressive Government House was Isaac Hildrith, a civil engineer who also did preliminary surveys for the Shubenacadie Canal. This early etching by John Elliott Woolford shows today's entrance on Barrington Street. The original entrance was located on the eastern side of the building facing Hollis Street. Government House was completed in 1805, and Lieutenant Governor Sir John Wentworth and Lady Wentworth were its first occupants. Built of Nova Scotia freestone, Government House was extensively renovated in the 1950s. Courtesy, National Archives of Canada

Queen Victoria's father.

Prince William visited Halifax from time to time on his ship, the HMS *Pegasus,* but the Duke of Kent's stay was longer due to his 1794 appointment as commander-in-chief of Nova Scotia, and he remained at Halifax until 1800. The lieutenant governor and his wife entertained both princes most royally, and it is partly because Lady Wentworth saw the need for a more regal Government House that Nova Scotia has the imposing residence on Barrington Street today. Its cornerstone was laid in 1800, and it took over five years to build, at a cost of about £30,000.

Children of Loyalists made their mark in the province as well. One was Joseph Howe, editor of the *Novascotian.* He deplored the fact that, in spite of having a representative government, the Executive Council was appointed for life by the lieutenant governor. So powerful was this body of men that it could simply veto legislation put forward by the Assembly if the legislation did not suit its purposes.

Howe first won notoriety when, in a libel case against his newspaper, he defended himself in court with a six-hour speech. He won his case, and also the case for free speech generally in the province. Following this success, he ran for office and, once elected, astutely guided the Reform party to defeat the overbearing Executive Council by a motion of non-confidence in 1848. Premier J.B. Uni-

Designed to house Nova Scotia's Legislative Council (or Upper House), this elegant room is usually referred to as the Red Chamber because of its colourful carpeting and upholstery. The room has been used for formal government receptions and meetings since the council voted itself out of existence in 1928. Courtesy, Nova Scotia Information Service

acke then chose a new council from his own party—the party in power—and the first responsible government in Canada was formed.

Howe was premier of Nova Scotia from 1860 to 1863, and was lieutenant governor for a brief three weeks when he died in office. A full-size bronze statue in the grounds of Province House shows Howe in a lifelike portrayal—right arm outstretched, left hand holding his lapel—his characteristic pose when giving an impassioned speech.

Today, a lieutenant governor, appointed by the governor general of Canada, is the Queen's representative in Nova Scotia. There are 52 seats in the Legislative Assembly, and the party with the majority of members forms the government. The leader of that party serves as premier and chooses as many members as he sees fit for the cabinet. The government may serve for five years before the premier must call another election. At present there are three active political parties in Nova Scotia—the Progressive Conservative, Liberal, and New Democrat parties.

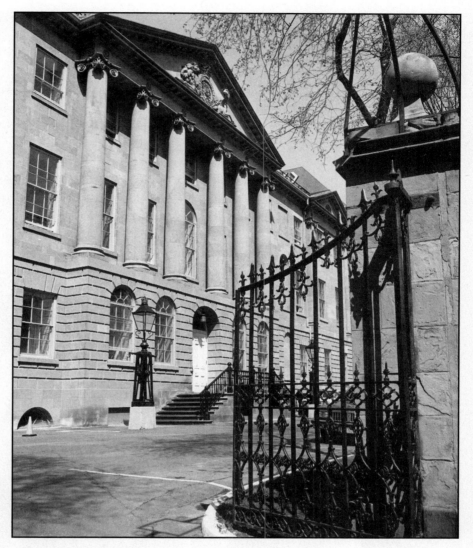

On August 12, 1811, the cornerstone of Province House was laid, but it was not until 1819 that it opened for the first sitting of the Legislature. The Hollis Street entrance with its semicircular drive is shown here. The lamp once stood on Waterloo Bridge in London, and the Ionic columns are surmounted by a gable end bearing a stone carving of Nova Scotia's coat-of-arms. Courtesy, Nova Scotia Information Service

The cabinet holds weekly meetings to discuss government business and the policies of its various departments. The entire Legislative Assembly meets once a year, usually beginning in February, and continues until the business of the session (which mainly consists of passing legislation) is finished.

Nova Scotia elects 11 members to the federal government House of Commons, and is represented in the Upper House by 10 senators.

Today, Nova Scotians and tourists find that the province's earliest and current seats of government prove to be fascinating places to visit. The replica of the Habitation at Port Royal draws thousands of visitors anxious to see the oldest European settlement in America north of the Gulf of Mexico, and which was once the capital of Acadia and Nova Scotia.

What a contrast it provides to the present capital city of Halifax, where Province House, home of the Legislature, has recently been beautifully restored by Nova Scotia craftsmen under the direction of English stonemasons. The building, a fine example of Adam architecture, was opened in 1819. When the government is in session, it is an impressive sight to sit in the Assembly chamber and reflect upon the history that has taken place there.

So, despite its often uncertain ownership through the years, and the exact extent of its boundaries, Nova Scotia today is a clearly defined Canadian province, with a democratic government which follows the principles of its model, the Parliament of Westminster.

A CULTURAL MOSAIC

Long before there were Micmac Indians in Nova Scotia, Paleo Indians wandered across the continent from Siberia following caribou herds. In 1963, at Debert, near Truro, archaeologists found stone tools belonging to these people that were said to be 11,000 years old.

Anthropologists have found evidence of ancient Indian villages in several Nova Scotia localities. One of the most recent discoveries was at Chegoggin near Yarmouth, the site of an archaeological dig in the summer of 1988. The village uncovered was said to be 4,000 years old.

By the time the first Europeans came to the area there were 35,000 to 40,000 Micmac Indians in what is now Nova Scotia. They spoke the Algonquian language

and lived by fishing and hunting, moving to the seacoast in the summer and back into the forest for the winter months. Their dwellings were lightweight birchbark wigwams, easily moved from one campsite to another. Birchbark was also used to make canoes and household utensils.

An excellent exhibit called "Elitekey: Micmac Material Culture from 1600 A.D. to the Present" was assembled by the Nova Scotia Museum in the early 1980s. Accompanied by a book of the same name, written by Ruth Holmes Whitehead, the exhibit travelled across Canada, showing the ingenuity of Micmac craftsmen. Examples of deerskin clothing with its fine embroidery, porcupine quillwork, decorative beadwork, and games made with bones gave a clear idea of the degree to which the culture of these native people had advanced.

When the French came to Port Royal in the early 1600s, friendly Micmacs educated them in the art of survival, showing them which wild berries and roots were edible, how to cure various ailments using herbs, and how to travel through deep snow on snowshoes.

Acadian priests converted many of the Micmac people to Roman Catholicism, but legends of the Indians' own god, Glooscap, have also survived to the present day—the subject of books, plays, puppet shows, and audio-visual productions.

Today most of Nova Scotia's Micmac people live on reservations in Hants County or on Cape Breton Island. Others have moved to urban areas. Their total population has dwindled to just over 5,000. Unemployment is a problem on the reservations, but there are successful business and professional people, university graduates, competent craftsmen, writers, and musicians who keep alive the proud heritage of the native people of Nova Scotia.

The earliest French settlements in the province had little success because of wars with the English. The first truly successful colonization effort was that of Isaac de Razilly, who brought 300 settlers to La Have. At de Razilly's death, his successor, D'Aulnay Charnisay, moved this settlement to Port Royal. From there, the Acadians gradually spread along the Annapolis Valley to Grand Pré, Minas (Horton), Piziquid (Windsor), Cobequid (Truro), Chignecto near Fort Beauséjour, and Tatamagouche. They built dikes and cultivated marshlands, eventually developing fine farms. It is estimated that by the time of the expulsion the Acadian population had grown to 10,000.

About 6,000 Acadians were deported to the 13 Colonies. Some escaped the deportation by fleeing into the woods, and others went to Cape Breton, which was still under French control. There they settled in the villages of St. Peter's, St. Ann's, Boularderie, and Louisbourg.

At the end of the Seven Years' War some of the homesick and deported Acadians made the long trek back to Nova Scotia from the 13 Colonies to settle on what is often referred to as "the French Shore," along the coast of Digby and Yarmouth counties. There are pockets of Acadians elsewhere, too, at Chezzetcook, Havre Boucher, Isle Madam, Cheticamp, Boularderie, and L'Ardoise.

The first large immigration of English settlers came when Halifax was founded in 1749. Their leader, Governor Edward Cornwallis, was not impressed with the abilities of the 2,500 inhabitants of the new capital, most of whom were discharged sailors and soldiers unacquainted with the skills needed for farming, fishing, or construction.

Between 1750 and 1753 a better equipped and more industrious group of settlers arrived—Germans and foreign Protestants. These people lived for a time in Halifax's north end, and on what was later called the Dutch Village Road on the western side of town. In 1753 they gathered together under command of Colonel Charles Lawrence and boarded 14 sailing ships to found a new town on the south shore—Lunenburg. These "Deutsch" people farmed, fished, learned the boat building trade, and eventually established one of the greatest fishing ports on the Atlantic seaboard.

After the capture of Louisbourg, Governor Lawrence was anxious to promote more immigration to Nova Scotia, so by various means he contacted New Englanders, offering free land (some of which included the fine agricultural land formerly occupied by the Acadians) to those who would settle in the province. The idea appealed to hundreds of families, and in 1760 and 1761 a total of about 5,000 of these "pre-Loyalists" sailed to ports along the south shore and the Bay of

OPPOSITE: Three of Nova Scotia's native Micmac Indian women are pictured here inside a birchbark wigwam, while outside at the water's edge, Indian men are seen by a birchbark canoe. Micmac wigwams and canoes were easily transported from one site to another because of their lightweight construction. Courtesy, Photograph Collection, Public Archives of Nova Scotia

Fundy. Those who came to farm were known as "planters," and they settled on Acadian lands in Annapolis, Cornwallis, Grand Pré, Horton, and Windsor. Fishermen chose to settle on the coast, resulting in the founding of communities on the south shore such as Yarmouth, Barrington, Liverpool, and Chester. Interestingly, some of these people were descendants of Americans who came over on the *Mayflower,* and today they are members of the Society of Mayflower Descendants.

Colonel Alexander McNutt, an emigrant agent, persuaded Presbyterian Irish from Ulster to settle near Truro and Londonderry in 1760, and they were joined by New Englanders with Irish roots. About the same time English settlers from Yorkshire came to Chignecto to take up grants of land on former Acadian farms there.

Because of Nova Scotia's name, flag, and coat-of-arms, there is a tendency to think of the province as being largely settled by Scots. However, after the failure of Sir William Alexander's colony at Port Royal and Lord Ochiltree's at Baleine, the next boatload of Scots did not arrive until 1773. In that year the *Hector* put in to Pictou Harbour after a miserable 11-week voyage from Scotland, carrying about 200 settlers. Many Nova Scotians trace their family's arrival in the province back to the *Hector,* much as do the *Mayflower* passengers' descendants in the United States.

During the Highland Clearances in Scotland (when English landlords drove people off the crofts and filled the land with more profitable and less bothersome sheep), hundreds of Scots flocked to Nova Scotia, settling in Pictou, Colchester, Antigonish, and Cape Breton. Many of this latter group kept their Gaelic language and customs alive in the Cape Breton Highlands.

Next came another wave of displaced people—United Empire Loyalists during the American Revolution. Over 22,000 Loyalists arrived in Nova Scotia between 1776 and 1783.

The Loyalists made their new homes throughout the province, swelling recently settled communities beyond their capacity to cope with the influx. Num-

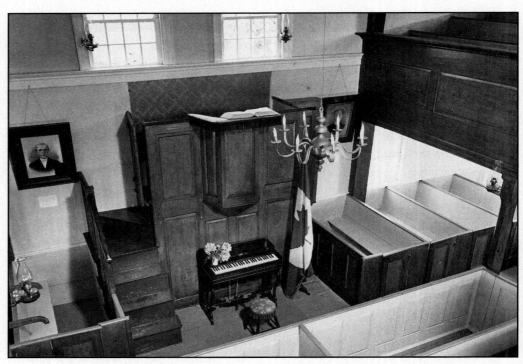

Located at the head of Chedabucto Bay, the waterfront village of Guysborough was founded by Nicholas Denys in 1654, but later fell to New Englanders in 1690. This beautiful engraving by E. Haberer depicts Guysborough in 1872—nearly 100 years after its Loyalist settlement in 1783. Courtesy, National Library of Canada

bers of them went to Guysborough County, where there had been French settlements in the 1600s. The most ambitious undertaking was the founding of Shelburne by 10,000 refugees, making it the second-largest settlement in all of British North America. However, it quickly diminished in number when the Loyalists discovered what a hard life lay ahead of them. Most of them were well educated—government officials, soldiers, professors, doctors, lawyers, engineers, ministers, accountants—and quite unable to deal with the problems of clearing land, building homes, farming, and fishing. Shelburne soon became almost a ghost town, as these people moved to Halifax or other towns in the province. Some went back to New England, while others crossed the Atlantic to England. However, the newcomers who did stay in Nova Scotia became leaders in their communities and many were elected to government positions.

About 1,600 Loyalists were blacks, most of them free men who had fought for the British. A few came with their masters as slaves or servants. The blacks were not given the same opportunities as the white Loyalists, with the result that when they were offered the chance to sail to Sierra Leone to found a new colony there, 1,200 of them left.

Another group of blacks came in 1796 when 500 Maroons from Jamaica were brought to Halifax and were given work improving the fort on Citadel Hill. The Maroons, too, chose to leave and settle in Sierra Leone after a relatively short stay in the province.

In 1802 a ship with almost 300 Scottish immigrants arrived in Sydney Harbour, the first of many such arrivals. The development of mining and a steel mill in Sydney attracted immigrants from Poland, the Ukraine, Italy, and the West Indies, and blacks from the southern United States.

The last major immigration of blacks occurred during the War of 1812, when about 2,000 came from the Chesapeake Bay area, mostly former slaves escaped from the United States on British warships. On their arrival in Nova Scotia they were given poor land, mostly in Halifax, Digby, Guysborough, and Hants counties. Today their descendants are scattered throughout the province, but the largest number live in Preston, a settlement originally laid out as a model New England township by Governor John Wentworth's Loyalist surveyor-friend, Theophilus Chamberlain.

During World War II, Nova Scotia welcomed Jewish refugees. After the war, farmers from the Netherlands settled throughout the province. Since then, at multicultural events, citizens have become aware of a dramatic rise in the numbers of people from Hungary, India, Pakistan, Lebanon, China, and African countries. Many of these people come to attend universities or teach in them. Their children attend public schools, adding colour (and competition) to classrooms which formerly were largely composed of pupils with British backgrounds.

Throughout the year, but especially in summer during the tourist season, almost every community in the province holds a festival of some kind. Many of these reflect the ethnic background of the community, and draw people of the same background to the celebrations. For instance there is the Glooscap Festival at Five Islands, and the Micmac Annual Pow Wow in Halifax. Acadian festivals take place in Halifax-Dartmouth, Wedgeport, Clare, L'Ardoise, Cheticamp, West Pubnico, Petit-de-Grat, and Pomquet.

At Bridgetown the Black Power Rendezvous takes place, and a Children's Festival is held at the Black Cultural Center in Westphal. Historic events are celebrated, like the Loyalist Garden Party at Shelburne, and the Sacking of Annapolis Royal at that memorable site. Scottish festivities include the Nova Scotia Tattoo in Halifax, Ceilidhs in Cape Breton, and Highland Game Days at Halifax, Antigonish, and Middleton.

Among the many popular sporting activities available in early Nova Scotia was the prominent sport of rowing. This lively illustration by E. J. Russell depicts the Digby races on July 10, 1872. Spectators lined up in rowboats to cheer the contestants who had come from as far away as Saint John, New Brunswick, to compete in the regatta. Courtesy, National Library of Canada

Each year there is a huge Multicultural Festival in the Halifax Metro area, with entertainment provided by groups representing many lands, while the aroma of exotic food from foreign cuisines lures visitors to sample their products.

Futhermore, there are chicken barbecues; cider, maple syrup, apple blossom, strawberry, and blueberry festivals; lobster, codfish, Solomon Gundy, and planked salmon suppers; horse pulls and ox pulls; a herring choker's picnic; and chowder challenges. All of these festivals make Nova Scotia a lively place for its citizens whether they be native Micmacs, 10th-generation Acadians, or newly arrived from India. Nova Scotia truly can be called a province of great ethnic diversity.

FOOD FOR THE MIND — RELIGIOUS AND SECULAR

When Samuel de Champlain and the Sieur de Monts first set out for Acadia in 1604, Champlain expressed concern that religion would cause difficulties in any settlement they might establish because de Monts was Protestant—a Huguenot and follower of John Calvin. Only six years previously, in 1598, Huguenots had been granted a degree of religious and political freedom in France by the Edict of Nantes, but feelings still ran high between Roman Catholics and Protestants. Although the problems Champlain envisioned did not occur immediately, his words were truly prophetic. From 1713 until the mid-1800s Nova Scotia was wracked by strife, at the root of which was religious discord.

In Acadia's earliest days, Jesuit and Recollet priests established missions, chiefly to convert the native Indians to Christianity. In 1610, 25 Indians were baptized at Port Royal along with their 100-year-old chief, Membertou. As new villages such as La Have, Minas, and Beaubassin came into existence, chapels were built and priests arrived to take care of their parishioners' spiritual and educational needs.

In 1633 Capuchin monks established a school for Indian boys at La Have. Before 1640 it was moved to Port Royal, after which Acadian boys were admitted as well, with the hope that their "more civilized" ways would serve as examples for the Indians. This idea proved too difficult to administer, and before long only Acadian pupils remained. A second school was established for girls, but both buildings were destroyed during skirmishes with the English in 1654.

From that time until the expulsion in 1755, education had a low priority in Acadian villages because of the constant threat of English attacks as well as the daily struggle for existence on isolated farms. In his work *L'enseignement,* Lionel Groulx wrote that the French king reminded the priests in 1665 that "The education of children is the principal duty of the fathers." This was all very well until the English captured Port Royal in 1710. After that time, the missionary priests allowed to remain were given new orders by their French monarchs, who sent them extra money with instructions to keep alive the Acadians' and Indians' love and loyalty to France and to preach hatred for the English conquerors.

Two French missionary priests in particular were active in this regard: Father Sebastian Rasle, a Jesuit whose chapel was at Norridgewock (now in Maine, but then part of Acadia), who rallied Abenaki, Malecite, and Micmac Indians to attack Annapolis Royal; and Abbé Jean-Louis Le Loutre, mentioned previously, who interfered so determinedly with the English settlement at Halifax. Major Paul Mascarene, president of the council at Annapolis Royal (and incidentally, a Huguenot) blamed Le Loutre for all of the troubles in Nova Scotia in 1746. Gov-

OPPOSITE: Even the military provided entertaining diversions for the sporting crowd of Halifax. A tented encampment and ladies with parasols indicate a shooting demonstration or contest is being held at the Bedford Rifle Range in this 1871 illustration. Courtesy, National Library of Canada

ernor Edward Cornwallis agreed, calling Le Loutre "a good for nothing scoundrel as ever lived."

There were peaceable French priests, however. The English allowed the Acadians to have their own churches at Annapolis, Cobequid, Piziquid, Minas, and Canard. Priests were supplied by the Bishop of Quebec, but before they were permitted to officiate or move from one parish to another they had to be approved by the Nova Scotian governor and the council at Annapolis Royal.

There was a chapel at Louisbourg (still under French control), and nuns kept both a day school and boarding school in the town. Like other priests, Antoine Simon Maillard, vicar general of Louisbourg and missionary to the Indians of Cape Breton and the mainland, initially urged his flock to harrass the English. But after the final capture of Louisbourg in 1758, he made peace with the English and urged the Acadians and Indians under his aegis to do likewise. Abbé Maillard spent his last years as priest to the Indians and Acadians in the vicinity of Halifax, where he died in 1762, well respected by Catholics and Protestants alike.

When Halifax was founded in 1749, shortly after the Battle of Culloden, the new government there was still influenced by the violent anti-Catholic bigotry that had been fanned by the Jacobite Rebellion. Added to the remembrance of that event was the fear of Roman Catholic settlers joining forces with the French in the event of war. The result was that the government at Halifax was every bit as strongly allied with the Church of England as were church and state in London.

Built in 1787 by the Reverend Ranna Cossit, the first Protestant minister assigned to permanent duty in Cape Breton, Cossit House is believed to be the oldest house in Sydney. It is one of many historic houses preserved, furnished, and operated through the assistance of the Nova Scotia Museum. Courtesy, Nova Scotia Information Service

It quickly became obvious which denomination would control the ecclesiastical and educational life of the province.

By 1750 St. Paul's Anglican Church in Halifax was open for services, with dissenters allowed its use until their own churches were built. Mathers Congregational Church, Hollis Street, opened soon after, and the "Little Dutch Church" (St. George's Lutheran) opened in 1755. It was built on Brunswick Street to accommodate the Germans who came with the foreign Protestants. Some of them had already moved to Lunenburg, where St. John's Anglican Church (built in 1754) became the second-oldest Protestant church in Canada. One of its early preachers was Rev. Jean Baptiste Moreau, who gave his services in English, German, or French, as the occasion warranted. Bridgewater's first church appeared that same year, originally serving all denominations; eventually, it was bought by the Baptists.

In England, the Anglican Society for the Propagation of the Gospel (S.P.G.) sent teachers to Halifax, Lunenburg, and Annapolis Royal, paying them a small stipend to set up schools in those towns. In 1766 Nova Scotia's first Education Act stated in part, "All teachers must be examined and approved by members of local clergy" (i.e., Church of England). It went even further to proclaim that "if any popish recusant, papist or person professing the popish religion, shall be so presumptive as to set up any school within this province, and be detected therein, such offender shall, for every such offence, suffer three months' imprisonment without bail or mainprize, and shall pay a fine to the King of ten pounds."

This edict created great dismay in Acadian parts of the province, as it resulted in fewer and fewer Acadians receiving any schooling whatsoever. Priests did what they could, but there were not many of them and their parishes were large. All rural communities had scanty educational opportunities, but the Acadian problem was unique due to their religion.

Soon after this, the arrival of pre-Loyalists and then Loyalists created the need for churches and schools in previously unsettled areas of the province, as well as in Cape Breton, which had recently formed its own government. New reli-

Truly founded upon a rock, St. John's Anglican Church stands on the solid granite that makes up much of well-known Peggy's Cove. Murals inside the church depict a local scene and an image of Christ calming the sea. They were both painted by William deGarthe, one of Canada's foremost marine artists, whose home was in Peggy's Cove. Courtesy, Nova Scotia Department of Tourism and Culture

gious groups appeared—Methodists in Halifax, Quakers in Dartmouth, Sandemanians in Preston, and New Light adherents in the Annapolis Valley and rural Nova Scotia. Churches, many of which are valued heritage buildings today, were constructed to accommodate the new communities: Barrington's Meeting House; Lower Granville's Meeting House, where the Baptist Association of Nova Scotia was organized in 1811; the Covenanters' Church at Grand Pré; and Anglican Churches in Shelburne, Sydney, Digby, and Middleton.

Irish Catholic immigrants naturally desired churches of their own, but even as late as 1780 Abbé Bailly (whose church in Halifax was strictly for the use of Acadians and Indians) was ordered to bar the door against Irish Catholics.

Laws against Roman Catholics were unbelievably restrictive—they were not allowed to own property, to vote, to build churches, or to sit in the Legislature. By 1784 these restrictions were eased somewhat, resulting in the construction of the first small St. Peter's Church in Halifax, today the site of St. Mary's Basilica.

The late eighteenth century was an extremely active period in the province for both religious and educational matters. Many clergymen worked in two capacities, spending their weekdays as schoolmasters or in efforts to create centres of learning for their flock. Five such men have become legendary figures for their cultural leadership at this time: Charles Inglis, D.D.; Abbé Jean-Mande

Signogne; Father Edmund Burke; Rev. Thomas McCulloch; and Rev. Norman MacLeod.

Charles Inglis, D.D., arrived in Halifax in 1787, having been appointed the first Anglican Bishop of the province. Soon after his arrival plans were made for the construction of King's Collegiate School, which was founded in Windsor and was followed by King's College in 1790. When in 1802 the latter became, by royal charter, a much needed degree-granting college, the general public was incensed to learn that "no member of the University shall frequent the Romish Mass or the meeting houses of Presbyterians, Baptists, or Methodists etc., or where Divine Service shall not be performed according to the liturgy of the Church of England." King's College, alas, was only for those of the Anglican faith.

Abbé Jean-Mande Signogne, known today as the "Apostle of the Acadians," was the only priest in southwest Nova Scotia for 20 years from the time of his arrival in 1799. He imbued his Acadian parishioners with a sense of self-esteem and pride of race, which they had lost at the time of their expulsion. Through a system of volunteer catechists he worked diligently to educate them, established a boarding school for boys at his rectory, and never flagged in his efforts to improve their living conditions.

Another notable priest was Father Edmund Burke (appointed first Roman Catholic Bishop of Nova Scotia in 1818), under whose guidance educational opportunities for Catholic children were begun, despite opposition from the government. He was a humanitarian, noted especially for his generosity to the oppressed. Shortly before his death in 1820, Bishop Burke laid the cornerstone of St. Mary's Cathedral.

Dalhousie University in Halifax has been educating students since Lieutenant Governor of the Province, Lord Dalhousie, laid the first cornerstone in 1820. Photo by Janet Dwyer/First Light

Meanwhile, in Pictou and Cape Breton large immigrations of Scots were inspired by such giants of Presbyterian clergymen as Dr. Thomas McCulloch and Rev. Norman MacLeod, who did far more than simply preach on Sundays. McCulloch's Pictou Academy and MacLeod's school at St. Ann's were examples of the Scottish reverence for education, and the determination of clergymen and parents alike to give the best possible grounding to their children. McCulloch's Pictou Academy graduated a phenomenal number of Nova Scotians who became leaders all across Canada, and McCulloch himself was appointed first president of Dalhousie College in 1838.

Gradually, over the years, education acts brought schools in the province to their present excellent standard. In 1808 an act encouraged the establishment of schools in every community. In 1811, 12 grammar schools were established. By 1832, elementary schools were compulsory in all villages. In 1833 there were reportedly 23 combined grammar and common schools in which instruction was given in classics and higher branches of knowledge. In 1841, a welcome act for the Acadian population ordered that any schools where instruction took place in French, Gaelic, or German become as equally entitled as English-speaking schools to funds from the government. And in 1864, Sir Charles Tupper's government passed the Free School Act, after which schools were supported by taxation.

Acadians were still having problems, because teacher training at the Normal College in Truro (established in 1855) was entirely in English, as were standard text books. Good French-speaking teachers, therefore, were very scarce. In 1882, "Royal Readers" were issued in French, and a 1902 Acadian Education Commission recommended further changes. These took years to be properly implemented, but today there are Acadian schools in French-speaking areas of the province, as well as in traditionally English-speaking areas to which French families have moved.

The province is also well served with consolidated high schools. Instead of small, one-room schools that previously served each little community, groups of communities co-operated to build larger schools to which students are bused. Consolidated high schools have the same advantages as urban high schools—good teachers, gymnasiums, libraries, and laboratory facilities. Vocational schools and institutes of technology (now called campuses of the community college) are located in all major communities, providing alternatives to university education.

Controversial King's College, Windsor, was eventually joined by others not so narrow in religious outlook. In May 1820, Lieutenant Governor of the Province, Lord Dalhousie, laid the cornerstone of Dalhousie College, saying, "Its doors will be open to all who profess the Christian religion. It is particularly intended for those who are excluded from Windsor." Today, of course, that too would be a narrow outlook, because in our shrinking world Dalhousie University's students include many who are not Christians. It is the major university of the province, offering a wide variety of undergraduate degrees as well as post-graduate degrees in the faculties of medicine, law, and dentistry.

Acadia College in Wolfville was founded in 1838. It is open to all, but does have a theological department for the training of Baptist ministers. Mount Allison College, with its Methodist tradition, opened its doors in 1840, just across the border in Sackville, New Brunswick.

That same year, in 1840, St. Mary's Seminary in Halifax began training young men for the priesthood. In 1970 it became an independent university located on its present south end campus. Another Roman Catholic university began in much the same way when St. Francis Xavier College first opened in Arichat, Cape Breton, in 1853; it moved to Antigonish in 1855. Today the College of Cape Breton and Nova Scotia Eastern Institute of Technology operate as satellites of St. Francis Xavier University. One of its faculty members, Dr. M.M. Coady, brought the university global recognition with his promotion of adult education courses, co-operatives, and credit unions.

Mount St. Vincent Academy, begun by the Sisters of Charity in 1873 in Rockingham, just outside of Halifax, is now Mount St. Vincent University. With a broad curriculum, it specializes in helping mature women to return to the work force.

Other important degree-granting universities in the province are the Atlantic School of Theology (founded in 1878 as Pine Hill Divinity Hall for the education of Presbyterian ministers), now graduating Anglican, Roman Catholic, and United Church clergymen; the Nova Scotia Agricultural College in Truro, founded in 1885; the Nova Scotia College of Art and Design, formerly the Victoria School of Art and Design, founded in 1887; and the Nova Scotia Technical College (now Technical University of Nova Scotia), founded in 1907.

Special mention must be made of Nova Scotia's bilingual facility, the Univer-

The many ports and harbours of Nova Scotia have played a major role in the province's industry and trade. Pictured here in this engraving by E. Haberer, which appeared in the Canadian Illustrated News *on May 20, 1871, is the International Coal Company shipping pier at Sydney, Cape Breton. Note the barge loaded with coal and the square-rigged ships awaiting their cargo. Courtesy, National Library of Canada*

sité Sainte-Anne, founded by the Eudist Order in 1890 at Church Point. It was incorporated as a degree granting institution in 1893, and gained university status in 1978. The first class of teachers graduating in the teacher training course emerged in 1974, ending the difficulty in obtaining good instruction for Acadian students in Clare, Argyle, and on Cape Breton Island. Located near the university is beautiful St. Mary's Church, built in 1905 and said to be the largest wooden church in North America. It is pleasing to think that the dedicated work of Abbé Jean-Mande Signogne in the eighteenth century has had this satisfying result.

Today in Nova Scotia there are many religious groups, and tolerance has replaced narrow-minded bigotry. Tradition often channels students to attend colleges founded on the faith of their fathers, but a spirit of ecumenism is evident in the fact that the province's universities are open to all. Students today are more likely to select a school that offers a degree in their chosen discipline rather than be influenced by its one-time religious affiliation. King's College, Windsor, which was originally such a disappointment to young dissenters in the province, marked its 200th anniversary in 1989. However, its founding had initiated an enthusiasm for educational institutions that culminated in the excellent facilities available to all students throughout Nova Scotia today.

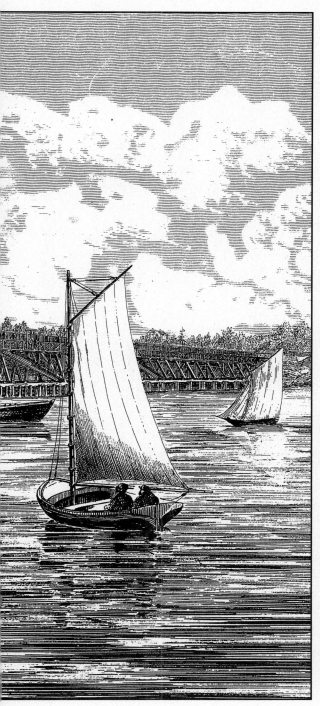

INDUSTRY, TRADE, AND COMMERCE

When the Acadians settled at Port Royal in 1605 they quickly took advantage of the friendliness of the Micmac Indians to learn the secrets of adapting to their new environment. Dressed in deerskins, Nova Scotia's native people were hunters and fishermen who survived on the bounties provided to them by nature throughout the year.

In *Acadia, the Geography of Early Nova Scotia to 1760,* Andrew Hall Clark wrote that one of the earliest French missionaries to the Indians, Father Biard, left a record of the Micmacs' seasonal activities.

In January they hunted seals; from February to mid-March their quarries were beaver, otter, bear, moose, and caribou; fishing season began in mid-March when smelt, herring, shad, sturgeon, and salmon were plentiful; and in the summer and early autumn months their diet consisted of birds and their eggs (especially pigeons and partridge), rabbits, hares, codfish, beechnuts, roots, and berries.

Another author, Laurie Lacey, in *Micmac Medicine—A Traditional Way of Health,* has documented a great variety of remedies from natural sources used to treat all manner of illnesses. The Acadians adopted these Indian methods of

The Acadian settlers of the early 1600s established their gardens near Port Royal at Lequille, where they grew their precious crops of grain. A grist mill was soon built to help grind the grain, making for more efficient productivity. This replica of the mill is the result of the imaginative 1967 Centennial project of the Nova Scotia Light & Power Company. No longer a functioning mill, this structure now houses a modern hydro-electric power plant. Courtesy, Nova Scotia Information Service

survival, and, in turn, their culture was introduced to the Micmacs. This led to trading: Indian furs for Acadian cloth; birds' eggs for beads; salmon for bread.

The marshy land along the Annapolis River and the Bay of Fundy was similar to diked farmland in parts of France, so the Acadians were able to convert this rich soil into arable growing areas. By 1686 it is estimated that there were 60 to 70 Acadian farms, growing wheat, peas, maize, hemp, flax, oats, barley, rye, cabbages, beets, and carrots. Apple and cherry trees had been brought from France, as well as animals and poultry—cattle, sheep, pigs, horses, hens, geese, and pigeons.

By 1755 the population around the Bay of Fundy was estimated at 10,000. Industries and crafts necessary for the daily life of each community had sprung up—carpentry and blacksmith shops, grist mills, saw mills, tanneries, and cobbler shops. Active trading took place between Acadia, New England, Louisbourg, and the West Indies.

Louisbourg, founded after the Treaty of Utrecht (1713) near the mouth of the St. Lawrence River, was closer to France than to Quebec and gradually became a trading centre of note. Christopher Moore, in *The Other Louisbourg*, reported that its codfish trade was worth three times Canada's (Quebec's) annual fur trade. Consequently, a merchant community developed with codfish as the exchange medium. As Louisbourg merchants grew ever more prosperous they were able to invest in their own ships, further increasing their trading ability. Soldiers from the fortress discovered coal seams in Port Morien, and thus started an industry which became the mainstay of the Cape Breton economy.

At the Public Archives of Nova Scotia, there is a copy of a letter addressed to the Earl of Macclesfield in England signed anonymously, "The Author"—an obvious enthusiast about the possibilities offered to colonists settling in Nova Scotia, "the nearest part of the American continent to any part

The railroad was an important aspect of Nova Scotia's economic growth in the 1800s, providing an efficient mode of transportation for the province's goods and products. Here, a Sydney & Louisbourg Railway train traverses the Mira River near Sydney and Glace Bay. Built for the railway and completed in the mid-1870s, this bridge boasted a centre section which lifted to accommodate the passage of ships. Courtesy, National Library of Canada

of Europe." The letter is undated, but appears to have been written shortly after the American Revolution.

"The Author" wrote that although the weather was sometimes cold, there was "abundant wood, coal and turf to warm the houses," even though "a want of labourers makes cutting and transport of wood and coal difficult." He described the crops grown, saying that the marshlands were "not exceeded by any in the world in point of richness and fertility." Next he told of the plentiful fish in rivers, lakes, and on the coasts—coasts free of ice before those of any other province. Lumber was available both for the construction of houses and public buildings, and for the past four or five years it had been used for masts. As for minerals, he listed silver, copper, iron and coal, grindstone, clay for bricks, tiles, and pottery works, and limestone for plaster of Paris.

For most of the latter half of the eighteenth century Nova Scotia was in turmoil. The expulsion of the Acadians, the final attacks on Louisbourg and Quebec, the arrival of the pre-Loyalists and Loyalists, the Napoleonic wars of 1793-1814, and the War of 1812 created a buzz of activity in the provincial capital of Halifax; this did not allow for efficient administration of the remainder of the province, or serene conditions for trade with the United States, England, and the West Indies.

At this time ship owners in the province reaped the benefits of this unrest by using their vessels as privateers. Nova Scotians like Simeon Perkins, Enos Collins, Joshua Mauger, Michael Francklin, and Malachi Salter became extremely wealthy, and were sometimes called upon to act as unofficial bankers. The first official bank, the Halifax Banking Company (now the Canadian Imperial Bank of Commerce), opened in 1825 in Enos Collins' Halifax building where Historic Properties is located today. The Bank of Nova Scotia followed in 1832. Many of the shareholders were men who had made their fortunes in privateering.

The pre-Loyalist "planters," who had been granted Acadian farmlands after the expulsion, repaired and maintained the original dikes and carried on with the mixed farming and orchards started by the Acadians. Gradually immigrants drifted to other good farming areas in the province: the Shubenacadie and Musquodoboit River valleys; sections of Yarmouth and Digby counties; the north shores of Cumberland, Colchester, and Pictou counties; and parts of Queens, Lunenburg, Antigonish, Inverness, and Cape Breton counties.

In the beginning settlers were only able to do subsistence farming. As they cleared land, they sold cut timber, resulting in combined farming-lumbering

incomes. Along the coasts, where rocky conditions made farming backbreaking work, it was often supplemented by fishing. Poor roads made transportation to markets difficult, but small coastal schooners provided an alternate means of delivery as well as transportation. In 1818 an Agricultural Society was formed, with Lieutenant Governor, Lord Dalhousie, as its president. Gradually more scientific methods of farming were adopted, resulting in higher yields.

Although family farms are still found throughout the province, large dairy and poultry farms, fruit orchards in the Annapolis Valley, and modern beef and hog producing operations are responsible for the bulk of agricultural income today.

Mining has been an important factor in Nova Scotia's economy ever since the first discovery of coal at Port Morien. Coalfields were also mined in Cumberland and Pictou counties, but by the 1980s they were nearly exhausted. Large deposits still exist in Cape Breton in the Sydney-Glace Bay area. For a short time in the 1970s it was feared that all coal mines would be shut down because of competition from oil. However, the worldwide panic that ensued when OPEC declared crude oil to be in short supply, artificially raising its price, created a new demand for coal. In 1986, 71 percent of Nova Scotia's electrical power was thermally generated, and in 1988 plans were announced to build an additional thermal power station adjacent to the Prince Mine at Point Aconi. The new Phalen

Some 500 feet from the main slope, these miners operate a core driller in an underground shaft at the Malagash Salt Mine in 1929. Courtesy, Nova Scotia Department of Mines and Energy

These miners worked above ground in the shaft house of the Baltimore and Nova Scotia Mining Company's gold mine at Caribou, Halifax County, around the turn of the century. Courtesy, Nova Scotia Department of Mines and Energy

Mine (near the Lingan Mine) in Cape Breton broke all former production records in 1988, yielding 1.8 million tonnes of coal.

Ever since farmer Peter Murray accidentally drilled a well of salt water, salt has been produced in great quantities in the province, first from a mine at Malagash in 1918. When it ceased operating in 1959, the present Pugwash mine replaced it, producing 1,000 tons of salt each day. At Nappan, the brine method of producing salt has been in operation since 1947.

The year 1860 marked the exciting discovery of gold. For many years gold mining was a thriving industry, and from time to time as new methods of extracting it are developed enthusiasm rides high once more—but all too often these schemes come to naught. According to *Gold in Nova Scotia* by Jennifer L.E. Bates, by 1982 nearly 1.2 million ounces of gold had been produced in the province.

Gypsum has been found in many areas, but today the largest supply comes from Hants and Inverness counties. It is shipped to the United States, where it is manufactured into wallboard, plaster of Paris, fertilizer, chalk, and paints. In 1988 plans were announced to locate an American-owned industry at Point Tupper to produce a special type of wallboard in which paper would strengthen the board internally rather than as a cover.

Extensive exploration for undersea oil and gas deposits took place off the Atlantic Coast of Nova Scotia starting in the late 1950s, and for a short while visions of future prosperity seemed about to come true. However, when world oil prices dropped, the high cost of recovering oil and gas from the offshore made the prospect unfeasible at present. The promising Venture gasfields off Sable Island were put on hold in 1988 and, according to the Atlantic Provinces Economic Council, "development of these reserves must await a suitable mixture of quite high and stable oil prices."

Many other types of minerals and construction materials have been found in the province. In addition to the ones already mentioned, those still in production are tin, limestone, dolomite, barite, celestite, clay, sandstone, granite, sand, and gravel.

There were fishing stations in Nova Scotia even before the founding of Port Royal in 1605, and the fishery has remained a vital part of the economy ever since. In sailing ships, and then in motorized craft of various sizes, Nova Scotia fishermen have landed enormous catches of cod, herring, haddock, mackerel, halibut, Atlantic salmon, and other less popular and remunerative species. Shellfish like lobster, scallops, shrimp, crab, and clams are becoming more and more popular, as dieticians and the health professions emphasize the benefits of low-fat diets. Modern refrigeration technology, too, has created a demand for frozen processed fish, while air cargo makes possible shipments of fresh fish to distant markets.

The discovery of gold in 1860 prompted a new and thriving industry in Nova Scotia. This detailed drawing depicts the gold mining settlement at Tangier in the late 1860s. Courtesy, Nova Scotia Department of Mines and Energy

Unfortunately, there is controversy and conflict in the fishing industry because of the imposition of quotas to prevent overfishing, as well as jealous rivalry between inshore and offshore fleets. At the same time, because of the demand for seafood more Nova Scotians are interested in participating in the industry. Intelligent and careful planning and negotiation will be needed to solve these problems.

Forest industries have always been important to Nova Scotia, at first largely for construction of buildings and ships, and for firewood. Sugar maple trees were valuable to supply early settlers with a sweetening agent. The mining industry created a need for pit props both within the province and for export. Pulp and paper making made further demands on the forests and is the biggest sector of the resource today. The Christmas tree business also thrives, with many growers profiting from exports to the United States.

Nova Scotia's famed wooden sailing ships gradually disappeared from its coastlines as steam power replaced canvas, and gasoline engines became common in smaller fishing boats. Industries in the province embraced steam power as well. From the mid-1800s foundries and machine shops in Yarmouth, Liverpool, Lunenburg, Halifax, and Dartmouth built steam engines and placed them in wooden-hulled ships. At the Nova Scotia Iron Works William Montgomery contracted to build 10 locomotives for the Intercolonial Railway. Every town had factories producing such items as lumber, footwear, furniture, wire, barrels and boxes, sashes and doors, carriages, pulp and paper, ships, woollen goods, rope, skates, harnesses, brushes, molasses, and sugar.

At the turn of the century, the huge steel industry in Sydney brought hundreds of immigrants to Cape Breton, and gave employment to a large work force in that area. By 1967, when fuel oil cut seriously into profits from the coal mines, the steel industry was also running into financial difficulties, partly because of its aging plant. Two crown corporations, Devco and Sysco, were formed to assist the coal and steel industries. Coal has since made a comeback, but after a short-lived recovery the steel plant proved to be an enormous drain on both federal and provincial funds. Between 1967 and 1988, $1.5 billion of government funds were sunk in efforts to rescue it. Now, in a do-or-die decision, $110 million is scheduled for Phase II of the plant's final modernization. Unfortunately, this will be at the cost of some job losses.

The Port Royal Habitation is a fun and exciting replica of Nova Scotia's first settlement. Photo by John Elk III

Many of the early industries that created vitality throughout the province disappeared through the latter half of the nineteenth century and the first half of the twentieth century due to various causes—the end of reciprocity with the United States in 1866, the emphasis Confederation placed on east-west trade, the increase in freight rates, competition with products from Quebec and Ontario, World War I, the Great Depression, and World War II. But today industry is making a comeback. Instead of foundries and shoe factories, almost every city, town, and district of any size has an industrial park. Incentive programs by federal and provincial governments have been responsible in encouraging entrepreneurs to develop a variety of new endeavours. While some of these, such as Clairtone and two heavy water plants in Cape Breton, have been failures,

others like Michelin and Volvo have succeeded and recently expanded their operations. Stil others—Novatron, Pratt and Whitney, and Litton Systems—are welcome new additions.

By 1986 manufacturing accounted for 12 to 13 percent of all employment in Nova Scotia. Industries included fish processing, pulp and paper, refineries, shipbuilding and repairing, steel rail manufacture, and tire production, along with many smaller endeavours. A good percentage of these latter industries involve high-technology projects.

Now, at the beginning of the Free Trade Agreement between Canada and the United States, it remains to be seen whether the outcome will be beneficial or detrimental to Nova Scotian industry. There are hopes that the prosperity of the mid-1800s will return to the province, with a greater volume of exports moving southward to large American markets.

Other significant influences on Nova Scotia's economy include: military bases throughout the province; service industries (N.S. Power Corporation, Maritime Telephone and Telegraph, radio and television stations, financial institutions, and merchandising outlets); professional services (i.e., medical, legal, engineering, and educational services); and government offices.

Nova Scotia's tourism industry has grown significantly in the 1970s and 1980s. In 1988 it was valued at $760 million. The province's main attractions are its magnificent scenery, the friendliness of its people, and its plentiful lakes and beaches. But more significant than all of these may be its colourful and lengthy history and the current enthusiasm for the study of genealogy. In the past, young Nova Scotians by the thousands have left their homes in search of employment, and today they and their descendants flock back to the province to visit the homes of their ancestors and to search for their roots. Here they find historical riches preserved in every corner of the land, for Nova Scotians are deeply aware of the value of their heritage in this storied province.

Sherbrooke Village transports visitors back to the lively time between 1860 and 1880, depicting the lives of early Nova Scotians. Photo by John Elk III

PRESERVING THE PAST, LOOKING TO THE FUTURE

Along Nova Scotia's jagged coastline there is scarcely a community which does not have a museum to commemorate some aspect of the province's history. From the first settlement at Port Royal, where a replica of the Habitation draws thousands of visitors each year, to the great Fortress of Louisbourg (the largest historical reconstruction project in Canada), every period of Nova Scotia's story has been well documented and preserved.

Yarmouth County Historical Society Museum is custodian of one of the most mysterious relics—a runic stone, found in Yarmouth County, which hints at the possibility of a Viking visit to Nova Scotia in the days of Leif Erikson. Micmac life is depicted in the Nova Scotia Museum in Halifax, as well as in small community museums, with displays of early tools, clothing, rock drawings, and other artifacts. Acadian life is remembered at the Nicholas Denys Museum at St. Peter's, La Vielle Maison at Meteghan, the Acadian Museum at West Pubnico, Le Musee Ste. Marie at Church Point, and at Grand Pré National Park.

Fort Anne, Windsor's old fort and blockhouse, and Halifax's Citadel (all with accompanying museums) survive as witnesses to the French-English struggle for domination of the province. The turbulent days that followed the captures of Louisbourg and Quebec are documented in the diary of Simeon Perkins of Liverpool. In his home there, preserved beside the Queens County Museum, Perkins wrote of the American Revolution, the arrival of British Empire Loyalists in Nova Scotia, and the privateering days of the south shore.

His diary has been published by the Champlain Society and is a remarkable historical record of early life in Nova Scotia.

Other memorials to this period of the province's history are the Covenanter's Church in Grand Pré, the Old Meeting House in Barrington, the County Museum and Ross-Thompson House in Shelburne, and the Quaker Whaler's House in Dartmouth. In Westphal, just outside Dartmouth, the Black Cultural Center tells the story of three separate black migrations to Nova Scotia, and of the continuing efforts of these people to establish themselves in their communities.

Under the aegis of the Nova Scotia Museum, historic homes throughout the province have been preserved and furnished according to their periods. They now reflect the lives of distinguished owners such as Attorney General Richard John Uniacke of Mount Uniacke; Judge Thomas Chandler Haliburton, creator of "Sam Slick," in Windsor; horticulturist Charles Prescott in Starr's Point; Rev. Thomas McCulloch, founder of Pictou Academy, in Pictou; and Rev. Ranna Cossit, who lived in what is now Sydney's oldest house.

In Baddeck, near the site of Alexander Graham Bell's summer home, the Aerial Experiment Association constructed the "Silver Dart," which made the first airplane flight in the British Empire on February 23, 1909. Today the mag-

The great Fortress of Louisbourg is Canada's largest historical reconstruction project. Photo by John Elk III

nificent Alexander Graham Bell Museum at Baddeck has exceptionally fine displays of early telephones, kites, plans for aviation and hydrofoil experiments, and a complete reproduction of the HD-4, Bell's successful hydrofoil craft.

The Maritime Museum of the Atlantic in Halifax touches upon all facets of Nova Scotia's involvement with the sea—fishing craft, pleasure boats, sailing ships, marine propulsion, ocean liners, naval vessels, and a preserved marine hardware shop complete with the aroma of tarred marlin. Restored ships are open to the public in the summer at the adjoining wharf.

This is not the only museum to depict the lives of working Nova Scotians. Sherbrooke Village has 20 buildings that take visitors back to the period between 1860 and 1880, showing an old post office and various shops at a time when that village was busy with lumbering, shipbuilding, and gold mining.

The Fisheries Museum at Lunenburg with its typical ships—a schooner, rumrunner, and dragger—brings to life the work of Lunenburg fishermen, and its aquarium displays the marine life of Nova Scotia's coasts.

At New Ross a working farm shows agricultural life in the nineteenth century at the Ross Farm Museum. The former workaday worlds of people throughout the province are demonstrated for visitors at miners' museums, a working water mill at Balmoral, a steam-powered saw mill at Denmark, a woollen mill at Barrington, and the Dean Wile carding mill at Bridgewater. A

Firefighters' Museum is at Yarmouth, and in the near future the Museum of Trades, Industry and Transportation will open its doors at Stellarton.

These are only some of the 124 museums listed in "Museums in Nova Scotia, 1981," a booklet published by the Nova Scotia Museum.

The Public Archives of Nova Scotia gives information and pleasure to thousands of Nova Scotians and out-of-province visitors each year. It features an extensive library, historical documents of all types, a vast newspaper collection, photographs, maps, charts, and a film library. The current enthusiasm for the study of genealogy as people search for their roots has been facilitated by microfilming of provincial and church records by the Church of the Latter-day Saints.

In June 1981 Nova Scotia's first provincial Heritage Property Act was passed, and since then several municipalities have formed Heritage Advisory Committees to register buildings of historical or architectural importance. As citizens realize the beauty and individuality of architecture throughout the province, enthusiasm is gradually growing in regard to our built heritage and the importance of preserving it for Nova Scotia's future generations.

Lest it be thought that the future of Nova Scotia is jeopardized by such keen interest in the preservation of the past, such is definitely not the case. In addition to the many universities in the province there are several research institutes where workers strive continually to solve the scientific problems of tomorrow. The Bedford Institute of Oceanography, a branch of the National Research Council, and the Nova Scotia Research Foundation are located in the Halifax-Dartmouth area. Dr. William B. Hamilton wrote in his book, *The Nova Scotia Traveller:*

Probably few visitors who stroll the Dalhousie campus or visit the Bedford Institute of Oceanography realize that the Twin Cities rank second to San Diego in North America in oceanographic research, or that all of the scientific investigation, inquiry, and research taken together makes the Halifax-Dartmouth area the third-largest scientific community in Canada, outranked only by Ottawa and Toronto.

At present the Nova Scotia government is actively working to improve environmental conditions. Scientists and engineers are making plans to treat the sewage that has run from surrounding communities directly into Halifax Harbour since their founding. The problems caused by acid rain, which affects vegetation and kills the fish in rivers, are being addressed, as are factors thought to destroy the ozone layer in the atmosphere.

These hopeful signs for the environmental future of the province correspond to the optimism presently felt regarding its economy as a result of free trade with the United States. With its temperate climate, natural resources, growing economy, proud history, varied scenery, and hardy people, Nova Scotia is blessed with so many advantages that future years can only continue to witness its growth.

This chapter on Nova Scotia began with an imaginary tapestry illustrating the glorious history of the province. At the turn of the twenty-first century, let us hope that environmental and economic conditions will have so greatly improved that needlewomen working on a contemporary panel will be able to create the most exquisitely embroidered scene of all to mark the anniversary of the province's first 400 years.

Early settlers were greeted with the radiating dawn light in their new homeland—a vision which still greets their descendants today. Photo by John de Visser/Masterfile

ABOVE: This charming church serves the coastal community of Canso—a settlement which dates back to the 1700s and the early years of Nova Scotia history. Photo by Mark Burnham/First Light

OPPOSITE: Today's Atlantic Provinces are rich with Acadian heritage. Photo by Greg Stott/Masterfile

85

ABOVE: An expert diver and underwater swimmer, the Atlantic Puffin is a brightly-coloured northern sea bird. Photo by Dawn Goss/First Light

LEFT: Splashes of autumn colour adorn the banks of New Brunswick's Shogomoc River. Photo by J.A. Kraulis/Masterfile

ABOVE: Winter settles over the rural port of South Rustico, Prince Edward Island. Photo by Barrett & Mac-Kay/Masterfile

OPPOSITE: Some traditional methods of food preservation and preparation are still in use today, such as this bright red shed used for smoking herring on Grand Manan Island, New Brunswick. Photo by Stephen Homer/First Light

ABOVE: The blush of cold winter air highlights the pink faces of these lively Newfoundland youngsters. Photo by Brian Milne/First Light

LEFT: These gleeful children proudly show their potato harvest, gathered from the rich farmland of Prince Edward Island. Photo by Brian Milne/First Light

FAR LEFT: Clam digging is a favourite seaside activity for those who enjoy the warm sun and wet feet. This group selected Malpeque Bay on Prince Edward Island for the day's dig. Photo by Lorraine C. Parow/First Light

ABOVE: This charming home in Cavendish, Prince Edward Island, was the inspiration for the internationally acclaimed Anne of Green Gables, written by Lucy Maud Montgomery in 1908. Photo by John Elk III

TOP: Laundry day in Petite Forte, Newfoundland, adds a touch of colour to the quiet afternoon scene. Photo by Stephen Homer/First Light

RIGHT: The Salem & Hillsborough Railroad traverses the New Brunswick country-side. Photo by John Elk III

ABOVE: The Celtic Lodge near the coastal community of Ingonish offers comfortable accomodations for those visiting the Cape Breton Highlands National Park in Nova Scotia. Photo by John Elk III

OPPOSITE: Agriculture still plays a crucial role in New Brunswick's economy. Photo by Brian Milne/First Light

ABOVE: Canoe making is a time-honoured tradition, still practiced in the Atlantic Provinces today. Photo by Stephen Homer/First Light

LEFT: The morning sun dawns bright over these Nova Scotian lobster traps. Photo by Ted Grant/Masterfile

OPPOSITE: Graceful sand dunes melt into the sea at Brackley Beach on Prince Edward Island. Photo by Jessie Parker/First Light

ABOVE: Moncton is a picturesque centre of business and industry in New Brunswick. Photo by John Elk III

LEFT: Charlottetown is the capital of Prince Edward Island and the most populated city on the Island. Photo by Barrett & MacKay/Masterfile

ABOVE: Low tide uncovers the ancient beach caves of St. Martins, New Brunswick. Photo by Jessie Parker/First Light

TOP: Sunbathers enjoy the sun and surf at Parlee Beach, New Brunswick. Photo by J. Gregory Dill/Sky Photo

RIGHT: Morning mist settles over Gros Morne National Park in Newfoundland, recalling the tranquil beauty of days past when Indians walked the land. Photo by Stephen Homer/FirstLight

ABOVE: Artist Kimberley Whitchurch and her vivid chalk drawings add a touch of colour to the streets of Halifax, Nova Scotia. Photo by Dawn Goss/First Light

RIGHT: Organ grinder John Witteveen and his frisky companion, "Susie," delight and entertain the people of Halifax, Nova Scotia. Photo by Dawn Goss/First Light

FAR RIGHT: The dramatic growth of Halifax is reflected in the harbour waters. Photo by J. Gregory Dill/Sky Photo

Nova Scotia's rugged coast-line is dotted with many har-bours, coves, and bays. Photo by Devries Mikkelsen/First Light

A Cape Breton fisherman prepares his net as the sun rises over the Gulf of St. Lawrence. Photo by Lorraine C. Parow/First Light

NEW BRUNSWICK
WATERWAYS TO THE WORLD

By Greg Marquis

Wedged between the Gulf of St. Lawrence and the state of Maine and capped by Quebec's Gaspé peninsula lies the province known since 1784 as New Brunswick. At present it contains just over 700,000 people. It is a difficult place to romanticize. The land is rugged, hardly a farmer's dream, and the climate, if not severe, is character-building. Physically, New Brunswick covers close to 30,000 square miles, much of it forest. As late as 1935, four of the largest counties consisted almost entirely of Crown Lands—timber land owned by the provincial government. Geography explains in large measure why the province will probably never develop the intense provincial loyalty that characterizes its Atlantic Canada neighbours. New Brunswick is dominated by two major river systems, the Saint John and the Miramichi; one flows into the Bay of Fundy, the other into the Gulf of St. Lawrence.

As the pioneer age passed, it became evident that two societies were growing within one political jurisdiction. The automobile, modern highways, and the mass media have not really counteracted this dualism. The southern society, oriented toward the Bay of Fundy and the Saint John watershed, has tended to be more populous, more urban, more wealthy, and more politically important than the sparsely settled northern society. The south developed as largely English speaking and Protestant, in contrast to the mainly Acadian and Roman Catholic north and northwest. (The dividing line runs diagonally from northwest to southeast.) The Miramichi, a region on the east coast containing a major river system of the same name, included a significant non-Acadian presence but it was definitely "northern." Thus the population has been divided by region, language, religion, and access to the levels of political and economic power.

New Brunswick is the only officially bilingual province. Section 16 (2) of *The Constitution Act of 1982* states: "English and French are the official languages of New Brunswick and have equality of status and equal rights and privileges as to their use in all institutions of the legislature and the government of New Brunswick." This occasionally uneasy dualism makes the province unique in Canada.

EARLY HISTORY
Although many New Brunswickers identify the Loyalists as the Founding Fathers,

---

The quaint and colonial aspects of Fredericton, the capital of New Brunswick, are well-rendered in this J.W. Giles lithograph from 1834. The city came alive during the winter months when the Legislature was in session. A highlight of the season was a ball sponsored by the governor. Courtesy, New Brunswick Museum

Pictorial Research by Peter Larocque

Micmac and Maliseet women frequently sold their crafts on the streets of Saint John and Fredericton in the 1800s. Renowned for quality, their baskets, brooms, and moccasins were often awarded prizes at agricultural exhibitions, which were held in the province after 1842. This John Stanton painting depicts the typical dress of native New Brunswickers in the mid-1800s. Courtesy, New Brunswick Museum

archaeologists have uncovered evidence of human activity going back 10,000 years. Stone tools and ancient campsites suggest that prehistoric people arrived from the south in search of caribou and other game animals. These small bands were not settlers but migratory hunters and gatherers, harvesting the resources of the forests and sea. The submerging coastline of the prehistoric period covered up most of their campsites and burial grounds, but evidence from neighbouring Maine makes it plausible that New Brunswick was visited by the Red Paint people, a seafaring culture that ranged between New England and Labrador until its disappearance 3,500 years ago. Later Ceramic period sites (2,500 to 1,500 years ago) have been found in both the northern and southern areas of the province.

At the time of European contact, circa A.D. 1500, the native inhabitants continued in their nomadic lifestyle of hunting, fishing, and gathering. With the exception of corn, there is little evidence that agriculture—one of the prerequisites of permanent civilization—was developed to any significant degree. The two major groups of Eastern Woodlands peoples in the area were the Micmac, who inhabited Nova Scotia and eastern and northern New Brunswick, and the linguistically related Maliseet, living to the south and the west, particularly in the Saint John and St. Croix valleys.

The native peoples used the rivers and lakes as their highways, and because personal or group wealth was not a priority, left behind no major buildings. The forest was both resource base and spiritual force. Clans or family groups practiced shamanism, a religion based on the notion that hunters, animals, and inanimate objects were part of a seamless web based on respect. The concept that individuals or clans could own land in the European sense was unknown. Together with the Abenaki of Maine, these cultures were the true masters of the region north of the Bay of Fundy until the eighteenth century.

For reasons that are not yet clear, native peoples and European visitors of the early colonial period enjoyed peaceful relations. Immense economic, social, and biological change resulted from the interaction of the aboriginal people and the newcomers. This interaction was largely negative for the Micmac and Maliseet

The indigenous peoples of New Brunswick produced many fine crafts. This place mat was made from porcupine quills woven into a birchbark backing. The motifs and design are typically Micmac Indian in origin. Courtesy, New Brunswick Museum

in the long run, and much of it, for example the impact of deadly European diseases, is not well documented. Portuguese explorers, cruising the coasts from Florida to Newfoundland, entered the Bay of Fundy as early as the 1520s. The Micmac word for codfish, *bacolos,* was adopted from the Portuguese, which says a lot about the concentration of European fishing activity in the area. Contact with seasonal European fishermen gave rise to a fur trade, first as a novelty, then as a large-scale business, that threatened to revolutionize aboriginal political relations and living standards.

By the early 1600s the Micmac had forced the Maliseet to move farther to the north and west and were challenging the Abenaki confederacy for control of European trade goods flowing to the west and furs coming from the interior. The native peoples overhunted furbearing animals and became increasingly dependent upon European tools, clothing, firearms, alcohol, and even imported food, and probably suffered periodic devastating population losses by epidemic disease.

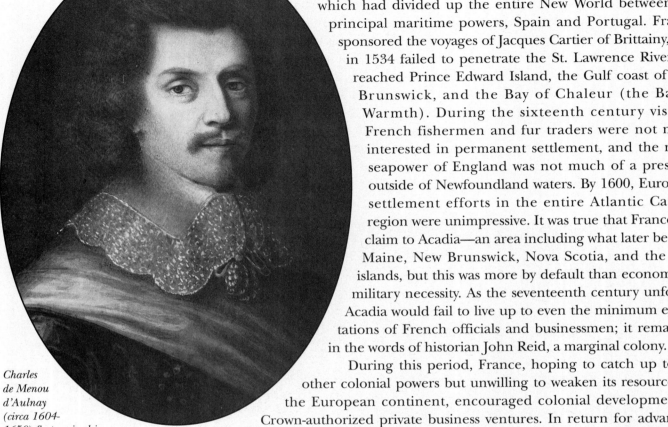

Charles de Menou d'Aulnay (circa 1604-1650) first arrived in Acadia in 1642 to serve as lieutenant to the governor. His duties made him responsible for much of the trade between the region and France. Responsible for the recapture of forts held by the English, d'Aulnay was appointed governor in 1647 as a reward for his successful ventures. Courtesy, New Brunswick Museum

THE FRENCH ERA

French activity in the region picked up after King Francis I convinced Pope Clement VII to modify a fifteenth-century treaty which had divided up the entire New World between the principal maritime powers, Spain and Portugal. Francis sponsored the voyages of Jacques Cartier of Brittainy, who in 1534 failed to penetrate the St. Lawrence River but reached Prince Edward Island, the Gulf coast of New Brunswick, and the Bay of Chaleur (the Bay of Warmth). During the sixteenth century visiting French fishermen and fur traders were not much interested in permanent settlement, and the rising seapower of England was not much of a presence outside of Newfoundland waters. By 1600, European settlement efforts in the entire Atlantic Canada region were unimpressive. It was true that France laid claim to Acadia—an area including what later became Maine, New Brunswick, Nova Scotia, and the Gulf islands, but this was more by default than economic or military necessity. As the seventeenth century unfolded Acadia would fail to live up to even the minimum expectations of French officials and businessmen; it remained, in the words of historian John Reid, a marginal colony.

During this period, France, hoping to catch up to the other colonial powers but unwilling to weaken its resources on the European continent, encouraged colonial development by Crown-authorized private business ventures. In return for advancing the interests of France, even if it meant merely showing the flag, nobleman Pierre du Guast, Sieur de Monts, in 1603 was granted a 10-year fur monopoly in Acadia. The first French settlement in New Brunswick, and one of the earliest European settlements in North America, was established on an island in the St. Croix River the next year. The men involved were not pioneering settlers hoping to build a new society but employees and members of a trading company who worked for wages or profits. The major accomplishment of the St. Croix Habitation was surviving the first winter, as nearly half of the employees died of scurvy, and facilitating the exploratory voyages of Samuel de Champlain, the famous navigator, cartographer, and author. The de Monts operation relocated to Port Royal, in the Annapolis Valley of Nova Scotia, in 1605. These early colonists included Roman Catholics as well as Huguenots—Protestants who were later officially excluded from Acadia.

Champlain soon departed for the St. Lawrence valley, where he launched the basis of the colony of New France. Acadia clung to its precarious existence; not only was it vulnerable to the dictates of nature, but also to intrigues at the French Court, the rising commercial and military power of New England to the south, and the infighting of French traders and fishermen. The Jesuit Order, which had already reached China and Japan, arrived in the Bay of Fundy region in 1611. The Catholic missions to the Micmac and Maliseet may partly explain the relatively good relations between the French and the native peoples; as well, the French and the Indians did not compete for land in Acadia, and thus there was less tension as compared to the New England frontier. The missionary effort extended up the Saint John and into Maine, encouraging the Jesuits to found a splinter colony near Mount Desert Island.

Following destructive raids by Samuel Argall of the Virginia Company, the long-term viability of Acadia was far from assured. It was, according to American historian Francis Parkman, "a wretched little colony," sustained by friendly native peoples, visiting fishing vessels, and, particularly by the 1630s, trade with the enemy, New England.

The Bay of Fundy and Gulf of St. Lawrence regions during the century and a half following the failure of the Habitation were the site of a diplomatic, commercial, and military struggle pitting Great Britain and New England against France and New France. Acadia and its small European population (a number of colonists were brought in during the seventeenth century) were of interest to officials at Versailles and Quebec because of strategic reasons and the potential of having the Micmac and Maliseet as allies against New England. New Englanders coveted the fisheries and fur trade of the Fundy region but were not interested in actually occupying Acadia. In the decades of struggle that ensued, the Saint John River was a potential military highway and Catholic missionaries served as political agents of the French Crown in western Acadia. Although the economic potential of the area was not insignificant, it was more valuable as a buffer zone between France and England in America than as a settlement colony. The small Acadian population developed as a border people.

Following the confirmation of French rights in Acadia by treaty in 1632, France's presence in the area continued to be minimal. Within a few years a struggle among French businessmen would bring more official attention to the colony. In the 1640s two rivals, Charles de la Tour, operating from his fort at the mouth of the Saint John, and Charles d'Aulnay, based at Port Royal, literally battled for commercial supremacy. Although a number of artisans, labourers, and families arrived from France in this period, the quarrel did little to advance the colony. D'Aulnay attempted to enforce a trading monopoly by destroying the fishing stations and posts of interlopers. La Tour, the chief French power in western Acadia, proved more adept than his rival in securing assistance from the Puritans of Massachusetts Bay. In 1643, with Massachusetts' support, he broke d'Aulnay's blockade of Fort la Tour and raided Port Royal. As every New Brunswick gradeschool student knows, d'Aulnay eventually captured Fort la Tour, despite the heroism of its commander, Madame la Tour, and executed the garrison. Madame la Tour soon died, according to legend, of a broken heart. Her widower had the last laugh by marrying d'Aulnay's widow in 1650 in order to consolidate his position in Acadia.

By this time, although Massachusetts fishermen dominated the Bay of Fundy, New England exhibited

After arriving in the New World in 1636, Jeanne Motin married Charles de Menou d'Aulnay, with whom she had eight children. After her husband's death in 1650, she attempted to maintain control of the properties d'Aulnay had held as governor. Unable to do so, a marriage of convenience with Charles de St. Etienne de la Tour was soon arranged. She is pictured here in costume as Bellona, the Goddess of War, after her marriage to la Tour. Courtesy, New Brunswick Museum

few territorial ambitions in the area; its traders were more than obliged by French middlemen. In 1654, however, the New Englanders drove the French military and trading presence out of the Fundy region and Acadia was run as an economic colony of Boston for the next 16 years. The new "governor," Massachusetts merchant Thomas Temple, extended his commercial stranglehold by building a trading post at Jemseg on the Saint John. Although the region was returned to French control in 1670 through the peculiarities of European diplomacy, the Bay of Fundy (*Baie Française* to the French) remained an English lake and Acadian posts at Pentagouet (Maine) and Jemseg proved vulnerable to attack. Indeed, an attack occurred in 1674, although from an improbable source: Jurriaen Aernoutsz, an officer in the Dutch navy, raided the post at Jemseg as part of a pillaging operation.

THE ACADIAN DILEMMA

During the next stage of Anglo-French conflict in America, King William's War (1689-1697), western Acadia became contested territory. Most of the fighting on this frontier was done by the Abenaki with the connivance of French officers, as the Acadians had little to do with the war. The French commander on the Saint John, with bases at Nashwaak and Jemseg, was Joseph Robinau de Villebon. Before the war had ended the French had repulsed an English attack at Fort Nashwaak, and had scored a major victory at the English strongpoint in Maine, Fort William Henry. The fort fell to the Sieur d'Iberville (the French Canadian officer who caused the English so much grief in Newfoundland and Hudson's Bay) and Acadian Indian allies. By spreading panic and anti-Catholic and anti-French sentiment along the New England frontier, these conflicts and the brutalities of Indian warfare placed the relatively inactive Acadian population in jeopardy.

Several years later, when the War of the Spanish Succession (1701-1713) erupted, the French, who had been claiming the Kennebecasis River as their western border, evacuated the Saint John. The Treaty of Utrecht (1713) ceded Acadia, with the exception of Isle Royale (Cape Breton) and Île Saint-Jean (Prince Edward Island) to the British, who attempted to found the new colony of Nova Scotia. The French, ever conscious of the strategic value of the New England-New Brunswick frontier, did not recognize the enemy claim to the territory north of the Bay of Fundy. They continued to lay claim to this wilderness while the British were confined to peninsular Nova Scotia, which contained the bulk of the Acadian population. A number of Acadian families had moved north to Chipoudy (Shepody), Petcoudiak (Petitcodiac), Memramcou (Memramcook), Gédaique (Shediac), and Cocagne, but most of the Acadians of Nova Scotia were loathe to leave their farms and start anew in French territory. Although they would enjoy three decades of peace, the sensitive nature of the Chignecto Isthmus border area and the question of the Acadians' ultimate loyalties made their situation precarious.

During the 30 years peace (1713-1744), officials in New France put pressure on the New England and Nova Scotia frontiers by supplying and remaining on good terms with the native peoples of Acadia and Maine. These Indians had good reason to remain friendly with the French, as New England had expanded into Maine, and, by 1750, the British had expanded into Nova Scotia. One result of this "secret war" was the establishment of a Catholic chapel at St. Anne's, the present site of Fredericton. By this time Acadia was of purely strategic value to the French authorities; few French officials were troubled by the fate of the Acadians. When the War of the Austrian Succession broke out in 1744, the French, operating out of Louisbourg, took the initiative in Atlantic Canada but once again the native peoples did most of the fighting on the frontier. The Treaty of Aix-la-Chapelle (1748) returned the captured fortress of Louisbourg to France but did little to persuade the Nova Scotia Acadians to swear unconditional loyalty to the British Crown. A new British base at Halifax and a new policy of sealing the frontier with Acadia indicated that a major showdown was in the works. New France, having opened up communications with the Saint John via Riviere-du-Loup and Lake Temiscouta, continued its secret war.

By 1751 the Chignecto Isthmus was militarized, with the French in possession of Fort Beauséjour to the east and Fort Gaspereaux at Baie Verte. Officers of New France forcibly removed Acadian families from Beaubassin, Nova Scotia, to

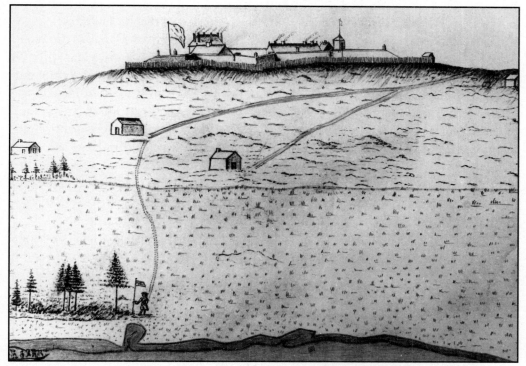

Built by the French between 1751 and 1755, under orders of de la Jonquiere, Fort Beauséjour was attacked by a combined British-New England expedition even before it was completed. The English force under the command of Colonel Robert Monckton captured the fort after French reinforcements failed to arrive from Louisbourg. The fort was renamed Fort Cumberland and withstood an attack by Colonel Jonathan Eddy during the American Revolution. Courtesy, New Brunswick Museum

north of Beauséjour. Nearby, the British maintained Fort Lawrence, from which they hoped to disrupt communications between the bulk of the Acadians and the French to the north and on Isle Royale. Following the outbreak of the Seven Years' War in 1754, a combined British-Massachusetts force defeated the French military presence at Chignecto. A couple of hundred armed Acadians were captured in Fort Beauséjour, but it is debatable if this influenced the momentous decision by the Halifax authorities to round up and deport the Acadian population, most of which had followed a policy of neutrality during the imperial conflicts and had regarded the area as their country. The unfortunate deportation was fairly successful from the point of view of the British, who also destroyed Acadian farms, but hundreds of Acadians managed to flee to the woods. The British, however, continued to hunt down and deport these refugees until 1763.

Taking advantage of superior seapower, the British consolidated their position by seizing the old French fort at the mouth of the Saint John and scouring the lower valley for Acadians. Any Acadian buildings along the Saint John and the Petitcodiac were razed and the sizeable village of St. Anne's was burned down in a ruthless night attack by New England rangers. Acadian refugees were picked up on the Miramichi and deported, and a force of Acadian and Indian guerilla fighters remained active during the declining years of the war. The last battle in the Acadian theatre, and the last major conflict in New Brunswick territory, took place in the spring of 1760 along the Restigouche River. Although Quebec had fallen, the British were worried that the French, who had not surrendered, would attempt to bring in reinforcements. The Royal Navy bottled up in the Bay of Chaleur a small French squadron consisting of one frigate, five transport vessels, and several hundred troops. Expecting the worst, the French commander retreated up the river and erected shore artillery batteries. The stronger British flotilla sailed in, destroyed the batteries, and sank or captured the ships. Charles de Boishébert, the commander of the Acadian and Indian partisans, could do little. With the Treaty of Paris in 1763 the territory later known as New Brunswick was annexed to Nova Scotia and placed under the authority of distant Halifax.

With the war over and the French military removed from Canada, the harsh British policy toward the Acadians was reversed in 1764, and a long and difficult process of re-establishment began. This heroic age of Acadian survival set the pattern for the nineteenth century. Denied political rights and unable to speak the language of the conqueror, the returning Acadians settled in remote areas, such as the upper Saint John, the north shore, and the Gulf coast. The economy along the coast was based on fishing and subsistence farming. Catholicism was legal under the new regime, but organizationally the Church did not prosper in the late eighteenth century; by the 1780s New Brunswick had only two resident priests. This situation improved by the turn of the century when new parishes, such as Caraquet, were founded.

Isolation and hardship were the price of linguistic and cultural integrity. During the nineteenth century, for example, Acadians were less likely to depart for greener pastures than were New Brunswickers of British origin. Some of the coastal villages benefited from employment opportunities provided by paternalistic Protestant fishing merchants who also controlled the local economy. To the west, the Madawaska district was ignored until pressure from Loyalists to the south prompted several pioneer Acadian families (joined by French Canadians from the north) to settle in the area. By 1800 New Brunswick's Acadians numbered around 4,000.

Throughout the 1770s privateers raided the coastline of New Brunswick and Nova Scotia. In order to protect the trading post at the mouth of the Saint John River, British troops under the command of Major Gilfred Studholme constructed Fort Howe on a hill overlooking the harbour. Pictured here in this 1781 illustration, the fort had the distinction of protecting the area without one shot ever having been fired. Courtesy, New Brunswick Museum

LOYALIST NEW BRUNSWICK

During the two decades between the Acadian deportation and the outbreak of the American Revolution, the new northern territory of Nova Scotia remained what it had been under the French—a backwater almost completely void of European settlers. The Micmac and Maliseet were still relatively independent of the white inhabitants. Officially the British were promoting the settlement of Nova Scotia by New England planters, but the movement of farmers and fishermen up the coast, when it happened at all, was directed to peninsular Nova Scotia. Nonetheless, New Brunswick did have agricultural potential and timber resources, especially pine. Thus, according to historian W.S. MacNutt, "virtually all the rich areas of the lower Saint John came under the control of speculators" —British officers stationed at Montréal. Two pre-Loyalist settlements were Sackville on the Chignecto Isthmus and the New England township of Maugerville on the lower Saint John. Named in honour of Joshua Mauger, the influential merchant who dominated the Nova Scotia economy, the settlement was linked to Massachusetts by the firm of Simonds, Hazen and White, whose lonely trading post guarded the mouth of the Saint John and did business with native people and fishermen. For the officials in Halifax, the territory north of Chignecto was *terra incognita*.

Maugerville's New England connections were underlined by the so-called Eddy Rebellion of 1776, a failed attempt by a few dissidents to throw off the yoke of British rule in Nova Scotia. With the help of a sympathetic minister, Jonathan Eddy, a renegade Nova Scotia Member of the Assembly, convinced the valley com-

The first United Empire Loyalists arrived in the Saint John River valley in the spring of 1783. The settlers were to receive 200 acres of land per person, provisions for one year, an allowance of warm clothing, farm implements, arms and ammunition, medicine, window glass, and other articles to help them build their new lives. By the end of 1784 nearly 30,000 Loyalists had arrived in New Brunswick and Nova Scotia. Courtesy, New Brunswick Museum

Ward Chipman (1754-1824) was a member of a distinguished Massachusetts family who emigrated to New Brunswick with other Loyalists after the American Revolution. Chipman was the first solicitor general of the province and became president of the Legislative Council in 1817. This portrait by Gilbert Stuart was completed during one of Chipman's many visits to Boston, where he replenished his supply of quality goods and renewed family contacts. Courtesy, New Brunswick Museum

munity to lend support to his small band of Americans, Indians, and Acadians. The resulting raid on Chignecto, while frightening the authorities, did not win over the "Neutral Yankees" of Nova Scotia to the American Revolutionary cause. It did prompt the British to establish a military presence on the Saint John and to win the Maliseet over to the Crown. Fort Howe was built on a rocky height above the operation of Simonds, Hazen and White, and a second post was established upriver at Oromocto.

By 1779 New York was a beleaguered city teeming with displaced and disgruntled Loyalists—Americans who refused to fight or speak out against the British Crown. The British commander-in-chief, Guy Carleton, encouraged the loyal Americans to organize group settlements in the safe colony of Nova Scotia. Hundreds sailed to the north where obvious tensions and jealousies soon surfaced between the new arrivals and the pre-Loyalist inhabitants and officials. In this agitated atmosphere, with the war going badly for the British, the idea of developing a distinctly Loyalist refuge in the north became increasingly attractive. One such scheme, which almost materialized, was New Ireland—a plan for a loyal British colony on the coast of Maine with a landholding elite and official status for the Church of England. New Ireland did not come to be, but the idea foreshadowed the creation of

a new colony reserved for the loyal Americans.

The establishment of New Brunswick, named in honour of the German lineage of King George III, was anything but a noble event, the sufferings of Loyalists notwithstanding. Hundreds of families, most of them in organized groups, arrived in the Bay of Fundy area in 1783 and 1784. In retrospect, the partition of Nova Scotia in 1784 was one of the boldest examples of political wirepulling in Canadian history. All refugees are unhappy and the Loyalists were no exception. The idea was to settle most of the refugees, starting with the Provincials (disbanded Loyalist troops), in the interior. Many did take up lands along the Saint John,

the Kennebecasis, Grand Lake, and Passamaquoddy Bay, and new urban centres sprang up: St. Stephen, St. George, St. Andrews, and, at the mouth of the Saint John, Carleton and Parrtown. Yet there was much criticism over delays in land allocation and problems associated with feeding and maintaining the refugees in the coastal centres.

Meanwhile, a small group of well-placed Loyalist gentlemen in New York and London convinced the British government to create a new colony in northern Nova Scotia and to put them in charge. This group included Edward Winslow, Ward Chipman, Jonathan Odell, Gabriel and George Ludlow, and George Sproule, who saw themselves as members of the natural ruling class. Few of them had ever set eyes upon New Brunswick. The first governor, Thomas Carleton, brother of Guy Carleton, was responsible for roughly 15,000 Loyalist refugees. These well-educated and somewhat authoritarian gentlemen hoped to build a model British colony based on loyalty to the Crown and the state church. Although the governor and his councillors were committed to popular elections—the first was held in 1785—they preferred a strong executive branch of government assisted by a class of rural justices of the peace. Personal ambition was a motivating factor behind the partition of Nova Scotia but, as a number of writers have pointed out, the founding of the Loyalist colony was also a matter of principle.

Because of the very human habit of glorifying one's ancestors, the popular image of the Loyalists is that of gentlemanly elite, the cream of eighteenth-centu-

This gentle vision of Saint John, New Brunswick, in 1814, painted by artist Joseph Brown Comingo, shows the city during a period when its population almost tripled. By 1820, with its ready access to British and American markets, Saint John was servicing a population which exceeded that of Upper and Lower Canada combined. Courtesy, New Brunswick Museum

ry colonial society. This romanticized view has been challenged by the writing of Esther Clark Wright and others. The New Brunswick Loyalist migration did include public figures, lawyers, Harvard graduates, wealthy merchants, and gentlemen, but in terms of social class, the refugees were a mixed lot. Most families were headed by farmers, artisans, or tradesmen who would have been insulted or amused by the genteel Loyalists of later history schoolbooks. The elite came principally from New England but the rank and file was from the middle colonies—New York, New Jersey, and Connecticut.

As historian David Bell has detailed, early Loyalist New Brunswick, particularly the rowdy part of Saint John (incorporated by royal charter in 1785) was marked by popular unrest and a demand for the rights and privileges of Englishmen. The government of gentlemen replied with repressive legislation and by locating the capital to Fredericton. They hoped to ensure stability through the Church of England, the law, and the development of education, but discontent and a distrust of centralized authority proved to be formidable obstacles. The first popular leader of note was Scottish lumber merchant James Glenie, who championed the rights of the people against the lieutenant governor and his capable councillors. Glenie so offended the Loyalist elite that he was challenged to a duel and was wounded by Revolutionary War hero John Coffin in 1797.

The first chartered bank in British North America was the Bank of New Brunswick, incorporated in 1820. Amidst the confusion of a myriad of currency being used—British pounds, American dollars, French francs—the urgent need for establishing professional banking services that could deal in foreign exchange and handle all manner of remittances was apparent. It was not until the 1860s that New Brunswick adopted the decimal system and minted its own money. Courtesy, New Brunswick Museum

THE TIMBER COLONY

By the early 1800s, the colony was not an economic success. The growing port of Saint John controlled trade with the interior and parts of Nova Scotia, but New Brunswick contained less than 25,000 people. One bright spot was the successful revolution of an attempted land grab by the Americans, who had insisted that the Magaguadavic River, not the St. Croix, was the true boundary on the coast. The boundary to the north, Madawaska for example, remained uncertain.

It was war—Britain's ongoing war with France—that boosted the local economy. By 1812 the international situation had precipitated war between Britain and the strong but disorganized United States. The Loyalist colony was defended by several hundred British regulars and an all but useless militia. Fortunately, the

Based on a drawing done by eyewitness Thomas H. Wentworth, this lithograph shows a view of the Great Conflagration on the night of January 14, 1837, when one-third of Saint John's commercial district became a heap of smouldering ashes. The reflection of the fire was seen past Fredericton, a distance of more than 90 miles. Burning paper and other materials were seen falling more than nine miles from the city. Courtesy, New Brunswick Museum

belligerents in this theatre of the war were, apart from a little privateering, more interested in trading and smuggling than in fighting. The New England states were less than enthusiastic supporters of the U.S. government and the Southern "War Hawks" ; partly as a result, New Brunswick had little fear of an invasion. In 1813 the New Brunswick militia was disbanded and the famous march of the 104th Regiment to Canada left the colony defenceless. One exception was the erection of a stone Martello tower on the west side of the harbour of Saint John. Merchants, fishermen, sailors, and vessel owners all prospered from a booming trade in British imports and American exports.

Relations with the United States after 1815 were fairly harmonious, with the exception of friction along the Maine border over timber areas. In 1839 Maine and New Brunswick almost went to war over the disputed Aroostook River valley north of Woodstock. The government of Maine, in defiance of its federal government, claimed timber lands in the valley, and there were several incidents that seemed to threaten New Brunswick's Madawaska area. The governor of Maine mobilized the militia in 1839, and the state legislature voted money for war. The northern boundary between Maine and New Brunswick had not yet been settled, and eventually the British backed down—Maine's claims were upheld.

The War of 1812 also brought a small black population to the colony. The British had liberated slaves during raids on the American southern states, and several hundred were accepted by the New Brunswick government and settled on marginal land at Loch Lomond, outside of Saint John. The government had abolished slavery by this time, but despite humanitarian impulses blacks were not accorded equal treatment with white settlers and labourers. Like the native peoples, they were regarded as an inferior and ultimately doomed race.

As New Brunswick passed from a frontier society to a wealthier, more sophisticated, and self-governing colony, the political class—merchants, lawyers, lumbermen, and prosperous farmers—was influenced by nineteenth-century reform ideas. One standard criticism was that the lieutenant governor (usually a military man) and his executive council threatened the liberties of the people. The reality was more complex. The independent and somewhat parochial "popular tribunes" of the Legislative Assembly effectively curbed executive action and prevented a more efficient use of public resources. Despite their speeches on executive tyranny, the evils of taxation, and the blessings of British liberty, politicians were fixated on local constituency matters such as the repair of roads. This political culture, based on family connection, ethnicity, religious affiliation, and personality rather than ideology, worked against the development of disciplined political parties until after Confederation. There was no Intellectual Awakening of satirical writers, reform orators, or political theorists; those clamouring for such abstractions as responsible government, like Lemuel Allen Wilmot and Charles Fisher, were in the minority. The electorate was largely rural, often illiterate, indebted to merchants and storekeepers, and deferential yet suspicious of social betters.

By the 1840s the lieutenant governor, although still officially the government leader, could not afford to alienate the leading power brokers of the Assembly, who controlled public revenues through a system of committees. The politicians saw themselves as loyal Britons, but they valued their independence; thus, Lord Durham's 1839 suggestion for a British North American colonial union received little support. By mid-century the government was "responsible" to the people in that an elected premier led a cabinet formed from a leading group in the Assembly, but the public took little notice of this constitutional innovation.

The engine of economic growth during the early nineteenth century was the export of a single staple—timber. Ample forest resources, an internal system of river navigation, and markets in industrializing Britain and later the United States made New Brunswick the timber colony of British North America. To obtain a

Trade with the United States and Great Britain encouraged the growth of shipping, shipbuilding, and the timber trade during the first half of the nineteenth century. By 1872 Saint John was the fourth-largest port in the British Empire. This 1830 oil portrait of the majestic ship David, *painted by William Clark of Greenock, Scotland, is the earliest painting to depict a New Brunswick vessel. Courtesy, New Brunswick Museum*

source of timber—a strategic resource in the age of wooden naval vessels—the British government enacted one of its last mercantilist policies, protecting colonial timber from foreign competition. Ignoring the dangers of relying on a single export commodity that was still dependent upon distant and volatile markets, New Brunswick embarked upon an orgy of timber harvesting. Lumbering relied upon British capital, a seasonal work force, and minimal government regulation. By the 1820s the timber trade dominated politics—when the Assembly acquired control of the Crown Lands, covering four-fifths of the colony, in 1839, the merchant class had within its grasp the major natural resource.

The fact that the colony was a net importer of foodstuffs suggested to critics that the timber trade was wasteful and retarded normal economic and social development, particularly agriculture. Social violence associated with woodworkers seemed to confirm these suspicions. For three decades following the War of 1812, the fortunes of most colonists were linked, directly or indirectly, to the timber sector. Sawmilling, particularly in the southwestern counties, was an important industrial employer by the 1840s, and in the following decade sawn lumber was shipped to the United States in significant quantities. The business by mid-century had taken on a pattern familiar to later generations of New Brunswickers: the monopolization of large tracts of land by a handful of large operators. Two of the biggest renters of Crown Lands (the price was a small fee) were based on the Miramichi—Joseph Cunard of Chatham and the Scottish firm of Gilmour, Rankin and Company.

COLONIAL SOCIETY

Because New Brunswick has not experienced any significant immigration in the last 120 years, the newcomers of 1815 to 1850 are of particular interest. Nineteenth-century immigrants came principally from the British Isles and many were only passing through. Thousands reached the colony each year following the Napoleonic Wars, most of them arriving in search of economic betterment. The peak year was 1847, when nearly 17,000 disembarked at New Brunswick ports. Most came as individuals, families, or small groups, and the government, other than assisting a number of charity organizations, did little to help them. Although settlers arrived from Scotland, England, and even Wales, the most significant group were the Irish.

Before 1840, most of the Irish who reached the colony were Protestant artisans and farmers of Scottish or English descent. The Protestant Irish, particularly in Charlotte country, blended in with the native majority, unlike their Roman Catholic counterparts, who were regarded as alien. The immigrants brought with them Old World customs and organizations such as the Loyal Orange Association, a militant Protestant secret society that spread like wildfire through the rural areas. The Catholic Irish, often unable to speak English, generally were poorer than their Protestant countrymen and gravitated to the Miramichi and the slums of Saint John, where they served as an urban proletariat. The host society viewed these immigrants with ambivalence; they were a source of cheap labour yet were also associated with poverty, crime, intemperance, and disease. The Irish who fled the great famine of 1846-1847, for example, brought deadly cholera and typhus. The coincidence of an Irish influx during the 1840s and the rise of an activist Catholic church and related institutions fed popular Protestant suspicions of Papal intrigue. Sectarian violence flared during this decade, particularly in

Saint John, where a clash between Orangemen and ghetto Catholics in 1849 took a number of lives. Recent studies indicate that the Catholic Irish in the Miramichi were more likely to keep to themselves socially and lagged behind economically and politically.

Religion and ethnicity appear to have been as important or even more important than social class or political theory in explaining nineteenth-century New Brunswick society. It was often difficult to divorce religion from public questions such as education. Even the growing movement for state-supported, non-sectarian schools had religious motivations, specifically the evangelical Protestant idea of the separation of church and state and the reform Christian desire to provide equality of educational opportunities.

One source of controversy was the special status, much of it informal, enjoyed by the Church of England and its adherents. Anglicans, for a number of reasons, appeared to monopolize public offices and ran a number of primary and grammar schools. They also ran King's College, Fredericton, founded in 1828. The Anglicans' monopoly (which was not monolithic) was partly formal and part-

ly informal. It was only gradually that British colonies such as New Brunswick got over the government's suspicion of non-Church of England sects, particularly the Methodists and Baptists. Most of the genteel types were Anglican or educated in Anglican settings; this began to change as the century progressed. Informal connections had to do with patronage and family connections; for example, the legal elite, which produced most of the judges in New Brunswick, was heavily Anglican.

The growing Catholic school system in the 1840s, which received government support, was another worry for evangelicals. Schooling largely was a luxury reserved for urban children—in the rural areas chores came first and the government did not dare to consider compulsory attendance. The Acadi-

an areas before Confederation probably sent less than one-fifth of their children to school. Most education reform was in the future, but the Legislature managed to secularize the administration of King's College, which became the University of New Brunswick in 1859. The Methodists were especially interested in education, having established an academy at Sackville in 1840. A Ladies college was added in 1854, and six years later the Mount Allison institution included a degree-granting college.

One of the great social questions in this period was the influence of alcohol. New Brunswick was not alone in being affected by temperance and prohibition, the most important and extensive social movements of the century. The Victorian fascination with the "liquor evil" stemmed from individualistic evangelical Protestantism, but was also boosted by puritanical Catholicism and scientific temperance that measured the physical effects of alcohol abuse. Temperance worked toward personal abstinence or moderation and a more stringent enforcement of liquor licensing laws, while the more radical prohibition approach called for an outright ban on the manufacture, sale, and consumption of spirits.

Women were fairly active in temperance and prohibition movements, but the leading organization was the all-male Sons of Temperance (it had women's and children's auxiliaries), which considered drink to be the root of most societal evil. In pre-industrial New Brunswick, beer was considered a type of food for the workingman, rum was cheap and plentiful, the rural inn was an important institution, workers were often partly paid with liquor, and legal and illegal grog shops flourished in urban centres. By mid-century the Sons of Temperance, who drew institutional and moral support from Maine, were politically powerful and poised to strike a death blow against the liquor traffic. A provincial law in 1853 attempted to make New Brunswick officially dry, but by the following year the enforcement of this legislation had divided the population. The Liberal politicians who supported prohibition, at least in principle, were nicknamed the Smashers, while their opponents were dubbed the Rummies. An even more stringent law in 1855 was met by widespread resistance, and the Smashers, despite the strength of evangelical opinion, admitted defeat soon after. Voluntary temperance, however, continued to be important in all religious denominations.

New Brunswick circa 1850, the eve of the railway age, has been described by historical geographer Graeme Wynn as still very much a wilderness. The 1851 census recorded that most of the population resided in the valleys of the Saint John and the Kennebecasis, the thriving city of Saint John and its suburbs, rural Charlotte country and its towns of St. Stephen, St. George, and St. Andrews, the south-

Situated on the fertile Tantramar marshes of Westmorland County, the Sackville area was first settled in the 1670s, and after the expulsion of the Acadians in 1755 it was resettled by New England and Yorkshire immigrants. The town of Sackville is dominated by Mount Allison University, which was established in 1840. Sackville was a busy port and railway centre by the 1870s, but business began to decline around the turn of the century. John W. Gray's 1872 view shows part of Sackville during one of its most prosperous eras. Courtesy, New Brunswick Museum

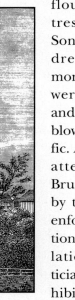

eastern coastal region, and the mouth of the Miramichi system. Mid-century government reports offer a colourful portrait of the fishermen of Grand Manan, Campobello, and the Western Isles, and confirm the folk tale that lobster was used to fertilize potato patches. A few small towns were found in the northern region, but most of the Acadians lived in coastal enclaves along the Gulf of St. Lawrence or the Bay of Chaleur. The interior was all but empty of settlers. Other than farms and cleared land, the major signs of human activity were roads, cut-over areas, and dams and ponds resulting from the timber trade.

Agriculture and timber trade were the largest employers and to a certain extent seasonally complementary. The fishermen were perhaps the poorest workers in the colony, usually under the thumb of local merchants who marketed their catch. The colony was still largely pre-industrial in that cash was in short supply, the middle class was small, residence and workplace were not usually separate, and employer-employee relations were marked more by paternalism than by class conflict. The little manufacturing that took place was produced by artisans or in large workshops for local consumption. The key economic players were the merchants of Saint John, who invested in the timber trade, shipping, and real estate, controlled the wholesale and retail sectors, and served as private bankers. This class had been agitated by the British move to free trade within the Empire during the 1840s, and by mid-century was keenly interested in the colony's economic and political future.

The interior of New Brunswick has long been renowned for its fertile hunting and fishing. E.B. Holmes of Brookline, Massachusetts, along with his guide, Arthur Pringle, bagged this majestic moose in the Miramichi region of the province in 1903. This photograph was one of many used by New Brunswick's tourism bureau to promote the region as a sporting centre. Courtesy, New Brunswick Museum

Built in 1851 by James Smith in Saint John and later sold to the Black Ball Line of Liverpool, England, the Marco Polo *was the largest and best-equipped emigrant packet in the world. After setting records for voyages between Australia and England, it became known as the "Fastest Ship in the World." The* Marco Polo*'s illustrious career came to a sudden end in 1883 when it was wrecked off Cavendish Beach on Prince Edward Island. Courtesy, New Brunswick Museum*

THE GOLDEN AGE

Because of locational factors, plentiful supplies of lumber, and the benefits of the British Imperial trading system, New Brunswick played an important role in the region's best known business venture, the construction and operation of ocean-going wooden sailing vessels. In terms of registered tonnage, the Maritimes by the 1870s had one of the largest merchant fleets in the world. Vessels, ranging from fishing boats and schooners to large ships such as the *Marco Polo*, were built not only around Saint John but also in St. Martins and Dorchester—wherever creeks and rivers were sufficiently deep. The larger vessels operated in the trans-Atlantic bulk carrying trade; after Confederation many were switched to newer, more distant carrying markets because of competition from steam power. In its heyday, the mainly locally owned Saint John fleet was the largest in the region, contributing to the city's reputation as the "Liverpool of North America." In the 1880s and 1890s, having over-invested in relatively cheap vessels for either sale or carrying cargo, the merchant owners switched to more predictable land-based investments rather than a modernized high seas fleet. Although the "golden age" of sailing produced a sense of pride and considerable wealth and employment for shipwrights, caulkers, and other tradesmen, it did little to further long-term economic diversification.

During the late 1840s and early 1850s, merchants and political leaders discussed a number of solutions for improving the commercial, agricultural, and industrial prospects of the colony. Some, in the wake of British Free Trade, advocated economic protectionism through higher tariffs on imports. Others suggested liberalizing trade relations with the United States. Largely because of Canada's interest and British diplomacy, a treaty was signed in 1854 that permitted reciprocal free trade between the U.S. and British North America in natural products such as timber, fish, and grain. Under the Reciprocity Treaty, Maine lumbermen were allowed to send timber down the Saint John duty-free. By 1866, the termination of the treaty, New Brunswick exports to the United States had increased in value 400 percent.

A second strategy was railway promotion: rail connections would give New Brunswick centres the potential to act as winter ports for American and Canadian freight. As early as the 1830s British and local businessmen had hoped to build a line north from St. Andrews into the interior. Saint John merchants were not adverse to this sort of land-based investment. Amidst talk of an Intercolonial Railway to link the Maritimes and the St. Lawrence valley, Saint John planned to connect with Maine by the European and North American Railway. By 1860 the ENAR ran from Saint John to Shediac and was so unprofitable that it had been taken over by the government. Southern New Brunswick hoped that the Western Extension, a line west to Maine, would bring economic salvation; northern interests, rival Halifax, and British officials were not so supportive. Because it would link New Brunswick with Maine, British officials worried about the political and military implications of the Western Extension.

John Warren Gray's sweeping mid-1860s panorama of the city and harbour of Saint John shows the development and activity of early New Brunswick. Note the sawmill smokestacks in the lower right corner, illustrating the flourishing business of lumber trade with foreign markets. Courtesy, New Brunswick Museum

CONFEDERATION

Because the Golden Age passed sometime after Confederation, it is tempting to conclude, as did many contemporaries, that the political union of the Maritimes and Upper and Lower Canada was a plot by the latter to reduce the former to marginal economic and political status. This is a gross simplification. The Confederation movement was based primarily on Canadian self-interest such as the need to solve a frustrating constitutional situation, but it also represented the working out of broader economic forces and British policy toward British North America. The initiative came from Canada, but political and economic allies were found in New Brunswick which, because of its geographic location, became the key to the Confederation struggle. The U.S. Civil War, which destabilized Anglo-American relations, was another factor contributing to Confederation. New Brunswick had strong trade, cultural, and family connections with New England, making it imperative that its press follow the war closely. In 1861 the Americans intercepted the British vessel *Trent* on the high seas, setting off a diplomatic crisis. Several

Located on the Maine-New Brunswick border, the community of McAdam was named after John McAdam, a local lumberman and politician. At the convergence of the European and North American Railway and the New Brunswick and Canada Railway, the town of McAdam served as a major connection point for American and Canadian rail lines. Courtesy, New Brunswick Museum

thousand British regulars were dispatched to Canada by sled through New Brunswick, an operation which accentuated the need for a safe rail link and coordinated colonial defence. Yet New Brunswick independence would not be given up easily.

Although under considerable pressure, for example, from Lieutenant Governor Arthur Hamilton Gordon, most local politicians were unwilling to hamper their freedom of action by entering into a federal union with the distant Canadians. By 1863, however, they were interested in discussing mutual regional problems such as railways, so it was agreed to

BY THE QUEEN!
A PROCLAMATION
For Uniting the Provinces of Canada, Nova Scotia, and New Brunswick, into one Dominion, under the name of CANADA.

VICTORIA R.

WHEREAS by an Act of Parliament, passed on the Twenty-ninth day of March, One Thousand Eight Hundred and Sixty-seven, in the Thirtieth year of Our reign, intituled, "An Act for the Union of Canada, Nova Scotia, and New Brunswick, and the Government thereof, and for purposes connected therewith." after divers recitals it is enacted that "it shall "be lawful for the Queen, by and with the advice of Her Majesty's "Most Honorable Privy Council, to declare, by Proclamation, that "on and after a day therein appointed, not being more than six "months after the passing of this Act, the Provinces of Canada, "Nova Scotia, and New Brunswick, shall form and be One Domi-"nion under the name of Canada, and on and after that day those "Three Provinces shall form and be One Dominion under that "Name accordingly;" and it is thereby further enacted, that "Such Persons shall be first summoned to the Senate as the Queen "by Warrant, under Her Majesty's Royal Sign Manual, thinks fit "to approve, and their Names shall be inserted in the Queen's "Proclamation of Union:"

We, therefore, by and with the advice of Our Privy Council, have thought fit to issue this Our Royal Proclamation, and We do ordain, declare, and command that on and after the First day of July, One Thousand Eight Hundred and Sixty-seven, the Provinces of Canada, Nova Scotia, and New Brunswick, shall form and be One Dominion, under the name of CANADA.

And we do further ordain and declare that the persons whose names are herein inserted and set forth are the persons of whom we have by Warrant under Our Royal Sign Manual thought fit to approve as the persons who shall be first summoned to the Senate of Canada.

Given at our Court, at Windsor Castle, this Twenty-second day of May, in the year of our Lord One Thousand Eight Hundred and Sixty-seven, and in the Thirtieth year of our reign.

GOD SAVE THE QUEEN.

hold a conference in Charlottetown under the fuzzy title "Maritime Union." The main supporter of Confederation, Saint John businessman and politician Leonard Tilley, was opposed by leaders such as Albert J. Smith ("The Lion of Westmorland") and Timothy Warren Anglin, an influential Irish Catholic politician and journalist. After a talented Canadian delegation won over the Charlottetown conference, New Brunswick was enthusiastic about the principle of a British North American union. However, when specific details were formulated, fears of losing local independence in a larger political unit curbed the enthusiasm, and the battle lines were drawn. Tilley's government was defeated in 1865 by Smith with Catholic support, yet the "Antis" lacked party discipline and a realistic alternative. This was particularly clear after the Americans announced termination of the Reciprocity Treaty and funding for the Western Extension failed to materialize.

Ironically, it was sensationalism surrounding the Fenian Brotherhood—Irish Americans dedicated to ending British rule in Ireland—that turned the tide for the Confederationists. During the 1866 election the Antis were discredited through an effective use of the loyalty cry by their opponents, who argued that New Brunswick independence was tantamount to disloyalty to the British Crown. Tilley secured a pro-Confederation resolution in the Assembly and went to London to help put the finishing touches on the new constitution, the British North America Act. In 1867 the colony became one of the four original provinces of the Dominion of Canada. New Brunswickers now had to learn to become Canadians.

The Dominion government, as promised, completed the Intercolonial Railway in the 1870s, along a north shore and Gulf coast route that benefited a place such as Moncton, which became the transportation hub of Atlantic Canada. But the economic results of Confederation were mixed. The imposition of the National Policy tariffs in 1879 initially was a boon, as it encouraged impressive industrialization in Saint John, Moncton, and St. Stephen. Alexander "Boss" Gibson, lumberman and railroadman, confidently founded a cotton-milling complex, complete with company houses for the workers, at Marysville. But most of these ventures, unfortunately, failed to survive overexpansion or the turn-of-the-century national corporate merger movement.

To make matters worse, local banks such as the Bank of St. Stephen went out of business or were bought out and, particularly after 1900, local wholesalers and retailers were challenged by national chains. Federal railway subsidies

The commercial centre of Saint John suffered from the economic decline of the early 1870s. James R. Woodburn's photograph of the Market Slip and Market Square, showing horses and slovens awaiting work and empty businesses along King Street, emphasizes the effects of the economic slump. "A world-wide depression crippled lumber exports and sharply curtailed trade for nearly 20 years after 1873," wrote historian George W. Schuyler. Courtesy, New Brunswick Museum

and public works spending did little to halt this decline, although they did help Saint John to modernize its port infrastructure. Despite the rhetoric of civic boosters, the port city, devastated by fire in 1877, never recovered from the passing of the Golden Age.

New Brunswick did not become the workshop of the Dominion, and remained a net importer of food and consumer goods. Shipbuilding and the shipping business were not replaced with any long-term growth base. Under these conditions, thousands of young people migrated to the United States, strengthening the province's ties with New England. It has been suggested that these migrants were often the more skilled and better educated. Between 1881 and 1891, the population was stagnant—a sign of outmigration—and over the next decade it rose by a miniscule percentage. The net result was a draining of the region's savings, profits, and human resources. These changes were largely because of market forces, but critics argued that the national government, preoccupied with the West, could have done more to lessen hardship.

ACADIAN RENAISSANCE
In the 1880s signs appeared indicating that the Acadians would not in the long run remain a politically passive minority. In the 1870s, Acadian areas had offered some of the strongest resistance to the Provincial government's attempt to pro-

vide state-supported, secular schooling at the expense of Catholic separate schools. Following violence at Caraquet in 1875, the government reached a compromise with the church on the issue. In the following decade, Acadians, or at least the educated elite, began to organize as a national group. Inspired by but distancing themselves from Quebec nationalism, they formed the Société National Assomption and adopted an Acadian flag (the French Tricolour with a Papal star), a national hymn ("Ave Maris Stella"), and a religious feast day (the Assumption, August 15). Institutions such as the College St. Joseph (Memramcook) and a number of convent schools stressed the spiritual side of Acadian life. Although this "renaissance" produced a number of political and cultural leaders such as Pascal Porier, Pierre Armand Landry, and Placide Gaudet, it did little to advance the economic plight of the average Acadian. The renaissance men offered a romanticized version of Acadian history, adopting Longfellow's epic poem

ABOVE: William Thomson (1818-1891) immigrated to New Brunswick with his parents in the 1820s, and started a business as a Saint John ship broker in the 1840s. His astute business sense helped him to found one of the most prosperous shipping empires in the province. Thomson was one of the first shipbuilders to construct steel steamers in the transitional age between sailing ships and steam-powered vessels. Courtesy, New Brunswick Museum

LEFT: British- and American-trained New Brunswick artist Charles Caleb Ward (1831-1896) painted from his studio in Rothesay. His 1891 painting, Path Through the Woods, reflects the romantic and sentimental influences found in the region's art at the end of the Victorian era. Courtesy, New Brunswick Museum

Evangeline as a basic cultural text, yet, like the Francophone press, they remained political partisans, Conservatives and Liberals. The Acadian minority would become more of a force with population increase; it grew from 15 percent of the population in 1871 to roughly 25 percent on the eve of World War I. Yet despite this growth and educational advances, Acadian nationalism was relatively latent during the early twentieth century.

THE TWENTIETH CENTURY

At the turn of the century, many New Brunswickers of British descent warmly supported the exploits of the British Empire. In 1911, however, a majority of the province's federal ridings returned Liberals, who as a national party opposed Canadian contributions to the Royal Navy. (One of the attractions in voting Liberal in 1911 was the possibility of a new Reciprocity agreement.) World War I produced a more patriotic response.

The *Busy East* magazine of Moncton stated in October 1914 what was obvious to loyal New Brunswickers: "GERMANY CAN NOT BE PERMITTED TO TRIUMPH NO MATTER WHAT THE COST." During the Great War, one of the province's most distinguished sons, Sir Max Aitken (Lord Beaverbrook), ran the British propaganda effort as minister of information. By 1916 several thousand volunteers, largely from English-speaking areas, had joined units such as the 8th Canadian Hussars and the Kent-Westmorland 145th Battalion. Although the 165th Acadian Battalion had been organized, it was believed by the majority in 1917 that the Acadians had failed to enlist in appropriate numbers. The 1917 federal "Conscription" election polarized the province on ethnic lines and drove the Acadians further into the Liberal fold. Despite the presence of the Acadian minority, the province's enlistment rate was roughly equal to that of Nova Scotia and Prince Edward Island.

One of the least appreciated historical developments in this period was the rise of the automobile, which brought new revenues to the provincial government, created a demand for a modern road and highway system, and helped to develop the tourism industry. In New Brunswick politics, roads, whether secondary roads or the Trans-Canada Highway, have been like patriotism—the last refuge of a scoundrel. The construction of roads and bridges (such as the province's distinctive wooden covered bridges) meant patronage opportunities for politicians such as Peter Veniot, public works minister in the early 1920s.

The provincial Liberals, responding to the presence of more than 11,000 autos by 1920, embarked on a trunk road building spree and were accused of neglecting local roads so necessary to farmers; a generation later Liberals were criticizing the Conservatives for similar extravagances. By the mid-1930s, however,

The central business district along Queen Street in Fredericton, New Brunswick's provincial capital, has changed little in the last century. It still retains the charm and organization displayed in this 1890 photograph by George T. Taylor, a prominent local photographer of the time. Courtesy, New Brunswick Museum

there were few roads of any description in the interior parts of Madawaska, Victoria, Restigouche, Northumberland, and Gloucester counties.

The automobile was quickly adopted by another product of the age—the rumrunner/bootlegger. This class benefited not only from local Prohibition (1920-1927) but also the American Volstead Act (in operation from 1920 to 1932), which created smuggling opportunities over the Canadian border. The Bay of Fundy and the New Brunswick-Maine border area in the 1920s and early 1930s were major conduits for supplying thirsty Americans. It was illegal to sell or consume liquor in the province, but legal to export it from warehouses. Runners used fishing vessels, automobiles, and trains to ship their contraband. Although the province remained officially dry until 1927, when government liquor outlets were established, it was possible to obtain legal "prescriptions" from doctors and druggists and illegal supplies from the local bootlegger. The opponents of the rum traffic were not all prudes or religious fanatics; many were well-meaning reformers concerned about issues such as rural depopulation or women's rights.

This informal grouping depicting the #10 Battery of the Royal Canadian Artillery of Her Majesty's Imperial Forces was photographed by George P. Roberts just before they withdrew from New Brunswick in 1871. Until Confederation, British North America depended upon Britain to supply troops for defence. After 1871 the New Brunswick volunteer militia filled this defence need. Courtesy, New Brunswick Museum

The United Farmers of New Brunswick, for example, who eventually organized more than 100 branches in the Saint John valley, endorsed Prohibition, and in the rural south dry sentiment lived on. A system of government control was established, but one legacy of this period by the 1950s was an illiberal liquor law system.

Women, as historians are beginning to discover, played an important role in New Brunswick history. They faced many obstacles. Unmarried women of property could vote by 1886, and a decade later each school board was required to include two women. But by the World War I era, the average woman was still unable to vote in federal and provincial elections and women as a group were shut out of most professions. In the rural economy, women's labour was indispensable. The same could be said of teaching and charity work. Denied the vote, women gravitated to organizations such as church groups, the Women's Christian Temperance Union, the Young Women's Christian Association, the Catholic Women's League, and the Ladies Orange Benevolent Association.

Many women's organizations were concerned with social questions such as temperance, public morality, health care, and child protection, but few of their members could be called "feminists." The Saint John Women's Enfranchisement Association, organized in the 1890s, was an exception. In 1912 it sponsored a visit by the militant British suffragist, Sylvia Pankhurst. New Brunswick poet Bliss Carman was particularly interested in the female question. As an advocate of "dress reform," he would have approved of the flapper of the 1920s:

There are women who would welcome martyrdom for what they believe to be the cause of personal freedom, who would not accept the freedom of their own bodies as a gift. Nothing could induce them to abandon their own absurd shoes and corsets.

In 1919 the Provincial franchise was extended to women, who also were able to vote in the 1921 federal election. They could not, however, run as provincial candidates until 1934, and by mid-century few had entered the political arena.

DEPRESSION AND WAR

Parts of the province went into an economic slump in the post-World War I period, several years before the Great Depression of the 1930s. There is disagreement as to the relative standard of living in New Brunswick during both decades, but economic conditions were rarely uniform across the province and among classes. During the 1920s the major productive sectors experienced a slump and once again New Brunswickers emigrated in large numbers. The recession gave vigor to an already growing sense of regional political and economic protest known as the

Between 1900 and 1918 the value of exports processed through the port of Saint John increased from almost $10 million to some $200 million. Federal, provincial, and municipal policies helped to reinforce New Brunswick's economy. Since Saint John had most of New Brunswick's manufacturing, along with control of both railway and ocean transportation facilities, the city's Board of Trade boasted that Saint John was the "Gateway to Canada." Courtesy, New Brunswick Museum

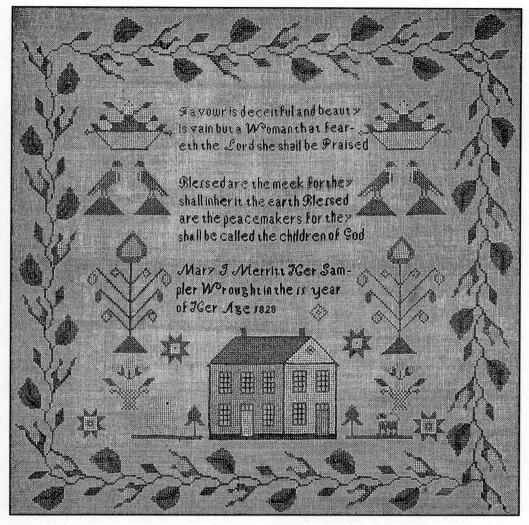

Needlework samplers, such as this 1828 example wrought by Mary Merrit, prepared young girls for future domestic tasks such as mending, darning, marking household linens, and creating decorative accessories. A child often worked her first sampler at the age of five or six and later moved on to more complex patterns and stitches. Samplers bring attention to the forgotten role women played in the history and economy of New Brunswick. Courtesy, New Brunswick Museum

Maritime Rights movement. Many groups and individuals, ranging from unions to journalists, were attracted to Maritime Rights. This approach to economic problems, based on a critique of federal railway and spending policies, placed little blame on local elites and also hampered the growth of stable farm and labour political parties. Regional discontent and political opportunism spurred the election of 10 Conservative New Brunswick Members of Parliament in 1925, and a similar number five years later following the outbreak of the Great Depression.

It has been argued (not by all authorities on the subject) that the province suffered greatly during the 1930s, and there is plenty of evidence of high unemployment rates, deteriorating health and educational services, and poor living conditions. In the north the decline of the fishing, lumbering, and sawmilling industries strained the relief capabilities of country and town councils. Premier J.B.M. Baxter promoted a "back to the land" strategy for the unemployed, which produced limited and highly inefficient results. Later in the decade Liberal Premier Alison Dysart attempted a more modern solution of abolishing the "dole" for the able-bodied and concentrating on public works projects such as highways. This enhanced the government's patronage relations and the status of local "contact men" —political organizers who served as unofficial employment agents.

The Second World War proved a short-term blessing for the ailing economy. In Saint John, harbour and air defences were improved and a small number of

corvettes were constructed for antisubmarine duties. Elsewhere, air strips were built and enemy prisoners of war were detained. The development of CFB Gagetown, a huge military training area in Queen's and Sunbury counties, would take place after the war. New Brunswickers fought with distinction in many of the war's battles, such as the Battle of the Atlantic and the bombing offensive over Germany. The 8th Hussars, now equipped with tanks, fought in some of the last actions of the war in Europe.

The conscription issue had surfaced again in 1940 when the federal government announced that nearly 30,000 New Brunswick males between the ages of 19

In the era of increasing public awareness and social responsibility during the late 1800s and early 1900s, many women's groups directed the efforts of their members toward social reform and women's rights. Religious organizations such as the Women's Auxiliary of the St. John Stone Church, pictured here circa 1910, provided the opportunity for participation in these areas of concern. Courtesy, New Brunswick Museum

and 45 were potential conscripts for home defence. In 1942, Ottawa, having pledged not to send conscripts overseas, staged a national plebiscite asking to be released from its promise. New Brunswick voted 35 percent against conscription, which indicated that the Acadians, like French Canadians in Quebec, did not approve of Ottawa's war plans. Because of strategic and political factors, ship-building and ship and aircraft repair were not promoted to the fullest in New Brunswick by the federal government. Despite high levels of employment and labour shortages in some trades, the war did not leave the province in great shape economically. Provincial politicians automatically blamed national policies, but

Richard Bedford Bennett (1870-1947) was New Brunswick's only native son to hold the position of Canada's prime minister, serving from 1930 to 1935 during one of the nation's most financially troubled times. This portrait by K.K. Forbes was presented to Bennett upon his retirement from the Conservative party of Canada in 1938. Bennett retired to England, and in 1941 was made Viscount Bennett of Mickleham, Calgary, and Hopewell. Courtesy, New Brunswick Museum

local political and economic elites were not without fault. A 1949 public welfare study noted that the province had the second highest infant mortality rate in Canada and that "Its people are poor, its sources of revenue meagre."

THE ECONOMY

The pulp and paper production industry, one of the most important new Canadian enterprises in the early twentieth century, was attracted to the province in the 1920s by plentiful softwood supplies, a work force skilled in woodwork, proximity to American markets, and the promise of cheap electrical power (the New Brunswick Hydro-Electric Commission was formed for political reasons as a public utility in 1920). Centres such as Campbellton, Dalhousie, and Edmundston benefited from a government policy that favoured the manufacture of pulp and paper rather than the mere export of pulp logs, and companies such as Fraser, Bathurst, and International Paper provided jobs and economic spin-offs in return for politically sensitive government concessions. There were also environmental and aesthetic trade-offs—it is not pleasant to live near a pulp mill. Nonetheless, the government and private woodlot owners benefited from this developing industry. Hydro-electric sites were developed at Musquash (NBEPC) and Grand Falls (private), but by World War II hydro was still not a major power source, placing well behind fossil fuel (including Minto coal).

In the postwar period pulp and paper continued to be important. Despite, or perhaps because of, rural electrification and the increased use of tractors and related equipment, the number of farmers, agricultural workers, and operating farms declined after 1945. Much of the cleared land was marginal. Two decades later many New Brunswickers lived in rural areas, but few could be described as farmers. The biggest jump in terms of the total work force came in the service sector, such as office work, the bureaucracy, and tourism.

In the 1950s and 1960s the provincial government planned economic development and diversification around the exploitation of natural resources. It was hoped that the significant deposits of non-ferrous ores in the Bathurst region would rescue the economy of the northeast and further hydro-electric development. In 1965 development of a controversial hydro site began at Mactaquac on the Saint John. The mining and smelting potential of the north was unlikely to be unlocked by local business, so the province worked at building a favourable investment climate. At present the mining of lead, copper, zinc, silver, and other metals employs several thousand and is worth, by way of example, 10 times the New Brunswick fisheries. According to New Brunswick historian E.R. Forbes, the forestry sector by the late 1970s "accounted for 14 percent of the jobs in the province, 38 percent of provincial exports and almost one-quarter of the goods produced."

The post-World War II boom in Canada, fed by American investment, did not bring spectacular benefits to the province. By the late 1950s, New Brunswick's per capita income was less than seven-tenths the national average. In this period Conservative Premier Hugh John Flemming was one of the strongest voices in demanding justice for the Atlantic region.

One of the most intriguing aspects of the province's recent history is the growth of the business empire of Kenneth Colin Irving, who was born in Buctouche at the turn of the century. "K.C." started out in 1923 with a small oil-delivery business in his hometown; by the 1960s it was easier to list what he did *not* own in New Brunswick, as his properties ranged from radio stations to much of the industrial landscape of Saint John. Tourists usually notice the most visible manifestations of this empire—the ubiquitous Irving service station—but residents like to speculate on the extent of the invisible empire. The Irving business

Under the proprietorship of World and Olympic speed skating champion Charles I. Gorman, the Avenue Service Station pictured here circa 1930 was one of the first stations in New Brunswick to use the Irving empire product—Primrose gasoline. Using advertising, shrewd investment, and sound management, the Irving companies now constitute the largest industry in New Brunswick. Courtesy, New Brunswick Museum

strategy, unimaginative but determined, is called vertical integration. For example, Irving service stations sell Irving-refined gasoline delivered by Irving trucks fitted with Irving tires, and so on. According to a recent article in *Forbes,* Irving may be worth more than $10 billion, which would make him one of the richest men in the world in terms of personal wealth. The family's operations are so secretive that government officials, business competitors, journalists, and historians often throw their hands up in frustration when attempting to deal with the Irvings. Unlike more civic-minded capitalists such as Lord Beaverbrook, the Irvings have been slow to appreciate the value of public relations, and thus there are few cultural or public facilities bearing the family name. This may change when the new generation takes over. Despite company rhetoric about serving the needs of New Brunswickers, in 1972 K.C. moved to Bermuda because of Canadian tax law, but he still spends several months of the year in the province.

EQUAL OPPORTUNITY

During the 1960s, the province experienced its own version of the American "War on Poverty" or Quebec's "Quiet Revolution," a controversial program of administrative, social, and economic modernization directed from Fredericton. The public policy of this decade, which also saw the political maturation of the Acadians, is best summed up by the official term "Equal Opportunity." An activist Liberal administration under the first elected Acadian premier, Louis J. Robichaud (1960-1970), aided by an able civil service and federal funding, set about to dismantle archaic local government and provide a basic level of social services to all parts of the province. In addition, the Liberals, working with federal regional development programs such as the Agricultural Rehabilitation and Development Act (ARDA) and the Fund for Rural Economic Development (FRED), tackled problems such as rural poverty and a weak industrial sector. During these years federal transfer payments became an important component of the economy and of the provincial budget.

Because Robichaud had the support of Acadian and "mixed" ridings and because the poorer areas tended to be both Francophone and northern, criticism was inevitable. Some charged that the Equal Opportunity Program was "Robbing Peter to Pay Pierre." Others disliked Fredericton's centralization of power: elected county councils were abolished, the number of school boards was cut dramatically and their powers shorn, and large consolidated schools, with long bus rides for students, began to replace the rural school house. The powerful Irving interests believed that the reforms jeopardized their taxation concessions and near monopoly in certain industries.

Centralization and equalization in education, health, and social services aimed to break down the province's north-south divisions. And despite their "welfare" image, the EOP planners were aiming for a more efficient use of labour and capital. Robichaud's biographer, Della M. Stanley, concluded that although Robichaud "overbuilt," the Equal Opportunity Program did improve the standard of living. It also proved that New Brunswick was not as backward as certain journalists and academics would have us believe.

THE ACADIANS COME OF AGE

During the 1960s the Acadian minority (nearly 40 percent of the 1961 population by origin) began to shed its second-class economic and political status. This was in part because of their own leaders, organizations, and educational advances and in part because of accommodative politicians. By mid-century Acadian institutions were gearing themselves more toward the state than the church, which necessitated a more openly political approach.

Group consciousness was boosted in 1963 by the foundation of the University de Moncton, which became the intellectual hub for the new "nationalism." Educational and media ties with Quebec and France strengthened this process, as did a keen interest in Acadian history and culture. New Brunswick native Antonine Maillet, creator of a number of strong female Acadian protagonists such as la Sagouine, is one of the best-known Francophone authors in the world. Student activism and ethnic tensions in the late 1960s made Moncton a lively place, as recorded in the documentary film *L'Acadie, L'Acadie.*

By 1967, Canada's centennial year, federal politics and Acadian political strength had created an official climate favourable to bilingualism—the provision

The old Province Hall in Fredericton, which housed the New Brunswick Legislature, became inadequate for the needs of the government by 1870. In March 1880 a competition was organized to hear proposals for a new building. Under the direction of J.C. Dumaresq, the Legislative Building was constructed of indigenous New Brunswick materials, such as finely tooled freestone from the Dorchester Quarry. It opened its doors in 1883. Courtesy, New Brunswick Museum

of bilingual government services and the right of choice for language of education. This would involve government jobs for Acadians and an extension of the French-language education apparatus. New Brunswick became officially bilingual in 1968, but the full provisions of the Official Languages Act were not proclaimed until a decade later.

Despite the confidence of the new Acadian elite of teachers, professors, civil servants, and business people, as well as a vibrant Acadian cultural scene, most New Brunswick Acadians subscribe to the politics of federalism, realizing, along

Explorers, surveyors, sportsmen, and even artists have been dependent upon the knowledge and skills of the native peoples for successful ventures into New Brunswick's interior. The birchbark canoe was a popular photographic subject for New Brunswick's first provincial photographer, George T. Taylor. And poets Sir Charles G.D. Roberts and Bliss Carman often travelled into the New Brunswick wilderness in canoes guided by the Maliseets. Courtesy, New Brunswick Museum

with their Anglophone neighbours, that it pays to have friends in high places, such as the federal cabinet. The 1970s separatist Parti Acadien, although garnering a share of the popular vote in Acadian constituencies, was little more than a protest movement along the lines of the more recent anti-bilingualism Confederation of Regions Party. Another force operating on Acadian unity is geography. New Brunswick Acadians live in three distinct areas: the northwest, the northeast, and the southeast.

The Progressive Conservative government of Richard Hatfield (1970-1987) inherited from its opponents a commitment to Equal Opportunity and bilingualism, not to mention a mounting provincial debt and fiscal reliance on Ottawa. Hatfield, a Protestant, was supported mainly by the Anglophone south, yet he attempted to rewrite the political rule book by courting the Acadians. This had to be done skillfully so as to avoid an Anglophone backlash such as that conducted on a miniature scale by the New Brunswick English Speaking Association in the early 1970s. This was complicated by the premier's outspoken defence of bilingualism and biculturalism in Canada as a whole, and by his desire to be a statesman when it came to the constitutional status of Quebec, characteristics not generally admired in New Brunswick's Bible Belt.

Some inroads were made, but provincial politics continued to be influenced by ethnicity. Apart from his flamboyant lifestyle, Hatfield's early stewardship was marred by the Bricklin debacle, whereby government money was pumped into an ill-advised scheme to produce a luxury sports car. The 1970s also were marked by a series of scandals and alleged scandals and by the launching of a "mega project," the Point Lepreau nuclear power plant, protested by few in job-hungry southern New Brunswick. The search for industry, assisted by the Federal Department of Regional Economic Expansion (DREE), continued. Parts of the province did well in the 1970s, yet the overall economic situation was uncertain and many business people became accustomed to depending on government grants, loans, and other forms of assistance.

Cultural and creative activities do not receive enough attention in New Brunswick, but the province has been associated with a number of important artists, writers, and musicians. Poets have included Sir Charles G.D. Roberts (1860-1943), one of Canada's founding poets; Bliss Carman (1861-1929); and Alden Nowlan (1933-1983). The works of Saint John native Miller Brittain (1912-1968), Tom Forrestall (1936-), and Alex Colville (1920-) constitute some of the best in Canadian painting. In the realm of popular entertainment, New Brunswick-born fiddler Don Messer (1909-1973), leader of the band Don Messer and the Islanders, was a figure of national prominence in post-World War II radio and television. More recently singer-songwriter Edith Butler (born at Paquetville in 1942) has done for Acadian music what Antonine Maillet has accomplished with her storytelling. The most significant new talent is Miramichi native David Adams Richards, a novelist whose stark depictions of rural and small town New Brunswick life have brought international attention and national recognition.

New Brunswick has a number of museums and historic sites and two major historic developments, the King's Landing historic village on the Saint John and the Acadian Village at Caraquet. The port city of Saint John has particularly exciting possibilities for the development of historic sites. The province's tourism potential has suffered from the lack of coordinated promotion, but hopefully tourists and residents alike will continue to explore New Brunswick's rich past.

A provincial museum was incorporated by the New Brunswick Legislature in 1929. Coinciding with the province's sesquicentennial in 1934, a neoclassical style building, housing a library, archives, natural science specimens, decorative art, and historical artifacts, was opened on Douglas Avenue in Saint John. Courtesy, New Brunswick Museum

CHAPTER FOUR

PRINCE EDWARD ISLAND

T H E   F A I R E S T   L A N D

By E. Boyde Beck

A sharp wind blows across a tundra landscape. It's cold here. On a rare summer day the temperature might climb above 11 degrees Celsius. The trees are short, stunted by the chill. Birch, willow, and alder, the tallest no more than three meters high, huddle around the rivers and lakes. The rest of the land is dominated by heath and sage. This is a land of lemming and ptarmigan, foxes and wolves. There are no humans.

Twenty-four thousand years ago, the great sheets of the Laurentide Glacier began to loose their grip on the Maritimes. Within 10,000 years they had freed Prince Edward Island. The high sea levels left by their passing would have seen several islands where P.E.I. now stands. Many modern-day hillsides—especially in Prince County—testify to the days when they were seashore. The landscape left by the retreat of the glaciers probably resembled the tundra found in the modern-day Arctic.

Eleven thousand years ago these high sea levels began to recede. Between 9000 and 6000 B.C. they dropped as much as 90 meters relative to modern levels. This exposed the Northumberland Strait, creating a land bridge archaeologist Greg Keenlyside calls "Northumbria." In Northumbria, the harsh skyline of the tundra era would have been softened with stands of cold-tolerant conifers: spruce, pine, fir, and larch. Into this gentler landscape came the caribou. Pursuing them—perhaps pushed from the south by population pressures—came the first humans on Prince Edward Island.

As with the rest of the Maritimes, archaeologists have divided the Island's first inhabitants into three cultural eras. The Paleo-Indian, or Fluted Point culture, was the first of these eras. Migrating probably from New England, this culture pursued the caribou north into the Maritimes. The culture inhabited the coastlines in the spring and summer, hunted caribou inland during the winter, and dominated the region from 8600 to 3500 B.C.

A stone point, found near present-day Tryon, suggests a Paleo-Indian familiarity with P.E.I. at least 8,000 years ago. A stone ulu, found off East Point, indicates habitation in an even earlier era.

The Paleo-Indian tradition faded out 5,500 years ago—it was either displaced

---

Built in the 1840s by architect Isaac Smith, Province House in Charlottetown was one of the colony's proudest possessions. Housing its legislature, courts, and public records, the Province House was at the heart of the Colony's administration. It is now renowned as one of the oldest legislatures in Canada, and as the scene of the first Confederation Conference in 1864. Courtesy, Public Archives of Prince Edward Island

Pictorial Research by E. Boyde Beck

by or evolved into a tradition now labelled the Archaic or Pre-Ceramic. Also called the Shellfish people, they have left few traces on P.E.I. As their name suggests, they developed a sea-based economy with a technology to hunt large fish and sea mammals. Unfortunately for archaeologists, sea levels around the Island began to resurge about 8,000 years ago. The sea has long since reclaimed the coasts inhabited by the Shellfish people, immersing the material evidence of their culture under 90 meters of water.

As the Shellfish people supplanted the Paleo-Indians, they were in turn replaced by Indians of the Algonquin cultural tradition. Again, it is not known if they were pushed out or absorbed. By either process, the Shellfish tradition was gone by 1000 B.C.

As these culture groups rose, then faded, the landscape continued to soften. Tundra gave way to taiga. This in turn gave way to timber. Three thousand years ago, when the Micmac began to make the region their own, the land had settled into the ecological pattern that greeted European settlers 300 years ago. Forests of pine, spruce, fir, and maple grew to the water's edge. The caribou had disappeared, but the forest was still home to large herbivores like deer and moose, as well as their predators: bears, wolves, and man.

A Jesuit missionary, Pierre Biard, described the Micmac as being of lighter build than Europeans, "but handsome and well-shaped; just as we would be if we continued in the same condition in which we were at the age of 25." There is no evidence they used horticulture. Rather, their economy was based on the ancient rhythms of the hunter-gatherer. They lived in a yearly cycle that exploited both the forest and the coastline.

After wintering in the interior, family groups would move to the coast every spring to harvest schools of fish so numerous "you could not put your hand into the water without encountering them." The Island in the summer could support a population through foraging for fish, shellfish, and edible plants. Every autumn, as the winds off the water grew sharper, these coastal populations would break into smaller groups and begin to move inland. Inland waters teemed with eels in the autumn, and winter was the time to hunt bear, otter, moose, and deer. In the spring, the population would return to the coast, and the cycle would begin again. "The land you sleep on is ours," a Micmac chief told Lord Cornwallis in 1765. "We sprang out of the earth like the trees, the grass, and the flowers." And so it must have seemed, to a culture living by the rhythm of the seasons and the richness of the land. From the Paleo-Indian culture through the Shellfish people to the Micmac, the land was theirs. There was no one to

The Micmac Indians followed the ancient rhythms of the seasons. Autumn and winter would find them inland where hunting was prosperous, and for the spring and summer months the Micmacs would return to the coast to partake of the vast fish harvest. Courtesy, Confederation Centre Art Gallery

dispute the fact. No one, until a summer day in 1534, when another, wholly alien culture came on the scene.

"THE FAIREST LAND . . . ."

On June 29, 1534, explorer Jacques Cartier sighted land beyond the sandbars that run along the north shore. "All the coast is low and flat," he wrote in his log, "but it is the fairest land 'tis possible to see, full of fine meadows and trees." As early as 1505, European mapmakers had supposed the existence of a St. John's Island somewhere around Cape Breton. Cartier's find was thus dubbed Isle St. Jean, mentioned briefly in Samuel de Champlain's 1604 *Des Sauvages*, and promptly forgotten. Despite Cartier's glowing assessment, there was little European interest in the Island for the next 150 years. English settlement concentrated far to the south, and the French were much more interested in settling the vital St. Lawrence River valley and occupying the rich marsh lands around the Bay of Fundy.

In the early years of the European era, the Island's main importance lay in its access to the Gulf of St. Lawrence fishery. As the Micmac and their predecessors had long been aware, P.E.I.'s north shore was an excellent fishing base. European fishermen also came to realize this. Though there are no records, it is logical to suppose that Isle St. Jean saw occasional use as a fishing station even before Cartier's sighting. By the mid-seventeenth century French fishing interests began to press for

Allies of the French in their wars against the English, Prince Edward Island's Micmac Indians did not fare well under British rule. By the time of Confederation in 1873 the Micmac population was estimated at little more than 300. Courtesy, Public Archives of Prince Edward Island

the establishment of a permanent, sedentary fishery based on the Island.

A sedentary fishery, in the French view, would not only enhance their economic presence in the area; it would also be the key to planting a permanent settlement. French populations had been firmly established in Quebec and Acadia by 1650. The Crown, however, was reluctant to accept the financial burden of establishing a similar colony on Isle St. Jean. Perhaps, it reasoned, private interests could be enticed to do so. The enticement: exclusive land and fishing rights to the Gulf of St. Lawrence. The price: all the expenses involved in founding and nurturing an infant colony.

The first such deal was struck with a group headed by Nicholas Denys. In 1654 Denys' company was granted sole ownership of Isle St. Jean, Isle Royale (Cape Breton), Newfoundland, and all of the smaller islands in the Gulf of St. Lawrence. In return, he promised to found several settlements "and labour for the conversion of the Indians." In 1663, Denys was accused of failing to fulfill his obligations. His grant was revoked and given to Francois Doublet. When Doublet was similarly unsuccessful, the grant was returned to Denys. In 1686 Denys lost it again, this time to Gabriel Gautier. Gautier in turn was revoked in favour of Sieur de Louvigny.

From this flurry of legal action, one thing was apparent; private investors were interested in Isle St. Jean only for the fish that could be caught from it—not for any settlement that might be founded there. Even aside from this, the ventures, under-planned and under-funded, seem to have been fated for failure. Until the government in France became more involved, there would be no major settlement on Isle St. Jean.

The incentive for this involvement came in 1713. Endeavouring to salvage an unsuccessful war (the War of the Spanish Succession) with a successful peace treaty, France ceded to the British most of its holdings in the Gulf of St. Lawrence. When the treaty was concluded, the French were left with their fortress on Isle Royale, the totally undeveloped Isle St. Jean, and the problem of relocating an Acadian population living in what had become British territory. With a powerful fortress and naval base at Louisbourg, and fertile Isle St. Jean to act as its provision base, France was confident it could soon reestablish its dominance of the gulf region. All it had to do was populate the two areas.

Immediately following the 1713 treaty, the French government hoped there would be a spontaneous mass migration from now-British Acadia to Isles Royale and St. Jean. Between 1713 and 1720, official policy favoured settling Isle Royale first. However, as the minister of marine wrote the governor of Isle Royale: "If the Acadians prefer to go to Isle St. Jean . . . they must not be refused; the great thing is that they should leave Acadia."

In 1711, following the fall of Port Royal, a few Acadian families did try to relocate to Isle St. Jean. There they found Louvigny's monopoly still in force and, unable to get clear title to land of their own, returned to Acadia. Though Louvigny's title was revoked in 1716, the French still found Acadians reluctant to relocate to Isle St. Jean. Many Acadians probably felt France would someday win the region back, and they were unwilling to abandon established farms while this possibility remained. Isle St. Jean was, moreover, quite unsuited to Acadian farming methods. The lush marshlands of the Fundy region were not to be found on Isle St. Jean. Farms there would have to be carved from the forest. Though Governor Jacques d'Espiet De Pensens later condemned the Acadians as "naturally lazy and

OPPOSITE: Fleeing deportation from their homeland in the 1750s, many of these Acadian refugees ended up on Isle St. Jean. Their respite proved to be short, however, when British rule extended to Isle St. Jean, and once again the Acadians were forced from their settlements in 1758. Courtesy, National Archives of Canada

accustomed to work only in easy marshes," it is not surprising that few would willingly trade comfortable settlements for a harder, more uncertain future.

As it became apparent there would be no exodus of Acadians to Isle St. Jean, the government fell back on an older method of arranging settlement. In 1719 the entire Island was granted to Compte de St. Pierre. In return for establishing 100 settlers in his first year, and at least 50 every year thereafter, St. Pierre was given exclusive fishing rights to both Isle Royale and Isle St. Jean. Unlike previous efforts, St. Pierre's settlement got off to a good start. In 1720, 100 settlers from Rochfort sailed into what is now Hillsborough Bay and founded a colonial capital: Port La Joie. Within the year settlement had spread to six more sites.

The possibility of a successful French colony on the Island was alarming to the English, who feared it might provide a springboard for the reconquest of Acadia. To disuade the English from attacking the infant colony, France dispatched a garrison of 25 men under Captain De Pensens. Arriving in 1726, De Pensens, though a reluctant governor, gave the Island the rudiments of a colonial administration. After this auspicious beginning, however, the St. Pierre venture began to go the way of its predecessors. By 1724 St. Pierre's company was destitute, and most of his settlers had left for Isle Royale. In 1725 his fishing rights were revoked. The entire grant was repealed in 1730, and Isle St. Jean returned to the royal domain. It consisted, in its entirety, of a crumbling capital with a tiny garrison, several thriving fishing ports, and a European population of 350.

Even though settlers were now free to obtain clear land grants on the Island, the colony continued to grow at an extremely slow pace. Immigration from

France, never great to begin with, dried up completely by 1734. Governor De Pensens, despairing that his career had foundered in such a backwater, spent as much time as he could in Louisbourg and France. Mice plagues, fire, and drought claimed three different harvests.

There were, however, some hopeful signs. The population, though small, was shifting its economy from fishing to farming, indicating that settlements were becoming firmly established. A new governor, Du Chambon, was appointed, and in 1740 he began to offer prospective Acadian settlers a year's provisions to help their relocation to Isle St. Jean. Five families came in 1741. Twenty more followed over the next three years. They came, in the words of historian D.C. Harvey, "in a careful, healthy manner; the younger Acadians moving over only after carefully spying out the land, and not in numbers too great to be absorbed." This time of slow, careful migration was soon to end. The long awaited flood from Acadia was about to begin.

In 1744 Du Chambon was promoted to governor of Isle Royale. His tenure there was short; within a year he was forced to surrender his domain to the British as a force of English and New England troops carried his fortress at Louisbourg. A British detachment was dispatched to dislodge the small garrison at Isle

Upon seizing Isle St. Jean, one of the first things the British did was commission a survey of their new possession. They chose Samuel Holland, one of their most accomplished surveyors. His map, shown here in its 1775 edition, was influential in shaping the future tone of Island history. The lots and townships he laid out became the focus of a century of bitter unrest over land and tenure. Courtesy, Public Archives of Prince Edward Island

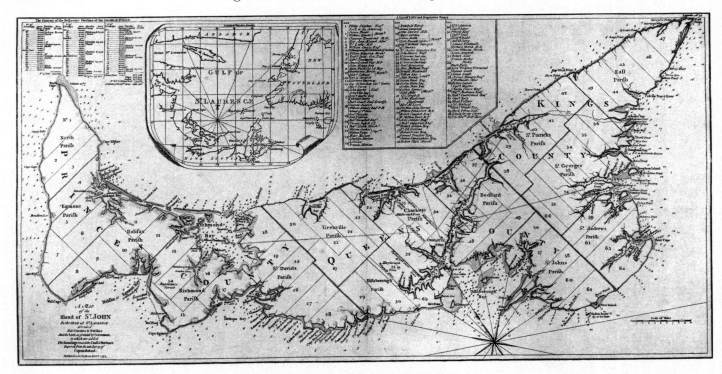

St. Jean. It destroyed the settlement at Three Rivers and, after a short battle, occupied Port La Joie. The war's hardship at first seemed to end here. The British, after a pledge of good behavior, agreed to leave the colony alone. In 1748 the peace of Aix-la-Chappelle returned the Island to French control. However, the war was to have a more far-reaching impact.

In the war's aftermath Great Britain decided to settle Acadia with its own subjects, and insisted that their Acadian settlers take an oath of allegiance. In 1749 Halifax was founded, effectively cutting Acadia off from Isle Royale. Acadians troubled by these political developments thus had only one place to flee: Isle St. Jean. The flood began.

Close to 1,000 Acadians decided to move in 1749. Another 500 followed in 1750. After a short lull, another 700 came in 1753-1754. In 1755, after the outbreak of the Seven Years' War and Britain's subsequent expulsion of its Acadian subjects, another 2,000 refugees fled to Isle St. Jean. Though 600 were immediately sent on to Quebec, the Island's population had swelled to 4,500—up from 650 seven years before.

This was no carefully planned resettlement, as had been the trickle of 1740-1744. It was the result of French, then British, policy. As in 1713, French policy in 1748 had been to entice settlers away from British-held Acadia. Again, it was hoped that a sound colony on Isle St. Jean would become the main supply base for the fortress at Louisbourg. When war resumed in 1755, British policy had been to expel from its sphere any settler who would not swear allegiance to them.

The result of these policies was an era of utter chaos on Isle St. Jean. The colony's system of granting land was not capable of dealing with the influx. Title was usually given verbally and this led to conflicts between new and old settlers over title and holdings. On a more ominous note, the colony endured three crop failures in the crucial years between 1752 and 1757. Acadian farmers grew wheat and peas, with the emphasis on wheat; instead of becoming the granary of Isle Royale, however, the colony was continually sending to Louisbourg for emergency provisions. At least those who fled between 1748 and 1757 had some time to prepare for life in their new homes. The refugees of the 1755 expulsion enjoyed no such luxury. They arrived in autumn, destitute and with few provisions to feed them. In 1757, when these latest refugees had barely been accommodated, the crop failed again. In 1758 the litany of disaster reached its climax. The British returned.

On July 26, Louisbourg fell for the final time to British forces. Within two weeks a British contingent of 500, commanded by Lord Rollo, landed at Port La Joie. This occupation would be quite different from that of 1743. Rollo had

As early as 1800 settlers discovered that the dense forest cover could be more than merely an obstacle to farming. Throughout the nineteenth century the timber boom provided one of the few means of earning cash wages on Prince Edward Island. During the Golden Age, lumber was the cargo of choice for shipbuilders sending vessels to the British market, and sawmills equalled shipyards in importance to the Island's economy. Courtesy, Heritage Foundation Collection, Public Archives of Prince Edward Island

ABOVE: In 1770 the Crown chose one of Prince Edward Island's own proprietors, Walter Patterson, to be its first governor. A difficult one at best, Patterson's administration was embroiled in bitter conflicts with fellow landowners until he was recalled in 1785. Courtesy, Public Archives of Prince Edward Island

OPPOSITE, BOTTOM: In winter, the only reliable link between Prince Edward Island and the mainland was by iceboat. Essentially a rowboat with an iron-shod keel, the iceboat was powered by a crew attached to its gunwales by leather harness. The crew would run with the boat across the ice until they fell through, then they would get back in the boat and row until they found more ice to traverse. Iceboats remained in service through the 1890s, carrying a precious cargo of passengers and mail. Courtesy, Public Archives of Prince Edward Island

orders to extend the expulsion policy to Isle St. Jean. His troops spread quickly to occupy the colony's various settlements, and British transports began to load French settlers. Many families, preferring to make their own way, fled in their own vessels. Port La Joie was leveled by a force of Micmac—former French allies determined to deny the capital to the British. A single enclave of 30 families, saved by their isolation, escaped the deportation. Within months it was over. As the forest began to reclaim abandoned French settlements, Isle St. Jean became St. John's Island. The British era had begun.

THE POLITICS OF LAND

Tangles of spruce and hardwood ran riot to the water's edge. Canopies of branches arched 20 to 30 meters over the forest floor, blotting out all but the fiercest sunlight. This was the sight that greeted the first British settlers landing on the Island: the forest from which they would have to hack homes and arable fields. It was a daunting prospect, especially for a people unschooled in the handling of an axe. As Lord Selkirk observed in 1805: "the settler set down in such a place feels the helplessness almost of a child."

Helpless or not, by 1800 an increasing number of settlers were arriving on the Island. It was a hopeful time for the infant British colony—a time of change and renewal. In 1799 it acquired a new name, Prince Edward Island, to both honour the Duke of Kent and ease the confusion of a region with so many "St. Johns" on its map. A timber boom was taking hold and, in 1804, the colony's shipyards launched its first full-rigged ship. And settlers were arriving. Mostly Scots, they were beginning to pour into the colony, swelling the population to 7,000 by 1805. At the turn of the nineteenth century Prince Edward Island was in need of a fresh start, for its first decades as a British possession had been anything but easy.

The British seemed unprepared for the windfall of colonies that followed the French collapse in North America. Beyond evicting the existing European population, they certainly did not know what to do with St. John's Island. In 1763 they added it to the domain of Nova Scotia. The following year they dispatched surveyors, who divided it into 67 lots of 20,000 acres each. Aside from this, they made no plans. Founding settlements was an expensive business—especially for a treasury depleted by seven years of war. London was too occupied with reconciling Quebec to life under its new masters to give much attention to tiny St. John's Island. The Island, however, was not totally ignored. In the 1760s there were other circles in Britain who took a vital interest in its development.

These were, mainly, individuals to whom the government owed political favours. They had heard, first from the French and later from their own sources, that St. John's Island was a place of great potential. The French had thought of the Island as the future "Granary of New France." British observers held there was not an acre in the place that could not be cultivated. It could easily support a population of 500,000, they predicted, and would quickly become a thriving agricultural community. In an age when agriculture still dominated most economies these were impressive characteristics. The Island gained an irresistible allure amongst the Whitehall favourseekers. From Lord Egmont—who wanted the whole thing—to hundreds of lesser claimants, requests for a piece of St. John's Island began to mount.

The Lords Commissioners of Trade and Plantations—precursor to the Colonial Office—saw in this clamour a simple solution to the problem of how to dispose of the new colony. In a variation on older French schemes, they decided to give the Island away. This time it would be granted not to a single company but to 67 interested proprietors—one for each lot. The colony would be split from Nova Scotia and set up with its own administration. The successful grantees would undertake to settle their lands with "foreign Protestants," thus avoiding a drain on Britain's own population. Generating revenue from lease fees, these proprietors would in turn remit annual quit rents to support the colony's civil administration. It was, in theory, a neat solution to the problem of creating a self-sufficient colony with minimal strain on the Crown's finances. And it had an added benefit; it would allow the Pitt administration to wipe a number of debts from its slate.

A list of worthwhile candidates was drawn up. On July 24, 1767, the successful grantees were chosen by lottery. "Thus was, the Island . . . given away in a day," one critic later commented. It was a significant day, for the ramifications of the land lottery would be felt for a century to come. The seeds sown that afternoon would grow to dominate almost every aspect of the colony's development: political, social, and even sectarian.

That the scheme was not going to work as well in reality as it did in theory was immediately apparent. More than one-quarter of the original grants quickly changed hands, indicating that many of the grantees were mere speculators. The "foreign Protestants" specified in the grants were not an easy commodity to secure, and the proprietors who were interested in developing their lots were forced to look in Britain for potential settlers. Settlement was further hampered

The land question politicized Prince Edward Island at a very early date. The escheat agitation of the 1780s and 1790s resulted in the development of the Loyal Electors—possibly the first organized political party in British North America. Pictured here is Angus MacAulay, one of the party's principal members. Courtesy, Public Archives of Prince Edward Island

by the outbreak of the American Revolution. Proprietors who had hoped to develop their grants and begin to draw revenue from them were thwarted by these difficulties. The remainder seemed more interested in merely holding their grants in hopes they would accrue in value even if undeveloped. Neither group could be persuaded to pay their quit rents. When the colony's first British governor, Walter Patterson, arrived in 1770, he found the proprietors had sent out fewer than 1,000 settlers, and that his treasury was all but empty.

That the colony had been set off on the wrong foot was apparent in more than its undeveloped lands and bankrupt administration. The land tenure system generated political strife as well. The proprietors soon settled into two groups. One group consisted of the wealthier grantees and those interested only in speculation who administered their lands from Great Britain. In the second group were the few proprietors who chose to emigrate to the new colony. The latter had a more personal stake in the development of the Island, and a voracious appetite for more land. In these endeavours they had an ally in Governor Patterson and a weapon in a process called escheat.

Escheat referred to the clause in each original grant that specified the grant could be revoked if the grantee failed to settle his lands properly or fell in arrears of his quit rents. Virtually every proprietor on the Island was liable to escheat, for none had filled his obligations to the letter. Though threatened on several occasions, escheat was first used in 1780. That year Governor Patterson seized several undeveloped lots and auctioned them to recover their rent arrears.

The landlords in England immediately mobilized a lobby to have the seized lands returned. A powerful group to begin with, they were able to capitalize on the fact that most of the escheated land ended up in the hands of Patterson and his political allies on the Island.

The Crown sided with the London lobby, returned the lots in question, and recalled Patterson in disgrace. It would not be the last time the politics of the land question would cause a rift between Britain and the Island, or the premature end of a governor's career.

Though it ended in defeat, the early escheat actions yielded several benefits for the Island. The British Parliament, admitting quit rents would never generate sufficient revenue, voted the colony's civil administration a yearly operating grant. More importantly, it led some of the less active proprietors to sell their lots to more interested parties. The benefit of this soon showed up in the increasing number of settlers landing on the Island.

They were coming mainly from Britain. Because of its land tenure system, and the fact it had no Crown lands to offer, very few Loyalists chose to relocate on the Island. By the time it changed its name to Prince Edward Island, the colony was being settled by a mix of Scots and Englishmen. The Scots were divided

The sight of American fishing schooners became commonplace in ports like Souris and Colville Bay, depicted in this circa 1825 engraving. Though technically banned from touching shore by the Convention of 1818, American skippers often landed to avoid bad weather, to buy bait, or to engage in contraband trade with local inhabitants. In later years, after the 1854 Reciprocity Treaty, as many as 600 American vessels would migrate yearly to fish off Prince Edward Island ports. Courtesy, Public Archives of Prince Edward Island

The Acadians who escaped deportation, and the many who made their way back to Prince Edward Island, succeeded in reviving many of their old communities and proceeded to establish new ones. Though often condemned by the British for lack of initiative (and for taking too many religious holidays), the Island's Acadians prospered through a blend of fishing and agriculture. Courtesy, Confederation Centre Art Gallery

Though sometimes considered a pursuit inferior to agriculture, the fishery was one of the most constant industries on Prince Edward Island. Until the 1880s, however, few Islanders aside from the Acadians made their living from the sea. Courtesy, Confederation Centre Art Gallery

William Cooper began his career as a land agent. In the 1830s, however, he abandoned that side of the land question and became the leader of the increasingly powerful Escheat party. After repeated attempts on the Island, Cooper took the question of land reform to London itself. Countered at every turn by the powerful proprietors lobby, Cooper and his Escheaters had to admit defeat by 1842. Courtesy, Public Archives of Prince Edward Island

OPPOSITE, BOTTOM: In the mid-1800s George Coles was one of a new breed of the economic elite on Prince Edward Island. A merchant and brewer, he made his money through commerce—not as a land agent or proprietor. Thus, when elected to the House of Assembly in 1845, Coles found himself tending to side with the reformers. In 1851, as premier of the first responsible government of Prince Edward Island, Coles embarked on an extensive program of social reforms. Courtesy, Public Archives of Prince Edward Island

between Protestant Lowlanders and Catholic Highlanders. Though the latter were not technically allowed to settle on P.E.I., the "Protestant" requirement of the original grants was long forgotten by 1800. The Lowlanders and Englishmen tended to come in communities of established farmers emigrating en masse—not to escape economic pressure but to capitalize on a perceived economic opportunity. The Highlanders, also coming in communities and in larger numbers, were literally being "sent out." There was a great deal of social and economic pressure on the traditions of the Highlanders. The English Parliament had passed laws designed to destroy their language and customs. In addition, the consolidation of large estates and enclosure of pasture lands had driven many small farmers from their leases. Reform-minded proprietors thought they could ease these problems by settling the Highlanders in the New World. Prince Edward Island, with its familiar, almost European landscape, was considered a better-than-usual place for such experiments. "This is an excellent poor man's country," trumpeted the *European Emigration Gazette.* "It is the Englishman's and Scotsman's and Irishman's friend—a shore for them to flock to when there is no food for them in their own country . . . If the poor in England did but know what advantages this Island holds forth, they would not stay and starve as they do."

Though they did not arrive in the thousands, as the promoters urged, they did arrive in significant numbers, despite the fact freehold land was rare and long-term leases difficult to secure. The population grew to 27,000 by 1828, 47,000 by 1841, and 71,000 by the 1850s. A far cry from the 500,000 predicted in the 1760s, but respectable in the circumstances.

The colony's economy grew apace. The Island was especially suited to Highland farming practices, once the intimidating forest had been brought under control. Accustomed to working small plots with hand tools, they were quite at home planting potatoes between the stumps of semi-cleared land and leaving their livestock free to forage. Though later condemned by more scientifically minded agriculturalists, these methods were very effective in their context, and served to secure a foothold on the land. By the 1830s Prince Edward Island had become a thriving agricultural settlement. It was not, however, an entirely content one. Settlers continued to chafe under the system of land tenure, and by the 1830s it was apparent that, once established, these tenant farmers would endeavour to improve their political fortunes as well.

As with Britain's other North American colonies, the 1830s and 1840s were times of political unrest on P.E.I. Unlike the other colonies, however, turmoil on the Island centred almost entirely on the politics of land ownership. In some ways, this agitation was similar to the conflicts of the eighteenth century. The battle lines were still drawn between resident Islanders and absentee proprietors. There were, though, significant changes. In the 1780s and 1790s, land reform was essentially a vehicle through which resident landlords sought to increase their holdings at the expense of their absentee rivals. The agitation of the 1830s was a more broad-based, agrarian movement. Ironically, it had its genesis in the fact

that the original proprietors had failed one, minor term in their grants.

At the time thousands of Scots Highlanders were being sent to P.E.I., the fact they were not the Protestant stock specified in 1767 was largely ignored. As poor, un-enfranchised Roman Catholics, they were considered the best available population for a colony crying for settlers. Their status changed in 1829. When London extended the franchise to Roman Catholics, the Island's electorate virtually doubled overnight. Suddenly, the colony's huge Highland population became one of its most significant political forces. In the 1830 elections for the House of Assembly, their votes, combined with the colony's other tenants and small landholders, installed a group of radical land reformers in the Legislature. The Island's tenants had decided the land they had cleared and improved should belong to those who worked it. They wanted more control, if not free title, to the lands they were forced to lease. Their leader was William Cooper, a former land agent turned land reformer. Their rallying point: the now traditional cry, "Escheat!"

Cooper's reformers, at first no more than a loose coalition of like-thinkers, soon coalesced into the Escheat party. They demanded that heavy taxes be levied on undeveloped lands, hoping this would force apathetic landlords to sell their properties. When this was disallowed they increased their demands, insisting a full-scale court of escheat be set up. They wanted each proprietor judged according to the literal terms of the original land grants. As it was widely admitted that no proprietor, good or bad, had met these terms, it meant a radical, almost revolutionary redistribution of property. Striding this platform, the Escheaters swept three successive elections. Under their leadership the tensions surrounding the land issue steadily grew. By the mid-1830s an active campaign of civil disobedience was mounting. Tenants were refusing to pay their rents, and so dominated many districts that the sheriff refused to

ABOVE: The advent of responsible government intensified activity in one of the Island's favourite pastimes—politics. An often volatile blend of religion and nationality contributed to some exciting polling days. The flourishing city of Charlottetown is shown here on one such election day in the mid-1800s. Courtesy, Confederation Centre Art Gallery

When the scientific agriculture movement gained momentum and cultivation grew more intensive, Prince Edward Island farmers became more concerned with maintaining the fertility of their fields. The most popular fertilizer used was mussel mud, formed by decaying shellfish beds. The mud was dredged from river bottoms in the winter and then sledded over frozen roads. As this late 1800s photograph shows, the annual mussel mud excursion was often a community event. Courtesy, Public Archives of Prince Edward Island

try and make them pay. They treaded the line, but did not cross into open rebellion. Their respect for the law was innate. They believed their cause would win, if only it was argued with enough persuasion. Unfortunately, there were few in London willing to listen to them, and many in active opposition.

Land reform was opposed at two levels. First, Prince Edward Island had its own version of the Family Compact—men who considered themselves patricians in a backwoods society. They believed power should be wielded only by those with proper education and breeding. Men, to be brief, like themselves. The Compact was strongly allied to proprietal interests. Indeed, many of the elites were land agents and most owned land themselves. To this element William Cooper and the Escheaters were democracy at its demagogic worst. Second, the elites had strong allies in London, where the proprietor lobby had grown more powerful since the 1780s. In addition to its political power, the proprietor lobby had the sanctity of private property on its side. Though escheat ruled the Island's Legislature, its opponents held more sway in the Colonial Office. Cooper's party could pass escheat legislation but had no way of making the Colonial Office assent to it. In 1838 Cooper himself went to London to argue the case for land reform—all to no avail. Worn down by a decade of frustration and refusal, the Escheat party began to fall into disarray. By 1842 it had ceased to function.

As in the 1780s, the defeat of land reform yielded benefits that were not immediately apparent. Lord Durham, dispatched by the British government to recommend reforms for the North American colonies, noted the unhappiness of the Island's tenantry. Discontent had grown so widespread that the Island was being compared to Ireland, and Durham recommended that steps be taken to ease the grip of the proprietors. More significantly, when the movement toward responsible government that Durham set in motion began to reach the Maritimes, the Island was ready with a core of reformers hardened in the battles over escheat.

By 1848 reform had rallied around a new leader—George Coles—and a new cause: responsible government. In 1851, when this was granted, the reformers swept back to power. Land reform reappeared, in muted guise, through an act empowering the government to purchase proprietal lands and resell them to resident tenants. As the decade progressed it appeared the "long, vexing land question" had found, if not an answer, than at least a more promising direction. At the same time the economy began to quicken. It appeared that Prince Edward Island's oft-predicted, long-awaited prosperity had finally arrived.

THE GOLDEN AGE

Shipbuilding, reciprocity, and a thriving agrarian economy—these were the essential components of the Island's golden age. Though a long time in coming, prosperity had hit full stride by the mid-1850s. Along with the experience of responsible government, it helped create a powerful sense of autonomy and

A sure sign of a conscientious farmer was the care he took of his land. Throughout the nineteenth century, the most popular method for revitalizing the soil was the application of mussel mud, dredged from the river bottoms in winter, when the ice was thick enough to support the equipment needed to load and transport the mud. Courtesy, Public Archives of Prince Edward Island

pride in the tiny colony—a fierce "sense of self" that would carry P.E.I. through the Confederation era, and a little beyond.

An observer of the colony's agriculture in 1850 would have been moved to note the sophistication that the pursuit had achieved since the 1830s. Gone were the days when crops were coaxed from partially cleared fields. The progress was slow, at least to those who preferred the label "agriculturalist" to "farmer." By 1850, however, the British "high farming" movement had filtered to the Island, bringing vast improvement to the colony's agriculture. Unsuitable crops like oats and wheat, which had been grown as much for tradition as for anything else, began to give way to root crops like potatoes and turnips, species better adapted to the Island's soil. Regardless of what was grown, suitable or not, the forest continued to give way to cleared land. Assaulted by the farmer on the one hand, and the shipbuilder on the other, the forest was in full retreat.

Shipbuilding had begun as an adjunct to the timber boom of the early 1800s. Though the end of the Napoleonic Wars curtailed the demand for timber, shipbuilding gained its own momentum. The Island was perfectly suited to the industry. The forest, a curse to settlers, offered an abundant stock of usable timber. The rivers offered coves by the hundred with grades suitable for receiving a keel and water deep enough to float the finished product. By the 1830s Prince Edward Island shipyards were gaining a reputation for turning out sturdy, if roughly built, vessels. By the 1850s they were launching 70 to 100 boats a year—more, per capita, than any other part of the British Empire. These were, as a local saying went, "the years of two fiddles and no plows."

The Island's carrying trade grew apace. Through the 1840s the colony had traded mainly with Great Britain and its fellow colonies in the Atlantic region. In the 1850s a third party came onto the scene. In 1854 Great Britain negotiated the Reciprocity Treaty between its Atlantic colonies and the United States. In return for fishing rights, the Island gained free access to the huge American market for its agricultural produce. To an agrarian society relying entirely on farm produce and shipping for its income, reciprocity was a profound advance. Charlottetown harbour sprouted a forest of masts as the United States became Prince Edward Island's main trading partner.

The 1850s saw P.E.I. develop a spiritual maturity to complement its material prosperity. Land long fought over engendered strong patriotism. Residents staunchly defended their colony's reputation as the most fertile in British North America. They were equally proud of their Legislature, now endowed with the power of semi-autonomy. In 1855 they incorporated their capital, Charlottetown, as their first city. Britain withdrew its garrison the same year, leaving an Island confident it could defend itself through its own militia. The colony boasted its own university—St. Dunstan's—and a free education system it considered unequalled by any other part of the Empire. The population, bolstered by its own birthrate and an influx of Irish immigrants, was nearing the 100,000 mark. To its own inhabitants, P.E.I. had become "our country" and they were extremely proud

Between 1840 and 1870 Island shipyards launched some 3,000 vessels. These were the years when shipbuilding was the heart of the Island's economy. In this circa 1860 photograph, shipwrights have completed the vessel's keel and ribs and are about to lay the floor. Courtesy, Public Archives of Prince Edward Island

of their "right little, tight little Island." The golden age was not without tarnish, however. Social and political tensions accompanied prosperity. Ironically, these tensions came to a head as prosperity reached its climax, and Islanders faced the biggest decision in their history.

THE CONFEDERATION ERA

"It is a question of self or no self," reckoned Cornelius Howat during the first round of Confederation debates. "We would be no better off than if we were Russian slaves." In 1865, as Islanders argued over their response to the question of Confederation, passions ran high. Most agreed with Howat, and considered the scheme a bad one for their country. A few, however, saw a possible solution to their local problems in a broad union of British North American colonies.

A major effect of the 1854 Reciprocity Treaty was a substantial increase in the Island's transport trade. This prosperity favoured some much more than others, since 80 percent of Prince Edward Island's cargo fleet was owned by no more than a dozen men. Courtesy, Public Archives of Prince Edward Island

The problems in question revolved around two issues, both as old as the colony itself. The first was the chronic land question. The Land Purchase Act had only eased, not erased, the tensions associated with land reform. The government of P.E.I. drew its revenue mostly from customs duties. Reluctant to borrow heavily, it could only slowly raise the money needed to buy out the proprietal estates. Besides, it considered the problem as mainly of Britain's making, and thus deserving Britain's assistance to remedy. In 1860 the Island government appealed to London for a grant to cover these purchases. When this was refused, tenant impatience began to boil over. As in the 1830s, a growing number refused to pay rent on land they considered their own. The more militant among them formed the Tenant League. By the mid-1860s the Island government so feared the agitation would explode into rebellion that it requested the return of a British garrison.

Adding to the strife of the land issue was a growing intolerance among the Island's religious groups. Through its first century as a British colony the Island

had attracted an even mix of Protestant and Roman Catholic settlers. Though there had been occasional expressions of ill will, the denominations had co-existed peacefully in the early years. It was simple to maintain good relations when communities were dispersed and isolated from each other. As these communities grew—and began to rub shoulders—religious intolerance became more commonplace. A compounding factor was that most proprietors were Protestant, and not above invoking religion to attract supporters and split their religiously mixed opponents. In the 1840s, following an influx of mostly Catholic southern Irish, the Protestant sects felt increasingly threatened. Agitation in the 1850s for denominational schools did little to calm their fears. By 1860 the Orange lodge was enjoying a growing membership and an anti-Papist newspaper even opened in Charlottetown.

Confederation, when first mooted, was considered a possible remedy for these ills. Perhaps, argued its supporters, the Island could forget its parochial

biases if part of a larger union. Perhaps this larger union could also advance the money the Island needed to buy out the proprietors. These were evocative arguments. They had to be, for the arguments brought against them were powerful indeed.

In many ways, the Confederation movement was a response to the growing power of the United States. At heart it was a customs union, designed to protect the infant industries of British North America and pro-

mote increased trade among the colonies. The Island, however, had no fears of the United States. Indeed, trade with the Americans had brought un-precedented prosperity to the colony. The shift in tariffs promoted by Confederation promised disaster for P.E.I. There was no industry, and little prospect of any materializing, so the Island had little interest in protective tariffs. Nor was free trade with Canada an appealing prospect. As one member of the Legislature put it: "Our imports from that colony are almost entirely of flour, and we export nothing to it save a few quintals of fish." Constitutional objections to the plan were even harder to counter. The semi-independence to which Islanders were just getting accustomed would be lost. "Talk about a local legislature?" anti-Confederates argued. "It would be a mere farce."

Prince Edward Island was willing to discuss the proposition, however. Following the first, promising series of meetings in Charlottetown, the Island sent seven of its best statesmen to Quebec for the second round of talks. After a week of negotiations even the staunchest Confederate among the P.E.I. delegation had to admit the other colonies would never come up with terms acceptable to the Island electorate.

In exchange for the complete reworking of the Island economy and loss of autonomy, Confederation offered what most dismissed as an inadequate annual operating grant. Union would not settle the land question, for the other colonies refused to guarantee the loan needed to buy out the proprietors. The hardest pill to swallow was that P.E.I. would have only five members in the new, 200-member House of Commons. Despite hints that the financial arrangements might be sweetened, and enormous pressure from the Colonial Office, Confederation had become a dead issue by 1865. The final rounds of nation building would go on without Prince Edward Island. Though the Island came out in opposition to the idea, these Confederation debates did convince Islanders they had to make some accommodation to ensure the continuation of their hard-won prosperity. The Colonial Office, keenly supportive of Confederation, voiced its displeasure at the Island's decision to remain aloof. Most Islanders agreed that the Mother Country would soon balk "at the expense of keeping up a protectorate over this patch of sandbank." Few Islanders realized how little leeway Britain intended to give them, or how quickly

the alternatives to Confederation would evaporate.

Some of the alternatives mooted were spectacular indeed. Correspondents to local newspapers touted the grand idea of an imperial union of all British colonies with a common parliament in London. Others suggested union with the United States—an idea that was often trotted out whenever an instance of British or Canadian nastiness was perceived. The course favoured by most Islanders was the status quo and

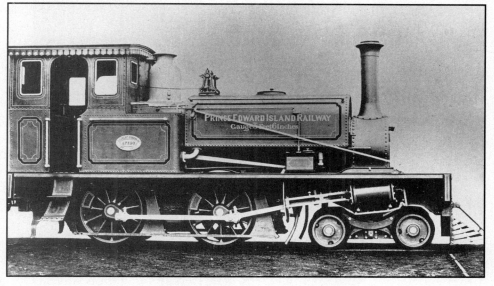

a return to reciprocity with the United States. The treaty had lapsed in the mid-1860s, and the Island, aware of how much of its prosperity had come to rest upon it, was eager to renew it. The United States, however, was too absorbed with recovering from its Civil War to contemplate renegotiating reciprocity with British North America. Seeing a chance to teach Britain and its upstart Dominion a lesson, it was willing to negotiate directly with P.E.I. In 1868 it sent a trade delegation to Charlottetown, and indicated a treaty between the Island and itself was possible. When the Colonial Office got wind of this it swiftly curtailed the proceedings, reminding the United States that the Island's foreign affairs were handled through London, not Charlottetown. Slapped down by the Mother Country, and refused the desperately needed reciprocity, the Island defiantly decided it would go it alone.

It soon found that pride and autonomy were easier to maintain in times of prosperity than in those of hardship. By 1871 a declining economy was proving a stern test. Steam engines and iron hulls were taking the bloom off the shipbuilding boom. In the absence of reciprocity, exports declined year by year. Markets

Lucy Maud Montgomery— by far the Island's best-known author— succeeded in capturing the spirit of late nineteenth-century Prince Edward Island. Her portrayals of the Island's proud, tightly-knit communities have enjoyed a sustained popularity both on and off the Island. Courtesy, Public Archives of Prince Edward Island

were more competitive and cash was in shorter supply.

The remedy, it was decided, was a railway. By 1871 the Island was fully in the grip of railway fever. Railway construction would employ thousands and inject needed cash into the economy. It would promote industry, foster farming, and attract tourists. A railway, argued its proponents, would improve the Island's prospects and prove to the world its ability to go it alone. When the Legislature passed railway legislation in 1871 Islanders literally cheered in the streets. The few who opposed it, shuddering at the huge risk the undertaking posed for the Island's fragile economy, were drowned out. Within a year, as the building costs soared to four times the original estimates, their fears seemed prophetic.

The Island's debt, hitherto minor, increased to $42 per head. As the railway debt mounted, the Legislature discovered no foreign institution would touch P.E.I. debentures or extend the huge loans needed to keep the work going. The Island's own banks began to falter under the strain. By 1873 Islanders faced the bitter fact: their country was on the verge of bankruptcy. The railway that was to be their saviour had turned into their downfall. The options were as exhausted as the treasury. Only Confederation remained. A delegation travelled to Ottawa and secured terms for an agreement. It was, considering the circumstances, a very generous deal. Canada increased its offer for an operating grant, advanced the money needed to buy out the proprietal lands, and agreed to assume the crushing railway debt. Though a few die-hards continued to oppose the deal, there was really no choice. Prince Edward Island would become Canada's seventh province. On July 1, 1873, a group of dignitaries and three observers turned out to hear the official proclamation read. The Island's century as a British colony, and its 20-year run of semi-independence, had come to an end.

ADJUSTING TO THE MODERN ERA

The mood was subdued as Prince Edward Island entered Confederation. "Make the best of it, for you go in as paupers," was the bitter warning of the anti-Confederates. The warning was well placed. If the 1850s and 1860s were intoxicating years, those that followed were sobering ones. As the twentieth century loomed, P.E.I. faced many changes to adjust to both the modern era and its role as Canada's smallest province.

Some of the most difficult adjustments to make were economic. The last quarter of the nineteenth century was tough on the Island's economy. Confederation wrought havoc on its traditional trading patterns. The new union stressed internal, east-west trading patterns—not the familiar arc between Great Britain, the Atlantic Provinces, and the United States. The National Policy, designed to protect Canada's infant industries, imposed severe hardships on resource-based economies like that of the Island. These developments, compounded by the general economic recessions of the 1870s and 1880s, conspired to destroy the few shreds of prosperity the Island had left.

The hardest adjustment to make was the loss of the shipbuilding industry. The decline that had been evident in the late 1860s quickly accelerated toward complete collapse. The causes of this were complex, but boiled down to two factors: rising costs and increasing competition. The rise of the steamship and decline of the Island's forests were telling blows, but not entirely accountable for the demise of the industry. Despite a century of clearing and exploitation, timber

Prince Edward Island's many tidal rivers, with their broad mouths and gently sloping banks, sprouted hundreds of shipyards throughout the nineteenth century. By the 1880s, however, increasing costs and declining markets drove most of these shipbuilders out of business. When this photograph of the schooner The Empress *was taken near the Montague shipyards at the turn of the century, the industry was moribund, and only a few yards remained in business. Courtesy, Public Archives of Prince Edward Island*

The Prince Edward Island lobster industry, which began in the 1860s, developed very slowly at first. However, improved transportation and refinements in technology resulted in an explosion of packing plants through the 1870s. Between 1873 and 1883 Islanders established more than 100 plants, like the one pictured here. This was the first time Islanders participated actively in their own fishery, and though the lobster industry declined in the 1900s, it has remained a mainstay of the Island's fishery. Courtesy, Public Archives of Prince Edward Island

was still plentiful in the 1870s. Rising costs, however, were forcing many yards to use cheaper, inferior grades. Compounding this was a shortage of "great timber" for masts and spars. The costs of importing these from New Brunswick and Nova Scotia added another obstacle to the industry's ability to compete. Though there was still a demand for ocean-going, wooden vessels, Island shipyards could not compete for it. One by one the great shipbuilders foundered. Although remnants remained until the 1920s, the industry was essentially dead by the 1890s.

Islanders were aware that they had lost one of the mainstays of their economy. Beginning in the 1870s, they tried frantically to find a replacement for it. They found it difficult, however, to find another industry so prominent, and so uniquely based on P.E.I.'s only natural resources: its land, its waters, and its people.

The waters could be tapped through the fishery. Until the late 1800s, Islanders had been bystanders to their own fishery—watching from the shore while American schooners exploited it offshore. Confederation and the end of reciprocity slowly closed the Gulf to the American fleet. Prince Edward Island filled its part of the subsequent vacuum by establishing its own, shore-based fishery.

One of the most spectacular instances of land use occurred at the turn of the twentieth century. At that time several Island farmers discovered how to breed the rare silver and black fox in captivity. With single pelts fetching as much as $3,000, and the Island enjoying a monopoly for several years, the economy experienced a fur boom that lasted through World War I. The boom, however, was short-lived. Fashion changed, and though more than a few fortunes were made, the industry collapsed as quickly as it arose.

A more enduring use of the land was the slow rise of tourism. Early travellers to Prince Edward Island were often struck by the contrast between it and its rugged neighbours in the Gulf of St. Lawrence. Their accounts rhapsodized on the softness of the landscape and general kindness of the climate. Throughout the first half of the nineteenth century these qualities were advertised to attract emigrants to the colony. But by the 1890s they were being incorporated into campaigns to attract more temporary visitors, and P.E.I. began to market itself as a tourist haven.

None of the successors to shipbuilding were able to equal its breadth and impact. The fishery, tourism, and fox farming took up some of the slack, but P.E.I.

Following the industry's sudden collapse in the 1920s, fox ranching could no longer sustain the large scale of its boom years. However, small farmers and breeders continued to raise foxes as a side-line. Courtesy, Public Archives of Prince Edward Island

In the early 1900s, Prince Edward Island was forced to seek economic alternatives to its fading shipbuilding industry. One of the most enduring was tourism. The Island's beaches and farmland, so unsuited to most industrial development, offered a refreshing and natural environment for vacationers. Courtesy, Public Archives of Prince Edward Island

remained essentially an agrarian society in an industrializing world. Because of this, its main export in the century following Confederation became its people. Unable to find enough employment at home, Islanders began to migrate. For the first time since the expulsion of the Acadians, the Island's population declined. From a high of 110,000 in 1867, it fell to 80,000 over the next 50 years. Perhaps the greatest single event of the post-Confederation era, it took the Island a full century to regain its 1867 population level.

The exodus has had several foci. At first the focus was the United States, especially the lumber woods of Maine and the factories of the "Boston States," as New England came to be called. As the industries of Upper Canada took root, the focus shifted there. More recently it has been on the Alberta oil fields. Fortunately for the Island, the post-Confederation decades brought some benefits to temper the ills of a declining economy and migrating population. The most significant of these was the resolution of the land question. In 1875 the Island Legislature made the provisions of the Land Purchase Act compulsory. With the help of Dominion grants, P.E.I. completed buying out the absentee proprietors. In essence, the Island bought its own Crown lands, which it then resold to those who worked it. It took a single afternoon to give the Island away, and more than a century to buy it back. By the 1890s the process was virtually complete, and more than 95 percent of the Island's

farmers could say they owned the land they worked.

With the turn of the twentieth century, it was evident that the Dominion government in Ottawa had replaced the absentee landlords as the favourite target of Islanders' ire. It was difficult to accept the marked decline that accompanied Confederation, but easy to perceive union as its cause. An Island premier, Thane Campbell, observed in the 1930s: "The citizens of this province have borne with patience a national policy which has been distinctly not beneficial; they see the citizens of other provinces grow rich at their expense; they see the best of their youth attracted to other provinces, just as they are entering the period when they might become an asset to the community." The Island has often considered Confederation a bad deal, and relations with the Dominion government have been characterized by arguments over its "rightful share" of the country's prosperity. Grievances over issues like transportation and transfer payments came to supplant earlier complaints about escheat and the proprietor lobby in London. Islanders, however, have generally conceded that participation in Canada was inevitable, and even preferable to facing on its own the hardships of economic decline. As Premier Campbell concluded: "Once committed to the union, there never was, nor is there now, any question of withdrawal."

Indeed, within a generation Islanders had managed to start cultivating an

A mounting concern about the harmful effects on roads and farm animals, supplemented by a general distrust of the newfangled, led the Prince Edward Island Legislature to ban automobiles from all Island roads. This prohibition was eased in 1913, allowing cars to travel every day except Sundays and market days, and was repealed entirely by 1918. Courtesy, Public Archives of Prince Edward Island

affection for their new country. This was especially apparent in the Island's reaction to the Dominion's military adventures. Beginning with the South African War in 1900, and continuing through the two world wars, Islanders have volunteered for service on a per capita basis far exceeding many other parts of the country. Admittedly, their motives were mixed. The possibility of adventure and a respected profession, especially when coupled to a reasonably decent pay cheque, have always had a special appeal in economically depressed areas. And their Canadian nationalism was tempered with a latent patriotism for Great Britain. However, it cannot be denied that they came to fight for their own, as well as their Mother Country, and in time transferred their old loyalties to their new country.

The main work of adjusting from colony to province has been complete for several decades now. The Island faces other challenges, and the issues of other generations often seem remote. Religious animosity, for instance, rarely rears its head anymore, and the old cries of "Escheat!" and "responsible government" have been committed to the history books. Some themes, however, continue to weave their way through the Island's development. The theme of the land remains constant. Farming is still the biggest single pursuit. Fewer people, however, now pursue it, and there has been a gradual drift away from the land. Since the 1930s the woods have actually been reclaiming a great deal of former farmland, and there is now far more forest than a century ago. With less reliance on the farm economy, population is now more concentrated in urban areas. Almost a third of the Island's population, for instance, now lives within the greater Charlottetown area. The ethos of society, however, remains predominantly rural, and Islanders pride themselves on retaining a "way of life" connected to the land.

For this reason Prince Edward Island is still vitally concerned with land use. A century ago Islanders debated what crops were best suited to the colony and its way of life. Now these arguments concern what sort of industries to plant, and

what impact they will have on an even more cherished way of life. The long agony of the land question also seems to have instilled in Islanders a determination to protect their land from "foreign" ownership. Regulations concerning not only the use to which land might be put, but also the extent to which non-residents might own it, reflect this determination.

Thus the Island's modern economy has been shaped by subjective, as well as economic, considerations. Traditional pursuits like farming and fishing are encouraged, as are spin-off industries like processing. Tourism is another industry based on the land and a rural way of life. It now ranks with farming, and ahead of fishing, in terms of impact and income generated. Larger, more "heavy" industries, though they are courted on occasion, find the Island's isolation and lack of a large work force unattractive, and tend to stay away. Islanders tend to appreciate this.

The landscape of modern Prince Edward Island would be hardly recognizable to the first humans who inhabited it. Since the last ice age freed it, cultures have flourished and faded; economies risen and failed; regimes come and gone. The Island has played host to many hopes and hardships. One constant, however, seems to run through every era. Residents, from the first to the current, have found a good place to live, and an easy place to love.

CHAPTER FIVE

PARTNERS IN PROGRESS

By Dorothy Dearborn, Marjorie Doyle, Brent King, and Bob Wall

F ish, furs, forests, and the desire for new opportunities drew settlers to the shores of Atlantic Canada. From its early days as a meagre shore base where fish destined for the markets of Europe were dried, it soon became a battleground as England and France wrestled for control of its abundant natural resources. Despite the wars, the activities of fishing, farming, lumbering, shipbuilding, mining, and trading flourished, and they quickly established the region as the commercial centre of the infant nation.

For more than a century Atlantic Canada dominated the mercantile life of the country. Fleets of tall-masted sailing ships fashioned from the area's virgin forests plied the seas carrying trade goods to ports worldwide. Like the tides that drive waves against its scenic shoreline, however, the fortunes of Atlantic Canada rose and fell with the times. As industry, forestry, and farming moved westward, the wealth of the ocean remained the one constant in the economic life of the region. As the region heads into the 1990s, even this small measure of stability is in doubt. These cycles of economic boom and bust demanded resourcefulness and vigor from the people of the area and resulted in a relatively diverse economy supported by a rich resource base.

The physical characteristics of the area are equally diverse. The manicured farms of Prince Edward Island contrast sharply with the rugged, craggy coast of Newfoundland and Labrador. The climate ranges from the arctic cold of northern Labrador to temperate weather throughout most of the three Maritime Provinces. And the sea that serves as the lifeline of the region also divides and scatters its people. Atlantic Canada has only 10 percent of the population of the country spread over an area equal in size to the province of Ontario. Fittingly, the three largest urban centres are port cities—Halifax-Dartmouth, Saint John, and St. John's.

Atlantic Canada has a rich history. The organizations whose histories appear on the following pages have chosen to participate in this literary project. The struggles of the people and organizations of the Atlantic Provinces have bred a depth of character that provides the strength to survive the bad times and prosper in the good. Coupled with this is a sense of community and a proud lifestyle that is the product of the heritage and natural attractions of the region. While economic and social adjustment admittedly take time, Atlantic Canada, with its legacy of perseverance, pride, and personal ingenuity, is well placed to meet and overcome the challenges of the new century.

Many militia units in New Brunswick required auxillary fund-raising activities to help supply equipment to the regiments. One popular event was the display of sword, bayonet, and rifle drill, and marching tactics performed by young women, such as this group pictured here circa 1895. Courtesy, New Brunswick Museum

ATLANTIC PROVINCES CHAMBER OF COMMERCE

(From left) Paul Connolly, Sandy Archibald, Al Rach, Jim Anderson, and Rick LeBlanc.

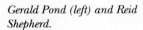

Gerald Pond (left) and Reid Shepherd.

The history of the Atlantic Provinces Chamber of Commerce is far from smooth sailing. It was born as the Maritime Board of Trade in Halifax, Nova Scotia, in October 1896 through the efforts of the Halifax and Saint John boards. The Atlantic Provinces Chamber of Commerce was frustrated at the overpowering dominance of Central Canada but nurtured by a desire to unite the provinces of Nova Scotia, New Brunswick, and Prince Edward Island to bolster the influence of those provinces on their own destiny.

A per capita tax of seven cents per member of the affiliated Maritime boards provided far from adequate financing. The Saint John Board withdrew its membership in 1909, claiming too much talk and too few results. The Saint John Board returned as a member at the first postwar meeting held in Moncton in the fall of 1919.

Once again Maritime union was the focus of discussion. An education program for the region as to the benefits of union was proposed. Earlier resolutions, such as those passed in 1905 for the construction of a railway tunnel under the Northumberland Strait and a committee to lead the British West Indies into the Canadian Confederation, reflect interests that continue to receive regular attention.

A major and recurring concern of the board was the independent railways in the region that members wanted united under the Intercolonial Railway. In 1908 a rift over the Canadian Pacific Railway was prompted by Nova Scotia's resolution stating the province had paid more than enough toward the original cost of the Intercolonial and wanted the CPR to have running rights over it. New Brunswick and Prince Edward Island board members believed this would lead to the demise of the Intercolonial, but Nova Scotia won the day.

In 1912 the board wanted the Dominion Railway Commission to compel the railways to charge the same passenger rates for west-east fares as was charged for east-west. It was not until the Transportation Commission was formed that any real success was achieved. The Maritime Freight Rates Act had its origins with this commission. Ultimately it became the Atlantic Provinces Transportation Commission and joined other such prestigious organizations as the Atlantic Provinces Economic Council and the Atlantic Canada Plus Association. In 1974 the Maritime Board joined with the Newfoundland and Labrador Chamber of Commerce to form what is now the Atlantic Provinces Chamber of Commerce.

The APCC has a direct corporate membership of 1,000 firms and represents more than 12,000 business and professional people in the region. Its primary objective is to represent the business community of the Atlantic Provinces on issues of regional significance to ensure fair government consideration, to foster economic development, and to enhance the quality of life.

The Atlantic Provinces Chamber of Commerce, located at 236 St. George Street, Suite 110, in Moncton, New Brunswick, is the only chamber in Canada that represents more than one province. In 1985 the provincial sections of the Atlantic Provinces Chamber of Commerce attained provincial chamber status, providing greater strength to the chamber movement at the provincial level. In 1989 the APCC joined provincial chambers across the country to launch the Canada Opportunities Investment Network (COIN), a national data base developed to introduce entrepreneurs to investors via the most sophisticated computer technology available.

DARTMOUTH CABLE TV LIMITED

When Dartmouth Cable TV Limited started airing programs in February 1971, viewers included its first subscriber, Mrs. Binnie Burgess, whose home was only 100 feet away from the facility.

Since then, that one installed link from the residence to the Victoria Road studio and headquarters has increased to more than 560 miles of subscriber cable. It's still growing by about 10 percent per year. Dartmouth Cable TV Limited, through its Dartmouth and Digby operations, has approximately 36,000 subscribers.

Along with the standard broadcasting content, the miles of cable carry hours and hours of varied community programming into subscribers' homes. "From the very beginning, we were one of the most prolific community programming studios in the cable TV industry in Canada," says president Charles Keating. His firm broadcasts 42 such hours weekly.

Keating views his community channel as a launching pad for young citizens of Dartmouth to get exposure to the TV medium through a public access TV facility. His studio organizes major annual fund-raising telethons for the Dartmouth Seniors Centre, the East Dartmouth Lions Club, the Nova Scotia Home for Coloured Children, and the Nova Scotia Kidney Foundation.

Keating's firm operates from a 14,000-square-foot former grocery store that he gutted and renovated. He spent $750,000 just to build a fully equipped soundproof production studio and control room for community programming. The staff began with five employees and has climbed to about 75.

Dartmouth Cable offers subscribers 28 channels of viewing in an area where only three are otherwise available. In the coming years, with improving technology such as fibre optics, up to 60 channels could be made available to subscribers. Programming currently includes English- and French-language CBC; the regional ATV, ASN, and MITV networks; the three major American networks plus PBS; discretionary pay channels; and an advertising channel.

To bring in the U.S. TV signals, Dartmouth Cable joined a co-operative venture with a handful of other cable companies (Chamcook Communications Limited) in Atlantic Canada. The consortium constructed the necessary head-end receiving station and antenna on Chamcook Mountain in New Brunswick near the Maine border.

In addition to serving Dartmouth and surrounding area, Dartmouth Cable provides a high-quality signal to the homes in Digby and communities of Tiverton, Freeport, and Westport, and has a substantial investment in Halifax Cablevision Limited and Kings Kable Limited.

Among a roster of memberships and directorships, Keating has twice served as the chairman of the Canadian Cable Television Association and has been chairman of the Atlantic Canada Plus Association, the Saint Francis Xavier University fund-raising campaign, and Loto Canada Inc.

Notwithstanding Charles Keating's community involvement, from the days of Binnie Burgess, the first cable customer, he has always strived to have Dartmouth Cable TV Limited provide the highest standard of service and quality programming signals to each and every subscriber.

The staff of Dartmouth Cable TV Limited in front of the original and current facility and its four satellite dishes.

The production department is the heart of the community channel.

PRICE WATERHOUSE

The chartered accounting firm of Price Waterhouse had a vital presence in Atlantic Canada long before it ever set up a permanent office in the region.

Members of the firm lent their help to a devastated Halifax following the December 1917 explosion when vessels *Mont Blanc* and *Imo* collided, caught fire, and exploded in the largest man-made blast before the atomic bomb. Price Waterhouse volunteered to organize the audit and financial departments of the Halifax Relief Commission set up to aid victims. The Montreal staff members were Harry F. Glass, F. O'Hearn, and A.B. Brodie. Price Waterhouse acted as auditor for the commission for its following 50-year existence.

Today, from waterfront office towers that view the ill-fated harbor narrows, the firm serves clients throughout the region. It carries on business that began in earnest in October 1954, when Price Waterhouse opened a Halifax office, the first national accounting firm to do so. Atlantic work had previously been handled from Montreal.

However, during the early 1950s the firm was carrying out projects for several major national clients, including Imperial Oil Limited and what was then the Dominion Steel & Coal Corporation (DOSCO). Such clients ensured a worthwhile local base of business, so Val Criddle founded the office in the Maritime Life Assurance Company building on Spring Garden Road.

The following years brought Price Waterhouse some major regional clients: In Nova Scotia, Stanfield's Limited, Volvo (Canada) Limited, Stora Forest Industries Limited, Nautical Electronics Laboratories Limited, and Scott Maritimes Limited, and, in New Brunswick, Rothesay Paper Limited. Prince Edward Island's clientele includes Maritime Electric Company Limited, while Newfoundland's includes Hotel Newfoundland and Abitibi-Price in Grand Falls.

Just as the firm's client mix has evolved—these days it ranges anywhere from a part-time bed-and-breakfast operation to companies with annual sales greater than $100 million—so has its services, extending well beyond traditional accounting and auditing. Full-time specialists now provide taxation, insolvency, financial planning, and management consulting services.

Under the direction of managing partner Peter Boomgaardt, the firm merged in 1987 with local management consulting firm Craig, O'Neil & Associates. The transaction bolstered the diversification strategy and added as partners Nova Scotia natives G. David Craig and J. Patrick O'Neil.

Price Waterhouse's Halifax office has consulted on projects from economic feasibility studies to strategic planning to market research. Assignments have encompassed mink oil, sauerkraut, frozen fruit bars, and textbooks.

Its staff has evaluated several job programs for disadvantaged minorities in Nova Scotia, undertaken a compensation study for the New Brunswick Medical Society, and researched the supply and demand of industrial land for Newfoundland's anticipated offshore oil development. Regionally Price Waterhouse has undertaken long-term policy work for Ottawa's Atlantic Canada Opportunities Agency, which has a total funding budget of one billion dollars targeted for the four provinces.

Halifax partners (from left) Peter Boomgaardt, David Craig, and Patrick O'Neil pose in front of the Halifax Explosion Memorial on a bright windy day 72 years after the event.

The Halifax Explosion Memorial Bell Tower commemorates the 1917 explosion when vessels Mont Blanc *and* Imo *collided. Price Waterhouse assisted in the relief effort.*

STANDARD PAVING MARITIME LIMITED

Whether an airport runway, a provincial highway, or even a home-owner's driveway, it's probably within the scope of projects that heavy-construction firm Standard Paving Maritime Limited has already completed somewhere in the region.

Since opening its first office in July 1931 in Halifax' old Capitol Theatre building, the firm has expanded operations to where it paves or repaves about 100 kilometres of asphalt (or concrete) streets and highways each year in Nova Scotia and New Brunswick.

Each of those projects calls for its own specifications and standards to suit the nature and flow of traffic. "There are always peculiarities. No jobs are the same," says J.D. "Dan" Arbing, president of the firm that employs up to 250 workers with an annual payroll of $3.5 million.

Standard Paving moved to its present Halifax headquarters and equipment yard, a former rock quarry overlooking Kearney Lake, during the late 1960s. Over a period of 15 years the firm drilled, blasted, and crushed some 6 million tons of rock, ending up with an area of roughly 10 hectares.

Historically, Standard Paving's projects have been as varied as the job sites throughout the two provinces. They have ranged from many jobs typically worth about $250,000 to those in the multimillion-dollar range. The firm has paved the approaches for Halifax' Angus L. Macdonald Bridge, put in $9 million of subdivision sewer and water services for the Rockingham North residential project, and contracted for $5 million for the present Halifax International Airport expansion, including runway and taxiway upgrading, aircraft apron extension, and car parking expansion. Other local contracts included work for industrial parks and containerized shipping terminals.

In downtown Halifax, Standard Paving notably worked on paving jobs in the early 1980s meant to enhance the restoration of buildings in the city core. It removed old tram rails and cobblestones and put down granite curbs. While the firm went with conventional pavement, it gave the surface a vintage reddish color by hauling special crushed stone from Folly Lake, more than 130 kilometres away. Likewise, the firm prepared concrete walkways with a special washing process to highlight the oldish look of rounded stones.

Elsewhere in Nova Scotia, major jobs have included main street improvements in Kentville, Amherst, and Parrsboro. In northern New Brunswick, a key project was a contract for a six-kilometre section of concrete highway.

Standard Paving's equipment fleet and physical plant have a replacement value of more than $20 million. The loaders, crushers, excavators, pavers, asphalt plants, and other equipment are divided among three Nova Scotia operations and one in New Brunswick.

In New Brunswick, especially, Standard Paving has been recycling pavement in recent years, reclaiming the used petroleum-based asphalt, stone, and gravel, then mixing it with fresh material.

Says Arbing, who joined the firm as a construction engineer in 1965: "We try to keep abreast of new technical developments by having a number of professional engineers on staff."

Standard Paving Maritime Limited's head office, machine shop, and asphalt plant on Lady Hammond Road, Halifax, in the early 1940s.

Construction is ready to begin on the approaches for Halifax' Angus L. MacDonald Bridge.

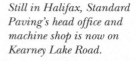

Still in Halifax, Standard Paving's head office and machine shop is now on Kearney Lake Road.

TRACTORS & EQUIPMENT (1962) LTD.

A Caterpillar RD4 tractor skids pulpwood to the landing in 1936.

A 280-horsepower Caterpillar wheel loader carries an 18m³ load of hog fuel to the stock pile.

It was the business hardship of the Great Depression that made possible the founding of Tractors & Equipment (1962) Ltd.

"Like a lot of things, it started in a very small way," recalls Chet Campbell, honorary chairman of Tractors & Equipment. "It didn't germinate from an idea but from an opportunity."

That opportunity came in 1932, when two Fredericton businessmen were willing to raise and risk a modest sum to buy a defunct Saint John firm that had sold Caterpillar tractors. John Neill ran a hardware business while his friend, Ashley Colter, had a lumber and contracting business. They borrowed $4,300 from the Bank of Montreal and contracted for the sales territory of New Brunswick from the visiting Caterpillar representative out of Peoria, Illinois.

With a strong vote of confidence from the Caterpillar representative, Neill and Colter started with a one-room office and warehouse on Fredericton's King Street, now the site of Kings Place.

Business was modest at first. The company sold a few machine parts to the provincial government as well as lumbermen and contractors who had tractors and pull-type graders. However, activity picked up nicely in the mid-1930s. The province's highway department undertook the first major road improvement program, boosting the demand for tractors, graders, concrete mixers, pumps, and crushers. At the same time the forestry industry became quite active.

When civil engineer Chet Campbell joined Tractors & Equipment in 1944, the expanding firm was badly in need of space for a shop and storeroom. The solution was to build on a seven-acre parcel on Smythe Street that the company bought from Imperial Oil. Although the swampy property almost claimed a tractor during construction, the company otherwise moved uneventfully into $250,000 premises in 1948.

Then, in 1967, to service the larger machines coming on the market, Tractors & Equipment beefed up shop facilities with an engine repair area and test equipment. In 1975 Tractors & Equipment installed a hydraulic test area for transmissions, controls, and pumps.

The firm had already actively serviced Caterpillar marine diesel engines out of Shippagan for 30 years when it opened a branch there in 1973. An estimated 90 percent of all vessels with more than 100 horsepower in the region's fishing fleet have Caterpillar

A Caterpillar V925 lift truck equipped with a container handler shuttles containers in Saint John, New Brunswick.

engines. The company next set up a branch in Bathurst to handle the province's mining industry. A separate material-handling division to look after forklift sales was founded out of a renovated building in 1980 on Saint John's Golden Mile.

Tractors & Equipment demonstrated its confidence over future business prospects yet again in 1982. Notwithstanding a slow economy, the firm celebrated its 50th anniversary by opening a modern facility in Moncton. Fortunately, business volume tripled during the 1980s, and the company had 185 employees throughout its branches.

Long established with a network of branches and a diverse Caterpillar product line, Tractors & Equipment merged operations with Halifax-based N.S. Tractors & Equipment Ltd. in 1989. The merger strengthened each dealership by sharing personnel resources as well as technical and marketing expertise. The two companies operate separately and independently in their own territories. The merger had benefits for customers and employees by introducing economies of scale and cost savings from co-operative technical training and product support.

Tractors & Equipment, for example, had experience with the forestry industry, where it had been involved with the mechanization of New Brunswick woodland operations. "The merger has given us the opportunity to more effectively respond to the needs of the forest industry," says Jack Craig, president and chief executive officer of Tractors & Equipment.

The firm had a strong niche in the forklift side of the Caterpillar product line in pulp and paper mills, food-processing operations, and warehouses. The Nova Scotia and New Brunswick lift truck operations have been merged to capitalize on the marketing and technical skills of Tractors & Equipment staff.

The company has a major thrust in the on-highway truck-engine business. Caterpillar engines have become the dominant power unit for highway trucks regionwide. About 40 percent of heavy-duty trucks in New Brunswick and Nova Scotia are powered by Caterpillar diesel engines.

Selling smaller equipment lines is another focus for Tractors & Equipment, especially Caterpillar's Century line of utility backhoes, excavators, tractors, and loaders.

Equipment-servicing needs have changed just as the range of Caterpillar models has increased. The Fredericton head office had a $500,000 warehouse overhaul and redesign in 1989. Tractors & Equipment carries 27,000 stock items worth $5 million at any given time.

"There is much more emphasis on servicing the equipment," says Craig. "There was a time when users could do most of their own repairs. Now with more sophisticated design for increased productivity, maintenance is very difficult and costly without factory-trained mechanics and specialized tools."

Caterpillar equipment will play a pivotal role in any large projects in New Brunswick. Reconstruction of the Trans Canada Highway across the province offers an excellent opportunity to Tractors & Equipment (1962) Ltd. The proposed fixed link or causeway crossing to Prince Edward Island would also likely involve Caterpillar products.

N.S. TRACTORS & EQUIPMENT LTD.

A Caterpillar D11 tractor, the largest in the world, with an impact ripper, replaces dynamite in the mining of gypsum in 1989.

Over the decades N.S. Tractors & Equipment Ltd. has modified its operations to better suit its clientele and keep up to date with advances in heavy machinery design and workings.

The exclusive Caterpillar dealer for Nova Scotia began in 1927. It was then the construction machinery division of William Stairs, Son and Morrow Ltd., a hardware firm that began in 1810 on Halifax' Lower Water Street. That division became N.S. Tractors in 1959, five years after the firm had moved to premises on Kempt Road.

In 1981 the firm set up an industrial and marine power division to custom build electrical power units from portables to industrial emergency standby power installations. The division sells marine engines and transmissions for vessels needing up to 6,000 horsepower. One notable customer of N.S. Tractors was the two-masted schooner *Bluenose II*. During a 1984 refit, Nova Scotia's world-famous sailing ambassador was equipped with a pair of Caterpillar auxiliary generators and made-to-order switch gear. Elsewhere, in the event of a power blackout, the Victoria General Hospital in Halifax would count on a generation plant supplied by N.S. Tractors. And the firm has supplied backup units for the newspaper offices and presses of Halifax Herald Ltd.

Caterpillar equipment plays a role in any number of projects: a new building, an improved road, removing snow, or installing bigger water mains. Recent years have brought Century Line products from the manufacturer. Century Line units tend to be smaller utility versions of the traditional equipment meant for large production projects. Century Line models include tractors, loaders, backhoes, and excavators starting at about 60 horsepower.

Continued growth has resulted in a multi-year project to build a new complex in Dartmouth's Burnside Industrial Park. Work on this project began in 1988 with the construction of a 22-bay engine facility. When all phases are completed, the 10-acre site will consolidate service, sales, parts inventory, and administration. N.S. Tractors has branches in Sydney and Yarmouth and 170 employees.

To further enhance customer service, N.S. Tractors merged with New Brunswick Caterpillar dealer Tractors & Equipment (1962)

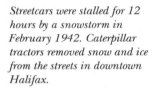

Streetcars were stalled for 12 hours by a snowstorm in February 1942. Caterpillar tractors removed snow and ice from the streets in downtown Halifax.

Ltd. in 1989. The two dealerships operate separately in each territory while co-operating in overall planning, marketing, and product support in New Brunswick and Nova Scotia.

"By merging operations we eliminated duplication and overlapping of training and personnel that now allows us to offer better product support and lower operating costs," says Jack Craig, president and general manager.

The two dealers call on their joint network of branches, service depots, and warehouse inventories. The firms share their technical and marketing expertise in the various industrial and commercial sectors of the two provinces. Collectively, Caterpillar equipment has applications in mining, forestry, marine, site development, home building, urban renewal, and a whole range of construction jobs. The firm also fills out its product line with Portec crushing and aggregate equipment and Grove hydraulic cranes.

N.S. Tractors' operating concept is to offer customers a good source of parts, servicing, and technical support throughout the life cycle of their machines. The firm trains employees through its classrooms, making use of video tapes, conference telephone calls, or live television classes beamed in via satellite from Caterpillar Inc.'s headquarters in Peoria, Illinois.

"The customers are very reliant on the dealer for a good source of parts, service, and technical support," says Craig, who is also president and chief executive officer of Tractors & Equipment. "Equipment is getting more sophisticated with complex hydraulics and electrical components, and the user can not afford to keep up to date, have the well-trained personnel, and [have the] special tooling and technology to provide the in-house support."

N.S. Tractors carries about 90 percent of the needed parts in stock and has computer links with Caterpillar dealers throughout North America. The firm's 30,000 line items run the whole gamut of Caterpillar machines that dig, push, rip, fell, lift, haul, level, grade, compact, load, and carry. For any part not on hand, N.S. Tractors can contact designated drawing sources in Canada and the United States. The firm has standing shipping orders from such geographically diverse Caterpillar sites as Denver, Miami, and Spokane. Most orders are shipped by air freight, and customers often get needed parts next day. Customers can contact the service department 24 hours per day.

The company's overall service philosophy is to take action before an equipment breakdown. The scheduled oil-sampling program is one example of the prevention approach. It is a service whereby technicians chemically analyze machine wear by regularly testing oil from engines, transmissions, and hydraulics. Detected impurities give a good picture of the engine or components and clues of future operating problems.

Other technical analyses are done in the field. N.S. Tractors & Equipment Ltd.'s product support services representatives inspect up to 100 checkpoints of a given piece of equipment. In the process representatives scrutinize identified key parts called critical indicators that are particularly important diagnostic areas. Owners can have their machines inspected during the winter so that any repairs or maintenance can be done when most convenient. Owners get a report of suggested repairs with a number of alternatives, all with firm prices so owners can control their operating costs.

Caterpillar-packaged electric generator sets, "Power of New Generation," on display at N.S. Tractors' 22,000-square-foot facility in Dartmouth, Nova Scotia.

A Caterpillar tractor with rear ripper carrying out initial excavation on the site of Scotia Square during the 1960s.

BEN'S LTD.

A child clutches a fresh loaf of Holsum bread from a Ben's home-delivery truck. Home delivery was a fact of everyday life until it was phased out in 1961.

Benjamin Moir started his bakery in 1907 and used a horse-drawn wagon to deliver 100 loaves of bread per day.

Ben's Ltd. can trace its bakery traditions, recipes, and even some customers back for two centuries. In 1790 Scottish-born tradesman Alexander Moir began selling his wife's homemade loaves to the nearby troop garrison in Halifax' Citadel Hill.

Today the firm still includes Department of National Defence military bases in Nova Scotia and New Brunswick among its 2,000 customers. Others include Sobeys Stores Ltd. and Atlantic Wholesalers Ltd. Until recent years there was a family continuity, too. The founder's great-grandson, Benjamin Moir, maintained the baking tradition, although with his own venture. In 1907 Benjamin Moir started his own bakery on Pepperell Street. It was a home bakery, and he used a horse-drawn wagon to deliver 100 loaves per day.

Ben's Ltd. of the 1990s can produce about 11,000 loaves in a single hour. That's the combined output of the Halifax and Moncton plants. Even the range of products has grown. "Never in the history of the bakery business has there been such a clamor for new varieties of breads," says Ed Stoddard, who joined the firm in 1927 and was secretary/treasurer for five decades.

In all, 500 Ben's Ltd. employees help produce, deliver, and sell 150 varieties of breads, rolls, cakes, and other baked goods. The product lines change with consumer demands. Low-calorie bread is geared to weight watchers. High-fibre bread is offered to the nutrition conscious; however, Ben's Holsum white bread has been a consistent product since 1938.

Whatever the recipe, there has been only a few times when Ben's Ltd. couldn't offer its baked goods. When the 1917 Halifax explosion levelled his bakery, Moir rebuilt it twice the size and, some years later, opened four metro retail outlets. Tragedy struck again in 1926, when fire destroyed that operation, causing $140,000 damage. Once again Moir came back. Within three months he was baking with modernized equipment.

In 1961 (around the time Ben's Ltd. phased out house-to-house delivery) Moir's son, Ben Jr., sold the firm. Then 61 years old and without a family member to run the business, Ben Jr. sold the bakery to Nova Scotia industrialist Roy Jodrey. A growth phase followed. Ben's Ltd. bought the Moncton bakery of Lane's Ltd. in 1981. A year later the firm added the Dartmouth bakery known as O'Malley's.

By the mid-1980s a consolidation phase was in the works. Ben's Ltd. unveiled a new logo (a smiling baker framed in an old-style oven) to refurbish its corporate look and unify the image of the three bakeries. It roughly coincided with the highly successful launching of Fibre Goodness bread.

Product packages themselves have aided in the firm's community-services program called Ben's Helping Kids. Through organized competitions, thousands of Maritime children from dozens of schools collect bread bags to help them buy equipment or take trips. Ben's Ltd. also continues to help raise funds for the Izaak Walton Killam Hospital for Children.

CASINO TAXI LTD.

Much like its president and owner, Warren Spicer, Casino Taxi Ltd. has always been impatient to progress and to lead. Long before he became sole owner of Halifax-based Casino in 1967, Spicer had accelerated his transportation career.

At the outbreak of World War II the Canning, Nova Scotia, native joined the Army at age 14, saying he was 21, and went overseas. He drove a tank, an armored gun carrier, a low-bed trailer truck—just about anything on wheels (except for motorcycles, which he did not have time to train on and test for). After the war Spicer drove a bus for seven years with the Maritime Bus Corp. out of Kentville. His first

years saw the company quickly grow to 35 cars. Having cast the die for moving forward, Casino has grown over the years to today's fleet of 225 owner-driver cars that handle around 1.5 million dispatched calls per year.

Steady growth for the firm made it economically feasible to radio equip his cabs—the first company to do so locally. It meant better customer service—always a priority in Spicer's long-term planning—since Casino drivers no longer had to rely on the system of taxi stands and pole-mounted, direct-line jig phones for calling the dispatcher for fares. Just prior, Casino had moved to a property on Isleville Street in 1968.

Other local firsts came as Spicer put pieces of

ABOVE: Warren Spicer, president and owner.

LEFT: Casino Taxi's entire fleet of five cabs and one ambulance in 1937—when a good cigar was five cents and a 50-cent fare would take you anywhere in the city. Clary Johnson, the owner of the firm at the time, is third from the right.

taxi stint in Halifax was in 1952 with Airline Limousine. At the start he did not know Barrington Street from Gottingen Street from Spring Garden Road. "I had to memorize every customer and every number of each house," Spicer recalls.

Later, while working for Canadian National Railways as a brakeman and conductor, Spicer began driving his family car part time for Three S Taxi in 1954. In the late 1950s, with a partner, he bought out Casino Taxi, then with five cars and located on the corner of Cornwallis and Gottingen streets. Initially a silent partner, Spicer then quit the railway to go with Casino permanently.

"I don't mind responsibility," says Spicer. "It's a challenge for me to do something and see it through." Expansion came as Casino acquired A-1 Taxi on Agricola Street, Stad Taxi on Gottingen Street, ABC Taxi on Hollis Street, and Scotia Taxi in the Trade Mart Building. Those

his unwritten but well thought through five-year business plans into place: among them a dress code for drivers; a stand-by diesel-powered electrical generator; a sophisticated, duplicate communications system; and a two-channel car-radio system so drivers and the dispatcher could separately receive and transmit.

Spicer himself has carried out his service credo many times. Once he drove a March of Dimes child from Halifax' Izaak Walton Killam Hospital for Children to her home in North Sydney. Another time he carried and drove a senior citizen in a wheelchair, plus a group of her friends, to the airport to catch a flight to Australia. When a new Casino Taxi Ltd. driver mixed up a night delivery to a bus terminal, Spicer drove the waylaid IBM typewriter to St. Francis Xavier University in Antigonish.

"Casino Taxi will remain a family business as long as they want it," says Spicer. Perhaps he planned it that way!

NEWFOUNDLAND BROADCASTING COMPANY LIMITED

Geoffrey W. Stirling, president and chairman of the board.

An artist's rendering of the building where CJON Radio first went on the air in 1951. CJON TV signed on from there when television came to Newfoundland in 1955. The painting is by Harold B. Goodridge.

In 1946 there was an unusual phenomenon at the Newfoundland ice fields. An airplane flew overhead periodically, and copies of *The Sunday Herald* were dropped to the sealers below. The importance of reading material to the isolated hunters can only be imagined.

The man with the flare for advertising his newspaper was 25-year-old Geoff Stirling, who had recently returned to Newfoundland from New York, where he had worked in an advertising agency. He busied himself with his newspaper, and during the battle for Confederation, he fought for economic union with the United States.

When Newfoundland entered Confederation in 1949, Stirling established Newfoundland Broadcasting Company Limited and applied for a radio licence. On October 10, 1951, from studios at Buckmaster's Circle in St. John's, CJON radio went on the air. Four years later, in September 1955, CJON TV also became a reality.

Stirling later bought radio and television stations in other parts of Canada, but he maintained the local company, which expanded greatly. CJON was the first local radio station to broadcast 24 hours per day. In 1963 the firm introduced commercial color television, and in 1977 the OZ FM Radio Network hit the airwaves—the first commercial FM station on the island. In 1988 television that was broadcasted in stereo was the company's newest advance. The firm also sponsored its own choir, the CJON Glee Club, which was active from 1956 to 1961.

Scott Stirling, the 38-year-old son of Geoff and executive president of the company, calls his father an innovator. "He likes to say that he finds the invisible—in other words, things that are there that no one has seen yet. They're vacuums or opportunities waiting to be exploited," says Scott.

Geoff Stirling is also a filmmaker. One of his films, *Waiting for Fidel* (1975) won Best Foreign Film at the Boston Film Festival. Stirling has created Captain Canada and Captain Newfoundland, print characters that have the potential to be developed in animation.

Newfoundland Broadcasting Company Limited moved to new quarters at Logy Bay Road in the mid-1980s. Today a staff of 70 people runs the Newfoundland Television Network and the OZ FM Radio Network. CJON Radio became a separate concern in 1977, when Stirling and Don Jamieson, his partner of 20 years, dissolved their partnership.

Jamieson, later a federal cabinet minister, is one of several former staff members who achieved national prominence. Others include the Honorable James McGrath, also a former federal cabinet minister and now lieutenant-governor of Newfoundland; Senator Gerry Ottenheimer; MP Brian Tobin; and national sports broadcaster Howie Meeker.

BLUNDEN CONSTRUCTION LIMITED

George Blunden, president of Blunden Construction Limited, remembers how modest the firm's first woodworking shop was; he helped his father build it in the winter of 1949.

They put up their structure with its barn-shaped roof on McLean Street in Halifax' south end, on a very irregularly shaped property leased from Canadian National. The property was once the site of an Army barracks and adjacent to the grain elevators.

Just out of high school, Blunden started as a carpenter's apprentice earning one dollar an hour with his father, Harry, a master craftsman and cabinetmaker. Employees shovelled wood shavings into a second-hand hot air furnace for

heat. (It had been removed from Fort Massey Church.) And when they ran the planer, the wood floor would shake up and down. That is how the company known as Blunden Supplies got its start in 1949.

Despite these Spartan premises and second-hand equipment, employees applied their woodworking skills to craft customized church altars, oak doors, communion rails, a hand-carved Bishop's throne, and an ark for a synagogue's Torah. Recalls Blunden, "It was a basic set-up, but we did a lot of nice work."

Business grew, and the firm went through eight expansions before March 1963, when it finally moved to its current location on Herring Cove Road in Spryfield. Further expansion came in June 1968. The Blunden operation (then called Blunden Supplies Limited) purchased and merged with the 100-year-old building supply firm Brookfield Bros. Limited. Management described the resulting Brookfield Bros. (1968) Limited as a "blending of the vigorous old firm with the dynamic younger company to form a revitalized organization."

At the same time Blunden Construction Limited was formed to carry on the general contracting business of the previous Blunden Supplies Ltd. and Brookfield Bros., the building supplies business. However, in September 1981 management wound down Brookfield Bros. owing to poor profitability and bleak industry prospects. Over the next three years at least 30 other building supply stores throughout Atlantic Canada went out of business due to the recession at that time.

These days a restructured and amalgamated Blunden Construction services a core of clients, concentrating on repeat contracts. The firm undertakes roughly $10 million worth of projects per year with 50 to 75 full-time employees. Acting as general contractor—it still does its own carpentry—Blunden says his firm gets the right people and puts the overall contract package together.

Blunden Construction

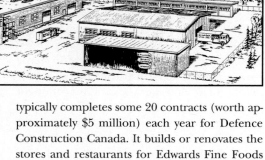

typically completes some 20 contracts (worth approximately $5 million) each year for Defence Construction Canada. It builds or renovates the stores and restaurants for Edwards Fine Foods Limited, which holds the franchise for Kentucky Fried Chicken in Halifax-Dartmouth and elsewhere in the province.

Renovation jobs of all types make up roughly one-half of the total work of Blunden Construction Limited. They might include redoing 144 bathrooms for the military housing complex at CFB Greenwood, rejuvenating a Halifax waterfront immigration building, or replacing the copper of St. Paul's Church steeple, whose main structure was erected in 1749. Concludes Blunden, "Renovation is our specialty. We have the expertise for it. After all, that's the way we started in 1943."

McLean Street, Halifax, 1960. The barn-shaped building in the centre was the original 1949 facility.

The current 519 Herring Cove Road location is depicted in this 1968 artist's rendering.

ROYAL BANK OF CANADA

Royal Bank of Canada, which today is a leading international institution with operations in more than 30 countries, was originally the Merchants Bank of Halifax, which arose out of the rousing commerce of the 1860s. The Civil War of the United States was at its peak, and blockade runners swarmed into Halifax, bringing their trade and a phenomenal burst of prosperity and profits. A group of seven influential Halifax businessmen, wishing to capitalize on those auspicious times, founded the Merchants Bank on May 2, 1864.

Their Bedford Row banking house was situated, appropriately, in rented space near the thriving wharves and warehouses of the waterfront. An advertisement of the time proclaimed the bank's scope of business "to discount promissory notes and acceptances, make advances on approved securities, purchase and sell bills of exchange, receive money on deposit, and transact all other business matters connected with a business establishment."

Things boded well for the first five years with the Merchants Bank averaging a 9-percent annual return. Along with Confederation in 1867 came the need for a bank reorganization under Ottawa's jurisdiction. Merchants Bank was federally chartered in June 1869 and the name changed to the Merchants Bank of Halifax. By fall the bank had more than 100 prominent Nova Scotians as shareholders and total assets of $729,163.

The earliest branches were in Pictou in 1870; Antigonish, Bridgewater, Lunenburg, Truro,

Royal Bank of Canada has its roots in Halifax as the Merchants Bank, established in 1864. Its first office was in this rented building on Bedford Row.

This 1907 photo is of Royal Bank's Sydney, Nova Scotia, main branch. Courtesy, Royal Bank Corporate Archives

and Weymouth in 1871; and Sydney in 1872. In 1873 the bank opened in Charlottetown. Sackville, New Brunswick, started up in 1882. In 1895 the Merchants Bank of Halifax in St. John's, Newfoundland, to provide financial services for the citizens whose two banks had failed. Bank notes of those two collapsed institutions made up most of the local currency.

"It is not hard to visualize the situation thus created," wrote one researcher. "Business was at a standstill and the people in a state of panic when the Canadian banks opened their doors."

Before the turn of the century the Merchants Bank of Halifax had defined and implemented a growth strategy with two prongs—south along the traditional Maritime trade route with the Caribbean and west following the new railroads into central Canada and on to the prairies. The first international branch was opened in Bermuda in 1882. By 1899 the Merchants Bank of Halifax operated 42 branches, encompassing Quebec, Ontario, and British Columbia as well as Havana, Cuba, and New York. Even then, two out of every three branches were outside Nova Scotia.

In keeping with expanding international interests, the bank was given parliamentary approval to become "national" and was renamed the Royal Bank of Canada in January 1901. The head office moved to Montreal in 1907, although there had been a branch in the city since 1887. A series of acquisitions followed: the Union Bank of Halifax in 1910, the Traders Bank of Canada in 1912, the Quebec Bank in 1917, the Northern Crown Bank in 1918, and the Union Bank of Canada in 1925. By 1929, following even more expansion, the Royal was the largest bank in Canada with assets of more than one billion dollars. And befitting the Royal's

aggressive expansion, the bank gets credit for the first modern highrise office tower in Halifax's downtown core. The 13-storey Royal Bank Tower opened on September 6, 1968.

The Royal employs more than 3,000 part-time and full-time people among its 143 branches in the four Atlantic Provinces. It is now the fifth-largest bank in North America and among the top 50 in the world. The Royal's total assets in 1989 surpassed $110 billion. It has 7 million customers and processes daily 4.4 million cheques, 1.1 million on-line savings and loan transactions from its branch computer terminals, and 840,000 credit card transactions.

Coming years will undoubtedly bring a variety of other Royal banking services as the federal government continues deregulating the financial industry. For example, the Royal has already broadened into investment services and securities. In 1988 it acquired Dominion Securities Ltd. and United Bond and Share Ltd. That same year Allan R. Taylor, chairman and chief executive officer, said, "We will be seeing our directions come even more sharply into focus as we continue our transition from being Canada's leading bank to becoming its leading provider of financial services.

"We have, over the past several years, become much more strategic in our approach, identifying with greater precision what we want to be, where we want to go, and how we want to get there, with the process being worked down to each business unit."

Yet all is not strictly business at the Royal. Its employees throughout Atlantic Canada are involved in many worthwhile endeavors for the benefit of their communities. Since 1985, for example, they have made one of their volunteer causes the Children's Miracle Network Telethon, raising more than $500,000 on their own initiative during a five-year period for The Isaak Walton Killam Children's Hospital in Halifax, Nova Scotia, and The Janeway Child Health Centre in St. John's, Newfoundland.

Royal Bank of Canada makes corporate donations totalling $8 million annually to such organizations as hospitals, universities, the arts, the handicapped, and 4-H clubs. Since Canada's Centennial in 1967, the Royal has sponsored a yearly award—now $100,000—to a Canadian who has made an outstanding contribution to human welfare and the common good. Award winners have come from the natural and social sciences, arts, humanities, business, and industry. Chosen by an independent selection committee, past Royal awards have honored such persons as a neurosurgeon, engineer, Cardinal, novelist, architect, actor, educator, humanitarian, scientist, and literary scholar.

Allan R. Taylor, chairman and chief executive officer.

CLARK, DRUMMIE & COMPANY

Clark, Drummie partners (seated left to right): Barry R. Morrison; M. Robert Jette; Donald F. MacGowan, Q.C.; Deno Pappas, Q.C.; Counsel George T. Clark, Q.C.; Thomas B. Drummie, Q.C.; Wallace S. Turnbull, Q.C.; Willard M. Jenkins; and Terrence W. Hutchinson. Standing (left to right): partners William B. Richards and L. Paul Zed; associate Sherrie R. Boyd; partner Frank P. Hamm; associates Donald J. Higgins, Frederick A. Welsford, and W. Andrew LeMesurier; partner Patrick J.P. Ervin; associates John M. McNair, James K. O'Connell, J. George Byrne, William M. Ryan, and Norman J. Bossé; and students Blair Drummie, John Warner, Tim Hopkins, and Karen Colpitts.

Clark, Drummie & Company developed from the merger of two Saint John law firms that traced their origins to the early 1920s. Drummie, Drummie, Clark & Pappas, and Ryan, MacGowan, Higgins & Case amalgamated on July 1, 1971, to continue a tradition of quality and professionalism dedicated to the single purpose of client satisfaction. Two years later, in 1973, the name was changed to Clark, Drummie & Company following the appointment of Henry E. Ryan as judge of the court of appeal.

Nearly 20 years later many of the original names remain on the company roster but the firm, and the stature of its partners and associates, continues to grow. Building on the reputations of its practitioners, Clark, Drummie has emerged as one of the largest firms in the region, with 12 partners and 10 associates. Founding partner George T. Clark, Q.C., continues to serve as counsel.

Because of its growth, Clark, Drummie took a unique step for a law firm. In 1976 the company decided to erect its own building at 40 Wellington Row, a quiet, tree-lined street within a few short blocks of the provincial and federal courts. The two-storey structure was designed to grow along with the partnership, and by 1988, when an increasing number of partners and associates indicated a need for expanded premises,

a third storey was added to accommodate them.

Throughout the firm's history a number of partners and former partners have served the community with distinction. George Clark, Q.C., served on the Saint John Common Council, and Robert J. Higgins, Q.C., became leader of the New Brunswick Liberal Party and is now a judge of the Court of Queen's Bench. David Case, Q.C., has recently been appointed vice-president/mergers and acquisitions for Bruncor Ltd.

In addition, the members of Clark, Drummie are active in many legal and community service organizations. Tom Drummie, Q.C., is a past president of the Saint John Law Society and Donald MacGowan, Q.C., served as national vice-president of the Canadian Cancer Society. Barry Morrison is chairman of the Saint John Environmental Consultation Committee; Wallace Turnbull, Q.C., is a director of Canada Ports Corporation; and Willard Jenkins is a national director of the Canadian Trotting Association. Other firm members take active roles in the Saint John Board of Trade, the Multicultural Association, and various service clubs.

In addition to their varied areas of specialization in corporate and commercial law, litigation, real estate, and administrative practice, a number of Clark, Drummie's senior partners have developed expertise in other specialties, particularly transportation (Motor Carrier Board), admiralty law, and securities regulation. In addition, the firm provides bilingual services for its clients.

Clark, Drummie & Company's Wellington Row headquarters in downtown Saint John.

FUNDY CABLE LTD. LTÉE

The 25-year history of Fundy Cable Ltd./Ltée of Saint John, New Brunswick, is synonymous with the story of a Fredericton-born electrical engineer, C. William Stanley.

In 1964 Stanley, just out of college, was managing Teleprompter cable system in Edmundston, and he was intrigued with what the seven-year-old cable industry could be in the future. Saint John businessman James F. MacMurray was also interested, and the two met to discuss the formation of a cable system for that city. The result of that meeting was the formation of Fundy Cablevision Ltd. in 1965. The original board of directors was C.W. Stanley, J.A. MacMurray, J.H. Turnbull, A.R.W. Lockhart, and the late Norwood Carter.

Unfortunately the Board of Broadcast Governors had a different idea about the future of cable; they froze cable's development in the region for the "foreseeable future," and the fledgling company had nowhere to go. Stanley spent the next five years in Kansas City where he became chief engineer and later vice-president/operations of United Transmissions Inc., a multiple systems operation that he bought, and then built 21 cable systems during that period.

In 1970 the Canadian Radio and Television Commission approved the use of microwave for cable systems, making cable a possibility for Saint John. Stanley returned to Canada, and, under the auspices of Fundy Broadcasting Ltd., he and the original group decided to try again—only this time in conjunction with four other groups. The CRTC also said, in 1970, that cable companies had to be 80-percent Canadian owned, and Stanley and MacMurray with Edmundston shareholders bought Teleprompter in Edmundston. On August 1, 1973, the CRTC licensed both Edmundston and Saint John to the Stanley/MacMurray companies.

"That got us off the ground," Stanley says, "but it took another 1.5 years to negotiate with NBTel and MT&T, owners of the microwave, and with about 30 other new licensees in the Maritimes, to ensure cable service throughout the Atlantic Region." Today the Stanley Formula, is still used as the industry's guideline for distant signal cost sharing throughout Atlantic Canada.

"We had 15,000 subscribers the first year; at one point Saint John people lined up around the block. In 1976 we created our first of several affiliated provincial companies, and then went through three major expansions in the early 1980s. Fundy Cable now serves more than 85,000 subscribers, 70 percent of New Brunswick subscribers, in 81 communities."

Stanley and MacMurray have continued in this partnership with MacMurray as chairman of the board of the Fundy Cable Group of Companies.

Stanley is vice-chairman and chief executive officer of The Fundy Cable Group of Companies, encompassing Fundy Cable Ltd./Ltée, Atlantic Canada's largest cable company; Cox Radio & TV; and Repairtec. Stanley is also chief executive officer of Fundy II Ltd., owner of radio stations CFBC AM and CJYC FM; Fundy II Real Estate Ltd., which operates Canada Trust Realtor franchises in Halifax, Dartmouth, and Lower Sackville, Nova Scotia, and Fredericton, Moncton, and Saint John, New Brunswick; Fundy Deer Farms Ltd.; and Briggs Communication Ltd. (operating in England). He also serves as president and director of Cable Management Ltd., a cable television and communications investment company that also owns NCA Microelectronics Inc., a research and development and light manufacturing firm.

Many of the group's 400 employees have recently exercised the option to become company shareholders.

C. William Stanley, chief executive officer.

The Fundy Cable Ltd./Ltée sign is lifted into position on the newly renovated studio in November 1988.

PAT KING GROUP LIMITED

The employee owners of Pat King Group Limited have combined the entrepreneurial flair of founder Patrick King with new innovative spirit to form one of Atlantic Canada's fastest growing companies.

What began as a small, one-person insurance company in Dartmouth in 1951 has grown to encompass more than 400 employees and a widely diversified range of subsidiary operations. By the early 1980s Pat King Real Estate had grown to the largest independent brokerage firm in Atlantic Canada with 19 offices. In 1984 he sold the company to several employees, and the business was consolidated into Pat King Group Limited. Management of the then seven Pat King companies formed a new board of directors, with longtime Pat King Limited employee Phillip Leverman assuming the role of chief executive officer.

With head office located on Dartmouth's Main Street, the company has continued to expand and diversify, already doubling its sales within a few years of the employee purchase.

Through its network of wholly owned subsidiaries, Pat King Group Limited provides a wide range of financial services to both business and individuals. The original make-up of services has grown to include property management and development, investment and equity funds, and venture capital. The company is also involved in areas that range from flooring products and electrical contracting to typesetting and printing services. Pat King Group Limited has

the region's largest fee appraisal company, which appraises and conducts feasibility studies on all types of real estate and equipment, including shopping centres, office towers, complexes, and subdivision developments.

In 1985 Pat King Group Limited became a part owner of nationally franchised HomeLife Realty Services Inc. with 260 offices nationwide. Pat King Group Limited is a HomeLife franchisor for the region and plans to expand HomeLife across Atlantic Canada. About 200 HomeLife Pat King Real Estate agents are already part of the system.

Pat King Group Limited's senior management credits the employees' young age for the firm's vibrant and ambitious outlook. Employees tend to be in their late twenties to early forties, and willing to tackle new ideas with an innovative approach. Consistent with its own business philosophy, Pat King Group Limited has begun funding awards programs at Saint Mary's University to encourage the growth and development of entrepreneurship in students at the high school and university level. The two programs, the Pat King Group Entrepreneurial Awards Program and the Entrepreneur of Tomorrow Scholarship, have garnered both attention from students and applause from the business community.

A solid history and foundation, the talents of today's young business minds, and the development of tomorrow's corporate leaders—all pillars of Pat King Group Limited's success.

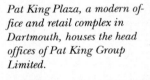

Pat King Plaza, a modern office and retail complex in Dartmouth, houses the head offices of Pat King Group Limited.

DOW CHEMICAL CANADA INC.

Small in numbers but large in service aptly describes the role of Dow Chemical Canada Inc.'s Atlantic region office. "We've had a full-time presence in the area for more than 30 years," says regional manager John Cattran. "Because we are essentially residents, rather than just salespeople who show up every six weeks or so, we're better able to provide for the needs of industry here."

Dow Chemical opened its first Atlantic sales office in Saint John, New Brunswick, in 1958 with a staff of three people, primarily to serve the province's budding pulp and paper industry. In the early 1970s Dow moved the office to Halifax to provide a central location for its expanding activities in the four Atlantic provinces.

Today, from his office overlooking the scenic Halifax harbor, Cattran oversees a staff of 11 employees, including people stationed in St. John's, Newfoundland, and Moncton and Fredericton, New Brunswick.

In addition to its sales activity, Dow Chemical owns approximately 1,000 acres of land in the Port Hawksbury area where a salt-brine mining operation was partially developed in the late 1960s. From its construction materials warehouse in Dartmouth, Dow serves a large sector of Nova Scotia, parts of Prince Edward Island, New Brunswick, and Newfoundland.

Although Dow does not manufacture chemicals in the region, its products are essential for making a wide variety of items that are part of the everyday lives of Atlantic Canadians. Dow plastic resins are the basis of the production of durable plastic bags found in grocery and department stores, among others. Most people will be familiar with products such as Saran Wrap® and Ziploc Bags®, as well as the Fantastic®-brand all-purpose cleaners. Styrofoam®, a registered trademark of Dow, is a familiar and effective

insulating material that adds warmth and comfort to homes and buildings in the long, cold Atlantic winters. In agriculture and the forest industry, Dow pesticides and herbicides are the backbone of modern large-scale production methods.

At the same time Dow is acutely aware of the need to provide environmentally safe chemical products to ensure the long-term health and safety of its workers and the public. With landfill sites rapidly reaching capacity, Dow Chemical Canada Inc. is co-operating in ventures to recycle plastics such as soft-drink bottles and the rigid high-density polystyrene containers that resist breakdown in ordinary landfills. "Our products contribute only about 6 percent of the total material that finds its way into the garbage," says Cattran. "But we are working on ways to reduce even that small figure because we recognize that we all have to do our part in protecting the environment."

Concrete-topped Styrofoam® insulation on the roof of the Loyola Building at Saint Mary's University, Halifax, Nova Scotia.

Extrusion of "film bubble" for polyethylene bags. Courtesy, Poly Cello—Amherst, Nova Scotia

McINNES COOPER & ROBERTSON

Pictured, left to right, are Messrs. Donald McInnes, Q.C.; George B. Robertson, Q.C.; and the Honourable A. Gordon Cooper.

The firm's offices are located at Cornwallis Place, said to be the possible landing site of Edward Cornwallis, founder of Halifax.

A forest of spars and masts signifying the prominent role of Halifax in world trade regularly lined the shores of the harbor when Jonathan McCully and Hiram Blanchard became partners in the practice of law in 1859. McCully, one of the fathers of confederation, and Blanchard, who later served as a premier of Nova Scotia, started an institution that endured and today is known as McInnes Cooper & Robertson.

Although McInnes Cooper & Robertson embodies 130 years of legal history, George Cooper sees it as young and growing. "Atlantic Canada is growing," he says. "Halifax is at the center of it, and we think there is a great future here."

With more than 50 lawyers the firm is one of the largest in the region. But as the firm has grown, so too has the complexity of society and its laws. "We're a full-service firm," says Cooper,

Lawyers at McInnes Cooper & Robertson are encouraged to give something back to their profession and to participate in community activities. Over the years 11 members of the firm headed the Nova Scotia Barristers' Society, and two served as national president of the Canadian Bar Association. Many have served on the various councils and committees of these organizations. Numerous members also take an active role in professional associations such as the Canadian Tax Foundation, the International Bar Association, and the American College of Trial Lawyers.

In the education field, two dozen lawyers from the firm have been part-time lecturers at Dalhousie Law School, and some teach regularly at other universities. Two served as chairman of the board of governors of Dalhousie University, two others as chairman of Mount St. Vincent University, and one as chairman of the Technical University of Nova Scotia.

Members of the firm have also been active in politics. Four were elected Member of Parliament for Halifax since World War II.

For more than 100 years McInnes Cooper &

"and in order to deal with the broad range of problems that people encounter in today's world, our services have expanded, and today we are highly diversified."

The firm has a number of practice groups, each of which works in a different area of law. Within each practice group there are several subgroups to cover specialties such as securities, admiralty, public utilities regulation, environmental law, and so on. But legal problems don't always land neatly in one category, so, when necessary, specialists in all relevant areas will team up to work for a resolution of a client's problem.

Robertson had its headquarters in the same location on Bedford Row near the harbor. But finally the archaic charm of the longtime home met face to face with the family that no longer fit within the walls. In 1988 the firm moved into the modern Cornwallis Place, at 1601 Lower Water Street, a building of which it is part owner. The eastern face of the building reminds the viewer of a ship's prow jutting out into the harbor. George Cooper likened the firm's boardroom on the sixth floor to the wheelhouse of a large ship—an apt allusion for a firm that has guided the affairs of so many Nova Scotians for so long.

REINFORCED PLASTIC SYSTEMS INC.

The distracting beauty of Mahone Bay makes it easy to drive past the headquarters of Reinforced Plastic Systems Inc. without a notice. Yet this unassuming facility nestled in a wooded hillside of the bay is home to the largest manufacturer of fibreglass-reinforced plastic piping systems in all of Canada.

The company traces its origin to the mid-1950s, when the use of fibreglass for the fishing industry and boat building was in its infancy. Paceship sailing yachts bearing the Eastwinds and Westwinds name and made in the plant can still be seen plying the waters of Mahone Bay and other scenic areas of Nova Scotia's south shore.

In 1965 the company began the move to the manufacture of specialized fibreglass-reinforced plastic pipe and fittings for industry. Using a process in which the fibreglass filament is wound rather than molded with fibreglass cloth or mat, it produced an eight-foot-diameter penstock (the huge pipe used to carry water from a reservoir to the turbine for generating electricity) for the Nova Scotia Power Corporation.

Production of fibreglass-reinforced-plastic pipe quickly expanded and became the major product of the organization. Recognizing the increased need in industry for pipe of all sizes that would withstand the ravages of corrosion and abrasion, company engineers, using a variety of special-purpose resins, successfully developed pipe to provide an economical solution in the handling of abrasive slurry consisting of fly ash and limestone.

This pipe became the heart line of scrubbing systems designed to remove sulfur dioxide caused by burning coal for electrical generation. It was first applied to flue gas desulfurization in 1971 for the Kansas Light and Power Company in the United States. In all more than 80 locations across the United States that installed flue gas desulfurization systems chose the fibreglass pipe developed and produced by Reinforced Plastic Systems in its unpresumptuous plant on the shore of Mahone Bay. By 1975 the success of this and other products had the plant bursting at the seams. Additional space was acquired, bringing the complex to more than 90,000 square feet. Today the company employs more than 150 workers.

With its ability to custom design and produce pipe to fit specific needs, Reinforced Plastic Systems has been able to serve a variety of industries in Canada and around the world. Pipe made in the plant can be found in Australia, East Germany, United States, Mexico, India, Saudi Arabia, Egypt, and Northern Ireland. In 1988 the firm filled the largest fibreglass pipe contract ever in North America by supplying corrosion-resistant pipe to a magnesium refinery in Quebec. And the emphasis that the company places on quality control allows its products to be used on critical nuclear power plant installations such as Point Lepreau in New Brunswick.

Reinforced Plastic Systems Inc. is continuing its commitment to the Atlantic region. In July 1989 the firm opened a new branch named the International Composites Division at the Burnside Industrial Park in Dartmouth.

This 24-inch-diameter pipe at Northern Indiana Public Service Company's flue gas desulfurization installation handles slurry at a coal-fired thermal electric plant.

LEFT: Process piping at Northern Indiana Public Service Company's flue gas desulfurization installation.

This seven-foot-diameter Minas Basin Penstock carries water from the reservoir to turbines at a small hydroelectric power station.

AIR NOVA

Air Nova took off on July 14, 1986, when flight number 812, a de Havilland Dash-8 with 17 passengers, made the 50-minute morning trip from Halifax to Sydney. Early that Monday, another Dash-8 inaugurated the Newfoundland route from St. John's to Deer Lake and Corner Brook.

Those champagne-and-orange-juice flights began Air Nova's operations with 2 aircraft, 5 destinations, and 46 employees. New aircraft on order will see the fleet grow to 26 aircraft by the early 1990s, serving a network of destinations. Air Nova will employ more than 500 people—mostly Atlantic Canadians—to manage, operate, and service its enterprise. That trans-

Joseph Randell (left), president and chief operating officer, and Harold Wareham, chairman and chief executive officer, in front of a de Havilland Dash-8, the type of aircraft that made Air Nova's inaugural flights on July 14, 1986. By the 1990s the Air Nova fleet will grow to 26 aircraft and carry one million passengers per year. Courtesy, Eric Hayes

lates into a targeted one million passengers per year and revenues of more than $100 million.

Air Nova's launching was made possible by airline deregulation. It started out from scratch simply as a concept in 1984, when the three founders saw the need for a higher calibre of air service in the region. An ongoing spirit of initiative and innovation has since made Air Nova a noteworthy air carrier.

One of the firm's earliest challenges was to prove the existing poor opinions of air travel throughout the region were no longer valid. Passengers had historically complained about the lack of frequent and nonstop flights, unreliability, and poor on-time performance.

To do away with those complaints, Air Nova extensively researched types of aircraft, travel patterns, market demand, and passenger needs before it started up. In particular, the firm wanted to make air travel more convenient for business executives and professionals, a vital category that makes up 60 percent of Air Nova's clientele.

The advance homework paid off. Within the first two months of operation, Air Nova outstripped its own optimistic passenger forecasts by 20 percent. More recent passenger opinion surveys confirm that Air Nova has turned around the old image. Frequent business travellers, some of whom have taken up to 80 flights in a 12-month period, have bestowed their wings of approval on the airline.

"Friendly people keep the freshness and excitement of a growing company alive," commented an executive originating from Bathurst, New Brunswick. "I was pleased with the introduction of the jet service to major cities," says a professional engineer flying out of Mount Pearl. "As a frequent traveller I prefer Air Nova for its on-time performance," notes a district retail manager out-bound from Dartmouth. "The variety of flights is a real plus," says a government employee from Conception Bay South. "I have flown Air Nova many times and have always been satisfied with the service," says a Halifax professor.

That customer satisfaction comes partly from Air Nova's business affiliation and meshed flight schedules with Air Canada. Air Nova signed an agreement as the first Liaison Air Canada Connector on May 20, 1986. Air Canada owns 49 percent of Air Nova while Atlantis Corporation of St. John's owns 51 percent.

The link with the national carrier offered Air Nova passengers co-operative flight scheduling, a frequent flyer program, joint and through fares, automatic baggage transfer, and the sharing of airport and computerized reservation services. Air Canada no longer had to fly large-capacity aircraft between routes where the passenger traffic did not justify such seat space. Residents in some of Canada's smallest communities had air links to a worldwide travel network through the

the regional and national carriers.

"In order to be successful in Atlantic Canada, you've got to cater to many different markets and tailor your product accordingly," Air Nova president Joseph Randell explains. "We make this a priority and work closely with the people in these markets."

Air Nova's growing number of routes and destinations has called for a carefully orchestrated build-up of its fleet of aircraft. Canadian-made de Havilland Dash-8s (37 passengers) and British Aerospace 146s (77 passengers) were the mainstays at the outset.

"In Atlantic Canada," says Randell, "we have a unique geography, consisting of low-density population centres separated by quite a distance and water barriers in some cases. The smaller aircraft offer our passengers the most advanced developments in aircraft technology, safety, and comfort while allowing us to offer in excess of 200 departures per day throughout our entire route network."

That will grow to 250 departures daily during the 1990s as Air Nova operates with main terminal hubs in Halifax, St. John's, and Montreal. To handle the firm's expansion, Air Nova has built a $5-million, 56,000-square-foot maintenance complex at the Halifax International Airport.

With its fleet makeup, and elsewhere, Air Nova still fosters the pioneering approach that led to its founding. It was the first Canadian airline to order Canadair's Regional Jets (50-passengers), an off-shoot of its executive jet. The 10 RJs will boost the number of Air Nova's long-distance, nonstop flights and help the firm adopt other prospective routes.

The passenger cabins of Air Nova's 146 jets have been modified to provide for a more extensive inflight service. For additional passenger comfort, the airline opted for the more spacious 2x3 seating configuration, rather than the usual 3x3 seating arrangement. Air Nova was the first Atlantic Canadian carrier to introduce Executive Class Service on its BAE 146 jets. Air Nova offers free ground coach service from the

Deer Lake airport to Corner Brook, about 30 miles away. For Halifax passengers, the firm installed an enclosed pedway in the first phase of a multimillion-dollar passenger check-in facility.

Air Nova's marketing efforts have been recognized for their "special ingenuity" by the Tourism Industry Association of Nova Scotia. The Atlantic Canadapass was an award-winning program. It is a travel package, along the lines of Europe's Eurail Pass, that offers passengers many destinations with scheduling flexibility and substantial savings in airfare. The program was co-sponsored by the four provincial governments in the region, and it is expected to increase tourism traffic and lengthen the tourism season.

Air Nova has contracted with Air Canada's tour packaging arm, Touram, to use its 146 jets to fly charters to Orlando and Miami. The airline has introduced the "cashless cabin," offering passengers free bar and beverage service on all flights.

Regionally, Air Nova has actively promoted the Marble Mountain ski resort near Corner Brook, becoming the official airline to serve that destination. "Now on the threshold of dramatic expansion, a recently announced $24-million development project has made Marble Mountain a success story of concerted public and private sector co-operation," says Bruce MacLellan, senior director of marketing at Air Nova. The airline is undertaking similar ski promotions for Crabbe Mountain in Fredericton, and the Laurentians and Monte Ste. Anne in Quebec.

Air Nova Inc. has supported the fund-raising efforts of more than 1,000 community organizations by donating travel passes. The airline is a member of the Mission Air mercy flight organization and gives more than 100 seats per year to seriously ill patients to fly to treatment centres.

To Air Nova president Joseph Randell, community support is a basic part of being a corporate citizen. "We accept the responsibility of helping to improve the quality of life in the communities in which we live and work. We are proud to be an Atlantic Canadian company."

One of Air Nova's 10 Regional Jets on order from Canadair. Air Nova will be the first Canadian carrier to fly the 50-passenger Regional Jet when it takes delivery in the 1990s.

LAWTON'S DRUG STORES LIMITED

Lawton's Drug Store, in Bell Island, Newfoundland, circa 1930.

A young Keith Lawton in his father's pharmacy in Newfoundland.

With 76 outlets at last count, Lawton's Drug Stores Limited is a dynamic Atlantic Canadian-owned retail chain. The growth, which is continuing at a healthy pace, is administered from the head office in Dartmouth's City of the Lakes Business Park. Lawton's strategy is to select pharmacists with a keen interest in business and give them management experience and the option to become owners. This is Lawton's winning formula.

"The stores are changing all the time," says founder and honorary chairman Keith Lawton. "I can't keep track of them all." Lawton attributes the firm's success to a little luck and a lot of forward thinking. Innovation, imaginative merchandising, and a vision for opportunities are hallmarks of the Lawton's formula.

Keith Lawton's broad concept for pharmacy was inherited from his father, who went to work in Harbour Grace, Newfoundland, at the age of 13. Six years later, in 1907, he opened a store in the Newfoundland mining community of Bell Island and carried on business there until retirement in 1966. Keith Lawton stayed on Bell Island until he went to Dalhousie University in 1939, and during these years the senior Lawton encouraged his son to increase his knowledge of pharmacy and the requirements of drugstore operations. Lawton reflects on the fact that these were pre-Confederation days and the bulk of supplies came from the United States and the United Kingdom rather than Canada, and the influences of American concepts and aggressive merchandising were found to work in a small, isolated mining town as well as in a large American city.

Lawton remembers piling up 200 gallons of chocolate syrup on the sidewalk—a summer's supply for the soda fountain—and later in Halifax selling 100 Ronson lighters in one day, driving a red-and-yellow delivery van when other stores used boys on bicycles, opening the first self-service store in the first shopping centre (Dartmouth) in Nova Scotia, and bringing the first ballpoint pens to Halifax (Reynolds at $19.50!). Lawton smiles when he recounts these and other "creative" activities and again credits his enthusiasm for adventurous innovation to his exposure to the American influence. He admits that there was considerable gambling, particularly in opening new stores, but with some few exceptions it paid off.

But to trace all the origins of Lawton's Drug Stores Limited, one has to go back to 1903. That year Enos MacLeod began his Halifax pharmacy career at the South End Pharmacy. Later he bought the store. In 1913 MacLeod became a partner with Samuel Balcom. Seven years later Foster Chittick joined the two partners, and the three formed MacLeod Balcom Ltd. with two stores. By 1949 more stores had been added, the management had changed, and the business was renamed Balcom-Chittick Ltd.

Ownership changed again in 1967 when the chain was bought by R.B. Cameron. Then, in 1969, the nine Balcom-Chittick stores were sold to Sobey-owned Canadian Shopping Centres Limited. Another Sobey venture, Empire Company Limited, acquired Keith Lawton's five remaining outlets in 1975. Paul D. Sobey, a grandson of the founder of the Empire Company, is chairman of the board of Lawton's.

Keith Lawton's drugstore chain had its own interesting evolution. Lawton graduated in 1942 from the Maritime College of Pharmacy and worked for two years at Fader's Pharmacy. When the owner of McFatridge's Drugs Ltd. on Gottingen Street died in 1944, Lawton arranged $5,000 financing to buy it. He renamed it Lawton's in 1950 and moved it across the street to the former Moir's bakery on the northeast corner of Gottingen and Cornwallis streets.

Lawton opened other stores as he identified good market prospects. When T. Eaton Realty Co. asked Lawton to set up a store in its new Halifax Shopping Centre, he accepted the invitation. He went to North Carolina to see the first enclosed shopping mall on the Atlantic seaboard. Two days later he knew exactly what he wanted. He opened in a high-traffic corner location with a sign the width of his store.

Therefore, the acquisition of Keith Lawton's drugstore chain was a key component of the re-sulting amalgamation. Ultimately the bold mor-tar-and-pestle logo and the Lawton's name have been used to proudly identify all the stores in the chain.

The current Lawton's master plan is to capitalize on expansion opportunities while developing a strong franchise and joint-venture program. President Tom Smith says a candidate for a franchise or a joint venture must be "a pharmacist with an entrepreneurial spirit." At Lawton's, pharmacists gain experience by carrying out regular professional duties. The emphasis on counselling customers about their prescription and medication needs, which has been the cornerstone of the firm's reputation, continues to be a priority at Lawton's. "We believe that meeting the service expectations of our customers is why the Lawton's formula is a formula for success," says president Tom Smith.

Pharmacists with an interest in developing their business skills are encouraged to work toward store management positions, and successful managers can be considered for the franchise or joint-venture program. Furthermore, the organization's policy of promoting from within gives its store management the opportunity to move into administrative positions in the head office. A company-subsidized continuing education program testifies to the commitment Lawton's Drug Stores Limited has made to its most important resource—its people.

The newest Lawton's outlet, on Cole Harbour Road in Dartmouth, Nova Scotia.

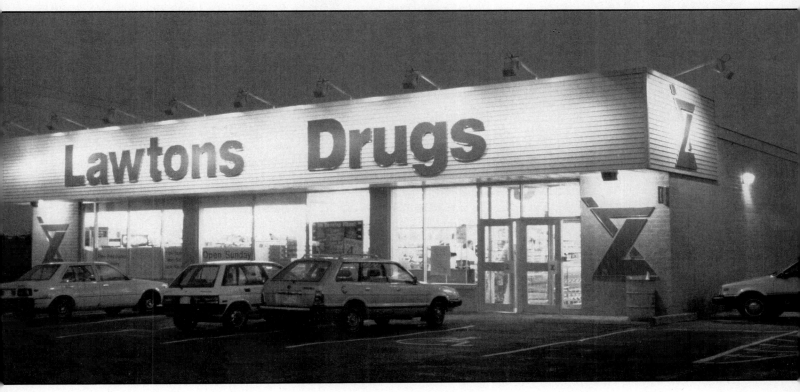

PORT OF HALIFAX

Halterm Container Terminal, one of the first container facilities in Canada, is a hub of activity as three gantry cranes are deployed for discharge and loading of the Orient Overseas Container Line (OOCL) vessel. The newly extended seawall at Halterm allows two vessels this size to be worked simultaneously.

The strategic significance of shipping to the port of Halifax has been documented since the very first permanent settlement encamped along its island-guarded shore. Mindful of the port's closeness to trading routes, Otis Little, an attorney at the time of the port's beginning, wrote that it was "more in the way of all ships passing to and from Europe to New England." In 1749 Halifax founder and Englishman Edward Cornwallis sailed into the harbor and recorded "all the officers agree the harbor is the finest they have ever seen." Five days after Cornwallis arrived on the sloop *Sphinx*, 13 transport vessels arrived bearing 2,576 settlers.

Summers before that nomadic Micmac Indians used to paddle birchbark canoes up the water they called Chebooktook, meaning "the greatest harbor," later known as Chebucto. And a French military engineer estimated in 1711 that the harbor and connected (Bedford) basin could hold 1,000 vessels.

Whether the port of Halifax has ever held 1,000 vessels is a moot point, but mariners in all types of craft have been busy there since the city's founding. In 1878 Halifax entrepreneur Samuel Cunard founded his famous shipping line that linked Halifax, New York, and London. During World War II the inner harbor of Bedford Basin was filled with naval vessels, tankers, and cargo ships being made up into convoys. About 1.25 million immigrants came to Canada through Halifax' Pier 21 between 1928 and 1971.

Today port-related activities account for $300 million per year in paycheques and 5,000 jobs from all the related support services. Halifax is located about 32 kilometres off the Great Circle shipping route between Europe and the U.S. East Coast, making it a gateway to North America. What makes the port equally attractive is its deep water, easy approach, and slight changes in tides. The port, 21 metres deep at low tide, is ice-free year round with an outer harbor six kilometres long and more than 1.5 kilometres wide.

Halifax has more sailings to more centres of maritime commerce than any other Canadian port. Total tonnage handled in 1988 exceeded 16 million tons. Goods and cargo vary as widely as the countries of origin and destination. There are commodities such as grain, crude and refined oil, gypsum, automobiles, and containerized cargo—even fish, apples, and blueberries. Bagged flour may go to Cuba, Yemen, Aqaba, or Morocco. Cargo too heavy or unwieldy for containers or pallets can also be shipped by roll-on/roll-off vessels. A vessel may carry a rock-crushing machine from Finland, compressor engine from Liverpool, or six-wheel tree-harvesting machine from Sweden. A Bell 212 helicopter, dismantled, may be consigned from Rotterdam.

Visiting shipping lines are equally varied. More than 30 steamship firms have regular scheduled service to Europe, the United Kingdom, the Mediterranean, the Far East, Australia, Africa, Iceland, the Middle East, the Caribbean, and the U.S. East and West coasts. Also luxury passenger liners call in as part of their cruises.

Growth in containerized cargo is especially healthy and projected to surpass four million tons in 1990. Container vessels make almost

1,000 calls to the port each year. Halterm, the port's first container pier, was built in 1969. A second container pier, operated by Cerescorp Inc., was built at Fairview Cove in 1982. Each terminal has mobile gantry cranes to handle a pair of the largest, latest-generation container vessels, some carrying 4,000, 20-foot containers. Since they began, the two terminals have increased the size of their operations, through increased wharf area and container storage space. A third container pier was added in 1989, and still another large separate container complex is being studied.

With its existing capabilities, the port of Halifax is in tune with the container trend. Larger container ships want to call at fewer ports and rely on the inland shipping connections of those selected ports. Halifax already services some of the largest container vessels: the *Marchen Maersk*, 294 metres long (4,000 containers), and the 292-metre Atlantic Container Line vessels (3,000 containers). Regular coastal feeder services can, in turn, ship to Newfoundland or the islands of St. Pierre and Miquelon. Boston is 380 nautical miles away, and New York is 600 miles away.

Cranes load containers directly from ship to rail. A container unloaded in Halifax can travel to Chicago (2,495 kilometres) or Detroit (2,255 kilometres) via Canadian National Railways' transcontinental connections faster than if that same container is unloaded in New York. About 70 percent of Halifax unloaded cargo is destined for inland customers in Montreal (1,300 kilometres) and Toronto (1,850 kilometres), so rail service is crucial.

Another Canadian National operation, Autoport, began in 1971. It handled its one-millionth car within 12 years, and now unloads and services up to 125,000 vehicles per year. Located outside of Dartmouth, the Autoport complex has a 200-metre floating dock, a 5-track rail siding, and a 40-hectare storage yard. Each year about 70 ships call at the Autoport.

In 1984 two organizations were formed to oversee and co-ordinate shipping business and development for the port. The Halifax Port Corporation administers harbor operations and carries out long-range planning and financial management. The Halifax-Dartmouth Port Development Commission promotes the port's facilities and co-operates with government, labor, and private organizations to keep the port efficient and competitive.

Halifax Harbour is the deep, ice-free body of water that separates the city of Dartmouth and the peninsula that is the city of Halifax. In the foreground is Ceres Container Terminal, and, almost directly in the distance, Halterm Container Terminal is visible. As can be seen from the photo, shipping lines calling Halifax have easy access to the port from the open ocean, which is a very short sail in protected waters.

FARMERS CO-OPERATIVE DAIRY LIMITED

The milk we pour on our cereal each morning, the cream in our tea or coffee, and the butter on our toast all look remarkably similar to those that our grandparents used, but the dairy industry that produces these items has changed dramatically over the years. Farmers Co-operative Dairy Limited has been a leader and innovator in the effort to provide wholesome dairy food products for the tables of Atlantic Canadians for more than 60 years.

Farmers traces its origins to the days when milkmen loaded cans of milk into horse-drawn wagons, drove to customers' doors, and ladled milk into any container that the customer offered. Today Farmers provides an array of more than 60 different dairy products, including ice cream, cheese, yogurt, and its long-shelf-life milk shakes. "If we counted all the different flavors and package sizes separately, we'd have a list of almost 800 products," says Bill MacLennan, a former president of Farmers and now an executive consultant to the firm.

In 1904 A.D. Johnson delivered milk the old-fashioned way to local Halifax households. He founded a family business called Maple Leaf Dairy, one of the forerunners of Farmers Co-operative Dairy Limited. In 1922 a group of dairy farmers joined to form a company called Farmers Limited to market their milk. During the 1920s processing innovations were introduced by local dairies to assure their customers a safe, nutritious supply of milk. Farmers Limited became the first local dairy to pasteurize its milk (treating raw milk with heat to

eliminate harmful bacteria) in order to ensure quality. And by 1938 Farmers had an automated operation that permitted its glass bottles to be washed and filled without being handled.

Maple Leaf Dairy and Farmers Limited prospered and expanded for nearly a half-century as the demand for milk products grew. Processing larger volumes and varieties of milk products required modern, more efficient plants and distribution networks. By the mid-1950s the familiar horse-drawn wagons that brought milk to the customers' doorsteps were completely replaced by motorized trucks. By the early 1960s the Farmers Limited dairy plant covered almost an entire city block at Windsor and North streets in Halifax and processed some 160,000 pounds of milk each weekday. At that point it was the

largest dairy in Eastern Canada. Maple Leaf Dairy was not far behind. It had outgrown its Chebucto Road plant and built an addition that increased the facility by 25 percent.

In 1961 the dairy farmers who supplied milk to Farmers Limited and Maple Leaf Dairy Limited formed a co-operative and negotiated the purchase of both dairies. The co-operative chose the name Twin Cities Co-operative Dairy Limited, after the new twin cities of Halifax and Dartmouth, but adopted the widely recognized Farmers brand name for all of its product lines. In response to soaring production costs that made centralized milk processing a necessity, 15 more dairies from Yarmouth to Truro joined the co-operative during the 1960s and 1970s.

In 1981 Farmers became a truly Atlantic Canada firm when it expanded again and acquired Central Dairies Limited of Newfoundland. Shortly thereafter the firm changed its name to Farmers Co-operative Dairy Limited in order to better identify the company with the familiar brand name carried by its products. Today the co-operative is owned by 250 Nova Scotia dairy farmers and employs more than 600 people in Atlantic Canada.

The co-operative business structure assures the continuation of local ownership and control. "We're directly responsible to the farmer/owners of the co-operative to make sure we market their milk and milk products in the best way possible," says Doug Bailey, president of Farmers. "But we are also responsible to each and every one of our customers to provide them with wholesome dairy foods that have an assurance of quality."

Over the years the co-operative has continued the spirit of innovation set by its predecessors. In 1966 it revived the Nova Scotia cheese industry. A cheddar cheese factory opened near Truro that year is still the only commercial cheese facility in the province. Almost 4 million pounds of cheddar are produced each year for sale throughout Atlantic Canada. In the 1970s the cheese factory expanded and began making powdered milk. The plant now processes most of the industrial milk products in the province and buys more than 37 million litres of industrial milk from Nova Scotia farmers.

Farmers has also been a pioneer in developing new products for the dairy industry. The introduction of spreads that combine butter with margarine—Farmers 20/80 and 50/50—was an industry first in Canada. The ultramodern dairy plant in Bedford was another innovation. Built in 1975 to replace the two plants in

Fond memories are evoked by this photo courtesy of Art Cox, who was office manager for Farmers Co-operative Dairy Limited during his years with the company from 1924 to 1973.

Halifax that Farmers had acquired 14 years earlier, the Bedford facility provides the latest in automation and technology for milk processing. Milk arriving at the 90-acre site in huge stainless-steel tank trucks is unloaded, graded, processed, and packaged automatically. Computerized controls direct the process while professional milk graders and dairy-lab chemists constantly oversee the operation to monitor product quality. Large portions of the plant are given over to storage areas that act as massive refrigerators for milk, ice cream, cottage cheese, yogurt, and other products. Almost 250,000 litres of dairy products and juices can be processed in the plant in a single day. Energy and water conservation systems add to the efficiency and economy of the plant.

In a move that put Farmers in the forefront of the international dairy industry, the co-operative added ultrahigh-temperature (UHT) equipment at its Bedford plant in 1983. The UHT facility, which cost more than $3 million, is an advancement on the traditional system of pasteurization. Milk and milk products are heated to much higher temperatures but for a shorter period of time. The process quickly eliminates the bacteria that causes milk to spoil. When combined with aseptic packaging, the UHT process results in dairy products that do not need refrigeration and have a shelf life of six months.

Farmers Shakes, prepackaged milk shakes in a variety of flavors and produced with the UHT process, are the "first fluid milk product in North America to be distributed coast to coast," according to Bailey. "The shakes offer a nutritious alternative to soft drinks, and the package makes it as portable as a pop can." Gary Sowerby and Tim Cahill, who completed the longest drive in the Western Hemisphere—from the tip of South America all the way to the coast of the Arctic Ocean in Alaska—used the shakes as a steady part of their diet on the epic trip.

Fruit juice, chocolate milk, and fruit-flavored yogurt beverages have also been added to Farmers' long list of products produced with the UHT process. The success of these and other Farmers products has resulted in annual sales of more than $110 million per year. The co-operative is now exporting its UHT products as far as Antigua and Bermuda.

While leaning toward innovation in its UHT line, Farmers continues to serve the individual consumers in the old-fashioned way. In Nova Scotia, where the per-capita consumption of milk is the highest in the country, door-to-door delivery of fresh milk still forms a substantial portion of Farmers' business. Mindful of the needs of health-conscious consumers, Farmers recently introduced milk with one-percent butterfat. "We found that some consumers wanted milk with more body and color than skim but with less fat content than 2 percent," Bailey notes. "So we moved to give them a product to fulfill that need."

The success enjoyed by Farmers is shared not only by the farmer/owners, but by employees as well. The company has a gain-sharing plan where an employee's level of productivity is calculated in dollars and cents. Bailey says that it makes sense to acknowledge individual productivity rather than just the firm's performance. This concern for its workers is one reason why Farmers Co-operative Dairy Limited earned a place on the *Financial Post*'s list of the best 100 companies to work for in Canada.

Pure Pak filling machines capable of filling 100, 250-millilitre, 500-millilitre, and one-litre cartons per minute. They possess the most advanced technology with enclosed filling chambers, bottom-up fill, and accurate weight control. These machines are built in Japan for Pure Pak Inc., a U.S. equipment supplier.

CHERUBINI METAL WORKS LTD.

In only 20 years Cherubini Metal Works Ltd. has grown from a three-man operation in a ramshackle garage on Main Street in Dartmouth to a multimillion-dollar structural steel and miscellaneous metal-fabrication company spread over 30,000 square feet in the Burnside Industrial Park.

"It was just a small shack with holes in the ceiling," recalls Bernice Lloyd, the firm's accountant for the past 10 years. "In the winter the snow would come in through the roof and land on the desk."

Renato and Danilo Gasparetto went to work for Cherubini when the business opened in 1967. They constructed and installed ornamental iron railings that were the sole product of the fledgling company. In 1972 the brothers bought the business and began to expand the operation. Six years later, still concentrating on small contracts for railings, they moved with 11 employees from the hopelessly overcrowded garage to a 10,000-square-foot plant in Burnside.

In the past 10 years the company has continued to grow and diversify to its present size with 65 full-time employees. The first step into large contracts came in 1981 with the supply and installation of the structural metals for the Annapolis Tidal Power project. Since then Cherubini has erected the steel frame work for a variety of well-known area buildings, including Torrington Place and the Woodside ferry terminal in Dartmouth, the Cole Harbour Sportsplex, and the Sun Office Tower in Bedford.

Jeff Kay, Cherubini's general manager, is enthusiastic about one of the firm's latest projects. "The new Grace Maternity Hospital that we're doing is the first stub girder system in a hospital in North America." A stub girder system binds concrete to the structural steel to allow a greater expanse of open space without columns.

But Kay is also proud of the smaller, specialized work the company does. "We fabricated and installed all of the beautiful brass railings in the Halifax World Trade and Convention Center. And we replaced the mirror-steel bearing plates on the Macdonald bridge that allow it to expand and contract with temperature changes. It was only a small contract, but it was interesting because we had to jack the bridge up to do the replacement," Kay says.

Although Cherubini now competes in the offshore market with projects already completed in Bermuda and Saint Pierre, it is very aware of its origins in Dartmouth. For two years running the employees have won the Burnside Challenge by raising more money for the Big Brother/Sister program than any firm in the industrial park.

Versatility and quality are the words that Kay uses to describe the work of Cherubini Metal Works Ltd. "Many of our original customers still come back to us years later when they want to replace or expand the railings we installed. We don't do much of that anymore," Kay remarks, "but we're proud to know that they think enough of our work to search us out when they want more."

Owners Renato Gasparetto (left) and Danilo Gasparetto look over plans for a new project.

MARINE ATLANTIC INC.

SS Prince Edward Island *was the first vessel to ply the Borden-Cape Tormentine route to Prince Edward Island, beginning in 1917.*

MV Joseph and Clara Smallwood, *delivered in December 1989, and her sister ship,* Caribou, *are Canada's largest ferries, operating between Newfoundland and Cape Breton.*

The mandate of Atlantic Canada's major ferry operator is simple but challenging: to provide reliable, cost-effective transportation links to the island provinces and Labrador, and highway alternatives across the Bay of Fundy.

Marine Atlantic Inc., an independent Crown corporation, maintains the vital services with a modernized fleet and reduced reliance on operating subsidies from the federal government. The corporation's 16 vessels carry more than 2.5 million passengers and one million vehicles each year.

Marine Atlantic's operations have a strong impact on the regional economy. The corporation employs approximately 3,000 people, buys area goods and services, and promotes tourism and hospitality. Marine Atlantic injects more than $100 million annually in wages and bene-

fits alone. For example, $20 million is paid to the 650 employees of the Prince Edward Island service, the heaviest used route of the system.

During the 1980s Marine Atlantic added five new Canadian-built vessels worth a total of $350 million. The super ferries *Caribou* (North Sydney to Port aux Basques) and *Joseph and Clara Smallwood* (North Sydney to Argentia) each carry 1,200 passengers and 350 automobiles. Ferry terminals were upgraded to make efficient use of the faster and higher capacity vessels, and employees were extensively trained in customer service and the use of new technology.

Marine Atlantic was officially renamed from CN Marine Inc. on September 4, 1986, following an act of Parliament that reconstituted it as a completely autonomous Crown corporation with its own board of directors. The firm had earlier streamlined its management structure and strengthened its presence in Charlottetown and St. John's to make it more sensitive and responsive to the needs of the island provinces.

The evolution of an independent ferry organization began in 1973 with the establishment of East Coast Marine and Ferry Service as an operating unit of Canadian National. CN Marine became a division in 1976 and a subsidiary two years later. Marine management consolidated operations, pooled expertise in the region, and achieved economics of scale. In 1984 the federal government decided the time had come for total separation from the railway company.

Regular ferry service between Borden and Cape Tormentine began in 1917 with the SS *Prince Edward Island.* Today Marine Atlantic vessels make more than 50 crossings per day between Prince Edward Island and New Brunswick at peak season. Service between Port aux Basques, Newfoundland, and North Sydney, Nova Scotia, was inaugurated by SS *Bruce* in 1898, and has been continuous ever since. Regular crossings of the Gulf of Maine between Yarmouth and Bar Harbor began in 1956. Service across the Bay of Fundy from Digby to Saint John, regular by 1827, was passed to Marine Atlantic Inc. from Canadian Pacific in 1976.

MOOSEHEAD BREWERIES LIMITED

More than a century of tradition is embodied in the Maritime beers of Canada's oldest privately owned brewery. Although the brands of Moosehead Breweries Limited have been adapted over generations, they owe their beginnings to Susannah Oland, who brewed a distinctive ale in her Dartmouth backyard during the summer of 1867.

The original Army and Navy Brewery was built on the Halifax Harbour in 1867 and destroyed by the Halifax Explosion in 1917.

Susannah and her husband, John James Oland, were approached by Captain Frances de Winton, aide to the Nova Scotia Governor General, who suggested turning the hobby into a business. In 1867 the Army and Navy Brewery began in Dartmouth. When her husband was killed in a riding accident in 1870, Susannah carried on the business, which was renamed S. Oland and Sons & Co. in 1877. More tragedies took place with fires in both the brewery and family residence. Susannah died in 1886, and in 1917 the brewery was finally completely destroyed by the Halifax Explosion.

The following year the Olands turned to brewing ventures in New Brunswick with the purchase of the Simeon Jones Brewery, which they renamed the Red Ball Brewery. This brewery and the Oland Brewery, which later opened in Halifax, eventually came under the control of the Halifax branch of the family. In 1928 Susannah's son, George W.C. Oland, and his son, George B. Oland, bought the James Ready Brewery, which they later renamed New Brunswick Breweries Limited. To ease the firm's entry into Nova Scotia, this brewery changed its name to Moosehead Breweries in 1947.

Moosehead's success carried on, and the firm erected a Dartmouth plant in 1964. Moosehead Breweries now employs about 350 workers in its two plants in Saint John, New Brunswick, and in Dartmouth, Nova Scotia, not far from the first Oland family brewery. It is fifth-generation family member Derek Oland, president and chief operating officer, who has guided Moosehead's international exporting coups.

In 1978 Moosehead was launched in the United States, where it immediately doubled the initial sales projections and has since impressively ranked itself as fifth most popular beer out of 400 imports. By 1985 Moosehead was available in Great Britain through a partnership with Whitbread & Co. PLC, London. In 1987 expansion came in Australia with Matilda Bay Brewing Co., Freemantle.

Moosehead Lager is exported to the United States and Australia, and is brewed under license in the United Kingdom by Whitbread. The company is currently exploring opportunities in Japan, Sweden, and New Zealand.

Moosehead's systematic marketing strategy of teaming up with long-term partners in other countries has made it a worldwide favorite. Millions of cases of Moosehead Lager are sold internationally each year. Moosehead's international image has gotten boosts from cameo product appearances in movies such as *The Three Fugitives,* starring Nick Nolte, and *Honeysuckle Rose,* starring Willie Nelson, and television episodes of "Dallas" and "Dynasty."

It all proves that a small company can find a winning niche in a mammoth industry by capitalizing on its strengths. Moosehead Lager's smooth, refreshing taste satisfies a wide range of palates. Domestically, Moosehead's other brands include Moosehead Light, Alpine, Alpine Lite, Ten Penny, Golden Light, and Molson Canadian.

Famous products of Moosehead Breweries Limited.

RAMSEN ENGINEERING ASSOCIATES INC.

Consulting engineering firm Ramsen Engineering Associates Inc. has won major contracts with a simple yet demanding business approach: Be flexible, mobile, inventive, persistent, and patient—some jobs take years to secure.

The firm began in 1980 in a one-room office located on the Halifax waterfront at Karlsen's Wharf, when engineers Richard Murray and Harold Henriksen left the business they worked for to go out on their own. Their strategy was to capitalize on their engineering experience as well as Murray's considerable business background and connections in the Caribbean. Their game plan was to supply construction projects there with shipload quantities of various building materials, from raw products to finished goods.

With some changes in the business course along the way, things have panned out. In 1981 an early contract was to supply and ship $25,000 of construction lumber to the Heywoods Holiday Village in Barbados. This led to 16 supply contracts on the Heywoods project. By 1986 Ramsen Engineering was bidding on and winning contracts such as a $1.7-million job to supply all the piping, pumps, and valves for a sewerage project in the Cayman Islands. Project values, export services offered, and the list of client countries have steadily grown.

Some of the exported commodities themselves are not exactly high technology—vessels of crushed stone, sand, cement, finished millwork, foundry pieces, and door and window fittings. However Ramsen Engineering's forte is in shopping the globe for the best quality and price of the specified materials, then arranging the logistics to get the cargo to its destination efficiently and in a cost-effective manner. At that stage the firm's engineering know-how kicks in. It can mean critical attention to details such as checking out charted harbor depths, tide tables, and shipping registries for cargo capacities and dimensions of bulk carriers.

"We rely on our engineering knowledge of particular construction processes to appreciate the goals of the contractor and developer," says Henriksen, vice-president. "We can offer alternatives that may be more economical or advantageous, which is different than most suppliers who just say 'You want a widget, here's a widget'."

Coming up with the winning edge for an overseas contract is vital given international competition, explains Ramsen Engineering Associates Inc. president Murray. "We get a lot of inspiration from travel, from being exposed to different countries and cultures and finding out the way they do things."

BELOW: The reception building of the Cayman Hyatt Regency Hotel. Ramsen supplied many architectural finishes throughout the 250-room resort hotel.

RIGHT: Unloading aggregates in Nassau, Bahamas, from the CSL Nanticoke. All 31,000 tons ordered were for Carnival's Crystal Palace Hotel. The cargo was unloaded in a record 5 hours and 50 minutes.

STEWART, McKELVEY, STIRLING, SCALES

McKelvey, Macaulay, Machum of Saint John, New Brunswick's largest and most widely known law firm, recently completed its merger with three prominent Atlantic law

Lawrence M. Machum, also an associate since 1953.

The predecessor firm, McKelvey, Macaulay, Machum, began its practice on May 1, 1955.

firms: Stewart, MacKeen & Covert of Halifax, Nova Scotia; Stirling Ryan of St. John's, Newfoundland; and Scales, Jenkins & McQuaid of Charlottetown, Prince Edward Island.

The New Brunswick offices of Stewart, McKelvey, Stirling, Scales now comprises 24 partners and nine associate practitioners. Its practice is in general civil law, corporate, tax, probate, labor, real estate, family, insurance, and admiralty law.

First known as Porter & Ritchie, the previous firm was formed in 1922 by Horace A. Porter and Louis McC. Ritchie, with offices in Saint John, New Brunswick.

In 1955, following Ritchie's appointment to the Exchequer Court of Canada, a new partnership was formed by E. Neil McKelvey, who had joined the firm in 1949 after war service overseas and graduation from Dalhousie Law School; Wallace D. Macaulay, a naval veteran and an associate since 1953; and

It was destined to thrive, growing steadily to the present day.

Through the years professional and community activities have been wide ranging. Neil McKelvey is a past president of both the Canadian and International Bar associations; Wallace Macaulay served as chairman of the Saint John Board of School Trustees; Wayne Chapman is a vice-president of the CBA and is to be president for 1990-1991; Levi Clain led recent work to establish new rules for civil procedure in New Brunswick; and many partners have been active in the Barristers' Society and the bar admission course.

For the future, in an era demanding ever-increasing specialization in the practice of law, members of the Stewart, McKelvey, Stirling, Scales team are fully confident of their capacity to serve their clientele well within the professional framework of a full-service legal group unique in the Atlantic region.

Principal partners in the Saint John office are (from left) E. Neil McKelvey, Q.C.; Wallace D. Macaulay, Q.C.; and Lawrence M. Machum, Q.C.

MARITIME BEVERAGES LIMITED

Just a small sample of the many flavors and product sizes offered by today's Maritime Beverages Limited.

Entrepreneur Simeon H. White of Sussex, New Brunswick, was having a well drilled on his property in 1894 when suddenly an underground reservoir was probed. Foul-smelling water gushed to the surface, and there was great speculation on whether it was fit to drink.

White promptly had it tested and learned that despite its odor and taste, it had "medicinal" properties. An astute man, he reasoned that once flavored and bottled it would have commercial value as well.

The rest, as they say, is history—the history of today's Maritime Beverages Limited of Saint John, New Brunswick.

In October 1895 the Sussex Mineral Spring Company commenced operations from a barn, offering no fewer than 17 flavors bearing such exotic names as Birch Champagne, Peruvian Beer, Pepsin Soda, Cherry Phosphate, Loganberry, and Tangerette.

By 1910 the firm had incorporated and built a modern 100-by-40-foot three-storey factory, employed 20 people, and was producing 5,000 bottles of its beverages per day.

But competition was hot on the Mineral

Spring Company's heels; in 1911 the Sussex Beverage Company opened its doors. J. Howard Pearn and G. Percy Bolton, both former employees of the Sussex Mineral Springs Company, were the ambitious proprietors. By 1912 they were producing in a former tinware plant and five years later were competing with their own brands, among them lime-juice soda, orangeade (which they sold by the gallon), ginger ale, Ironola, sarsaparilla, hop ale, root beer, herb brew, and ginger beer.

G.P. Bolton, whose mandate was sales for the new company, established a tradition that has continued throughout its history. Actively involved in the sporting community, particularly senior hockey, his contributions as an administrator resulted in the Sussex Amateur Athletic Clubs of 1920 to 1925 being inducted into the New Brunswick Sports Hall of Fame.

For 17 years Sussex Mineral Springs and the Sussex Beverage Company remained rivals. Then, in 1929, James MacMurray, Sr., of Saint John spearheaded union of the two, resulting in the formation of Sussex Ginger Ale Limited.

Capacity was doubled, and, in spite of setbacks resulting from the Great Depression, Sussex Ginger Ale branched out from the town of Sussex for the first time. Warehouses were opened in Saint John, Fredericton, and Moncton.

Consumer demand for Sussex products kept growing and so did the company, acquiring bottling sites in Halifax and Fredericton and licensed distributors throughout New Brunswick and Nova Scotia.

World War II sugar rationing found the company restricting its variety of flavors. Nineteen varieties now became only six; golden ginger ale, orangeade, root beer, ginger beer, lime rickey, and dry ginger ale.

Following the war Sussex Ginger Ale burgeoned once again. A major development was the 1961 purchase of Seven-Up (Maritimes)

Soft drink delivery in turn-of-the-century Saint John.

Limited resulting in Seven-Up Sussex Limited, with head offices in Saint John. This company inherited the franchising rights for most of the Maritimes and the Pepsi-Cola franchise for portions of southern New Brunswick.

Seven-Up Sussex Limited entered the 1970s as the largest manufacturer and distributor of carbonated beverages in the Atlantic Provinces.

Throughout the 1970s Seven-Up Sussex widened its range of products and territories. This growth was reflected in the birth of Maritime Beverages Limited on December 6, 1972.

Emphasis now was on national brands, which included Pepsi-Cola, Crush/Hires, and Canada Dry. Expansion continued, and today the firm operates soft drink bottling and canning plants in Moncton and Grand Falls, New Brunswick, and Dartmouth, Nova Scotia, and distribution plants in Saint John and Fredericton, New Brunswick, and Liverpool, New Glasgow, and Weymouth, Nova Scotia. Maritime Beverages Limited has a staff of 500 and continues to be the largest independent soft drink producer in Eastern Canada. On November 7, 1986, Maritime Beverages was sold to U.S. interests.

In January 1989 the company purchased Coffee Break and Vending Ltd. of Moncton, New Brunswick. In mid-1989 Chapman Brothers Limited of Amherst, Nova Scotia, was also added to Maritime Beverages Limited's holdings, and early in 1990 the company purchased 100 percent interest in Sparkling Spring Water Limited, supplier of Sparkling Springs bottled water.

Maritime Beverages' soft drink and juice labels today include Pepsi-Cola, Seven-Up, Crush, Canada Dry, Hires, Sussex, Country Time Lemonade, and Caribbean Select.

Throughout its steady growth over nearly 100 years Maritime Beverages has continued to serve the community from local to national levels through involvement in sports, including the Canada Games Aquatic Centre program for youth, sponsoring of local sports teams such as the Pepsi Midgets hockey team, and support for the YM-YWCA.

In addition, Maritime Beverages Limited provides support to the South End Day Care Centre in Saint John, the Izaak Walton Killam Children's Hospital, Junior Achievement, and the United Way, and contributes to such cultural institutions as the Beaverbrook Art Gallery and the New Brunswick Youth Orchestra.

As a continuing symbol of its concern for youth Maritime Beverages Foundation Inc., incorporated on January 31, 1985, established the Hugh H. Mackay-James A. MacMurray scholarships, which are open to residents of New Brunswick and Nova Scotia. Several scholarships of $2,000 each, renewable to a total of $8,000, are awarded annually.

Hugh H. Mackay was vice-president of Maritime Beverages Limited for nearly 30 years. James A. MacMurray served as both president and chairman of the board of the company.

The earliest soft drink bottles were sealed with a cork and shipped upside down.

The Fredericton warehouse and fleet of Sussex Ginger Ale Limited, circa 1949.

ALLSCO BUILDING SUPPLIES LTD.

ABOVE: Don Lahanky, president of Allsco Building Supplies, Moncton.

ABOVE RIGHT: The new headquarters for Allsco Building Supplies at Moncton Industrial Park.

When Don Lahanky first started in the aluminum-window business in 1957 in Sydney, Nova Scotia, with a company called Alsco, he was office manager. Two years later he moved with them to Moncton. By 1964 he had bought out the owner. "The Maritimes were a good area for aluminum windows; it was a natural," Lahanky says from his office in the Moncton Industrial Park, where a solid wall of windows looks out over a large stand of evergreens and birch trees.

"We were affiliated with Alcan, and in 1970 that firm wanted to buy us out. We were bought out by Alcan, but they assured me that if I would stay on with the company I would receive 25 percent of the profit annually. By 1975 business had expanded, and my 25 percent was much greater. It was then decided that they would change their name from Alsco to Alcan. By doing that they were no longer obliged to share 25 percent of their profit with me, and I would only be a manager on salary. Furthermore, they would not agree to give me any good will. I collected my 25 percent and resigned my position. Within two months I had started my own company.

"But there was an irony there. Because they wouldn't pay me for the good will of the company, I was able to register the company again with only a slight name change, and in December 1975 Allsco—with a double "L"—Building Supplies Ltd. was born at 194 Barker Street in Moncton."

Allsco's business continued to be primarily aluminum windows and doors and aluminum siding. Lahanky negotiated a dealership with Reynolds Aluminum, an Alcan competitor. In 1976 he was offered a Maritime Provinces dealership in vinyl siding by a company called Daymond Vinyl.

"It wasn't a very well-known product so I said I would like to wait and see how it sold. They agreed to work with me on a consignment basis. I bought 2,000 squares of vinyl siding in 1977. In 1988 I bought 87,000 squares. For the past 10 years Allsco has been the leader in the sales of vinyl siding in the Maritimes. In 1986 we started manufacturing vinyl windows in Moncton, and we are now the largest manufacturer of vinyl windows in the Maritimes. In 1989 we started manufacturing steel doors at our plant in Moncton."

Lahanky is constantly trying out new ideas and adding new products to the Allsco line of vinyl and aluminum siding, siding accessories, gutters, and shutters. Allsco advertises one-stop shopping for all exterior building supplies. "About four years ago I noticed the louvres in houses were aluminum, and they often didn't look good on a house that was nicely built and finished with vinyl siding. We went to the engineering department at the University of New Brunswick and asked them to work on a design for us that would go with the siding. They did, and now we are selling our louvres across Canada. Anyone building a house can now have their louvres the exact color to match their siding.

Another line added to the Allsco name is steel doors and fibreglass and vinyl patio doors that are assembled in the firm's plant in Moncton. "It is a sideline, but it means there are 10 more jobs here."

Similarly Lahanky's decision to make shutters has met a demand in the construction industry. "To make the shutters we buy random lengths of vinyl extrusion from the United States."

Allsco began manufacturing thermo panes on Halifax Street in 1986. The firm also started rolling coil stock and manufacturing aluminum soffit and accessories at Eaton Street.

Allsco continues to use aluminum in some of its products, but the vinyl production at its plants has tripled, and the company has expanded at a rapid pace. The Industrial Park site has 33,500 square feet; the wholesale site at Eaton Street has 26,000 square feet; the Halifax Street site has 9,500 square feet; the Barker Street premises has 16,000 square feet; and the Dartmouth site has 10,000 square feet—for a total of 95,000 square feet.

Allsco vinyl window plants are computerized. "Computers make production more efficient," Lahanky explains, demonstrating how a sheet of glass is fed onto the cutting table. The computer measures the size of sections needed and then cuts the glass to the exact size from information entered into the computer from tapes made by the engineer. The first time man touches the glass is to separate the sections and to move them from

the table on to the next section of the process.

Allsco's 90 employees, who range from engineers and accountants to glass cutters and assembly line workers, know that rather than reducing jobs, increased efficiency creates more jobs as new ideas and concepts come into play. Allsco has more than 500 dealers and distributors throughout the Maritime Provinces. Each of these dealers usually has at least six people working for them. That means that Allsco has helped maintain at least 3,000 jobs in the Maritimes in addition to its 90 in-house employees.

Allsco's workers also share in the company's profits. "Last year [1988] we shared $155,000 with our employees, on top of their salaries. They have the choice of taking the cash or reinvesting it in the company." Lahanky says when the employees reinvest he can give them a 20-percent return on the investment.

Lahanky is working with other local business people to provide venture capital to entrepreneurs. "I think it is important that people with ideas get help in developing them, but I think they also must realize that you have to learn to crawl before you walk. You may have lots of ideas but if you overextend yourself when you are just starting out, you could be out of business. Now that I have established myself in the business, I can afford my ideas!"

Lahanky is entering the U.S. market, setting up a branch near Boston in 1990. "It's a market of 25 million people, and a lot of them build houses," he says. "In Canada, we are ahead of the United States with our vinyl products, windows in particular. I think we will do very well down there."

The story of Allsco Building Supplies Ltd.'s growth since 1975 is amazing in itself. It becomes even more amazing with the realization that Don Lahanky came to Canada in 1949 unable to speak a word of English.

A Ukrainian living in Polish-occupied Ukraine, Lahanky lived through World War II in terror, aware that his parents were hiding their Jewish friends from the Nazis. He escaped in 1944 and joined the British Eighth Army, Second Polish Corps, in Italy. In 1946 Lahanky moved to England.

An uncle brought the 24-year-old Lahanky to Sydney, Nova Scotia, in 1949. He had been trained as an accountant, but it took him some time to learn English and get a job. Today three of his children have joined him in his multimillion-dollar business. Daughter Danica is manager of the wholesale division; Terry, his oldest son, has been manager of the factory for 11 years; and Gordon, a business administration graduate, recently joined the firm.

Both Don Lahanky and his company, Allsco Building Supplies Ltd., have been recipients of business awards. Lahanky was named Entrepreneur of the Year in 1985, and two years later Allsco was presented with an Award of Distinction by the Vinyl Council of Canada for the work done on a building at 1299 Main Street, Moncton, which was deemed to be the outstanding project produced by a Canadian manufacturer using vinyl siding. As a result of hard work and careful planning, it is clear that Don Lahanky possesses true entrepreneurial spirit.

New Brunswick lieutenant-governor George Stanley presents the Entrepreneur of the Year Award for 1985 to Allsco president Don Lahanky.

Allsco vinyl window and door frames are produced in the Moncton Industrial Park plant, one of the company's three Atlantic Canada locations.

THE FEDERAL BUSINESS DEVELOPMENT BANK

The Federal Business Development Bank (known until 1975 as the Industrial Development Bank) has become, during its corporate history, firmly entrenched as an important resource for Atlantic Canadian business. In 1944 Canada was faced with an imminent return from the heavy industry of wartime to a more traditional business base. A pressing need was apparent for some form of financial assistance for new and developing businesses—a resource that could provide loans over longer terms than those to which the chartered banks were generally limited.

In establishing an institution focussed on small- and medium-size businesses and mandated to complement other lenders, the Government of Canada created an asset for Atlantic business that would change and grow with the times. The Halifax office, opened in 1956, was followed by offices in Saint John in 1959, St. John's in 1961, Moncton in 1962, Charlottetown in 1971, and Sydney and Corner Brook in 1973. By 1975 the FBDB was represented in all Canadian provinces, with the Atlantic region sharing in a success story that had seen 65,000 loans, worth $3 billion, authorized for 48,000 businesses from coast to coast—businesses that would have been unable to obtain conventional financing on reasonable terms and conditions. These businesses had, in turn, responded with a repayment rate of 90 percent.

When the new corporate identity as FBDB was legislated in 1975, the original mandate was broadened to include the provision of management and other non-financial services for small businesses, and the aim of working toward regional parity was intensified. Since then FBDB's presence in Atlantic Canada has grown even more. Thirteen branches are now co-ordinated by the Regional Office in Halifax, including Moncton, Bathurst, Saint John, Edmundston, Fredericton, Charlottetown, St. John's, Grand Falls, Corner Brook, Halifax, Sydney, Bridgewater, and Truro. The bank employs 130 Atlantic Canadians.

As a result, the FBDB's effect on life in the region is increasingly evident. A manufacturer of small machine parts adds significantly to employment in the local area; an aquaculture operation diversifies the economy of a fishing cove; a rural silversmith breaks into the export market, creating dozens of new jobs—each year about 15,000 Atlantic enterprises are assisted by FBDB.

About 5 percent of all Atlantic Canadian businesses are loan clients of the bank, but financing is only one of the many FBDB services that helps Atlantic enterprises to establish, to grow, and to become more effective. Financial planning, management training, counselling, publications, and even do-it-yourself kits for small business owners are part of the bank's grass-roots approach to fostering entrepreneurship throughout the region.

FBDB statistics for the Atlantic region confirm the bank's concentration on small- and medium-size operations. Over the past decade FBDB authorized approximately 10,000 loans totalling almost $600 million. The majority of these loans were made to businesses with fewer than 10 workers, and almost half had been in operation for five years or less. Four out of five loan customers were located in rural communities.

The sectors on which the bank concentrates its efforts are manufacturing, wholesale and retail trade, and the tourist industry, which together account for 60 percent of lending activity. The rest is divided among commercial properties, construction, transportation, and other areas.

"The small business sector is dynamic," says John Ryan, vice-president and regional general manager of the bank. "It will be responsible in the future, as it has been in the past, for a major share of Atlantic Canada's economic growth. The FBDB will continue to develop new services to meet emerging business needs while still providing the basic financial and management services this sector requires."

Some of the highly effective programs and

When the Federal Business Development Bank first established its presence in Atlantic Canada in the late 1950s, the regional office was located in Halifax in the Bank of Canada building on Hollis Street. Today both the Halifax District office and the Atlantic Regional Office are located in Halifax, in Cogswell Tower.

services resulting from this commitment have been in the area of lending policy. For instance, the FBDB offers term loans to clients to buy fixed assets such as land, buildings, and equipment, with repayment terms worked out to meet the client's individual needs. The bank also assists with management buyouts, refinancing, expansions, and replenishment of working capital.

But initiatives in many non-lending categories have also been developed in response to changing needs of small business. As an example, the bank's Counselling Assistance to Small Enterprises (CASE) program uses scores of highly experienced retired business people who, for exceptionally modest fees, closely counsel some 1,000 individual Atlantic entrepreneurs every year.

Through its Community Business Initiatives program, started in 1986, FBDB provides business management training to community business groups, designed to cover specific training needs that members have identified. The business owners participate in a yearlong series of workshops, and later receive follow-up counselling to help them implement what they've learned. Typical of reaction to the program is the response of one participant: "It was a totally

worthwhile experience, and the material presented was invaluable."

Some FBDB programs have been developed in response to the special requirements of various groups. In Halifax, FBDB formed a 26-member multicultural business advisory committee to identify the needs of the rapidly expanding multicultural business community and to work on ways to satisfy those needs. In the Truro, Nova Scotia, area, a pilot project was undertaken with Mic Mac Indians to help them take their business ideas through all the planning stages and then to actually implement them. Another special endeavor was devoted to training laid-off industrial workers in Cape Breton in how to start their own small business.

Female entrepreneurs, as a fast-growing presence in Atlantic Canadian business, have been the focus of special attention from FBDB as well, including the formation of a 13-member committee of successful female entrepreneurs from Newfoundland and Labrador. This group undertook important studies on what barriers exist against women wishing to become small business owners, and how they can be overcome.

Creativity, adaptability, and energy are among the prime characteristics of successful entrepreneurs everywhere; in Atlantic Canada, the Federal Business Development Bank applies those same qualities to supporting the financial, counselling, and training needs of entrepreneurial clients of all kinds. The vital role of FBDB in Atlantic Canada will continue to be based on an open-door policy—a willingness to offer complementary banking services to business owners with sound ideas and special requirements. The bank's developmental assistance to small- and medium-size businesses in the region very often continues through the long term, as clients grow, prosper, and take a prominent place in the economic mainstream.

The diversity of FBDB's economic base is clearly reflected in a sampling of some long-standing FBDB clients: A Nova Scotian sawmill operation undertook an FBDB strategic plan to identify its future course of action (above), photo by Albert Lee; a Newfoundland fish plant acquired a new fish pump with an FBDB loan and expanded operations (left); and through FBDB assistance, a manufacturer supplies a wide variety of nuts and bolts to the Atlantic Canadian market (above left), photo by Albert Lee. These FBDB clients have made a solid contribution to the prosperity of the Atlantic Canadian economy.

ADI LIMITED

When first built in 1964, the ADI building (right) was considered to be daringly located on the outskirts of town. ADI grew and so did Fredericton; now the building is part of Fredericton's Prospect Street business district. In 1986, needing more space, ADI moved next door to a modern office complex (below).

Since 1945 the engineering consultants at ADI Limited of Fredericton have been "rolling up their sleeves and getting the job done," according to John R. Dean, P. Eng., company president.

Initially called Moore and Beattie, Civic and Structural Engineers, after its founders, two University of New Brunswick professors, the firm, in 1952, included additional partners and changed its name to Associated Designers and Inspectors to reflect the growth and the expansion of services offered. At the time the partnership was comprised of I.M. Beattie, P. Eng.; H.W. McFarlane, P. Eng.; R.H.B. McLaughlin, P. Eng.; A.M. Stevens, P. Eng.; and O.I. Logue, P. Eng. It remained a partnership with associates until the late 1960s, when John Dean joined the company as the 10th partner.

A mechanical engineer, Dean brought considerable management skills to the firm from his successful career as manager of production for NB Power. The partners had been looking for a different style of management arrangement; they got it from Dean. The company was incorporated as ADI Limited in 1969.

Five of the original 10 partners are still active in the company: Dean as president; K.O. Bartlett, P. Eng., as vice-president; W.L. McNamara, P. Eng., as secretary/treasurer; and C.A. Ponder, P. Eng., and J.H. Collyer, MRAIC, as directors. Always an employee-owned firm, ADI now has 26 shareholders, including the five former partners.

"ADI has never been a one-person company, but rather a broadly based firm with many areas of expertise," says Dean. "Providing service has always been a group effort. When a client comes in the door with any job to do with design or consulting services, we have someone right here to address that particular sector.

"We will always be a hands-on company," he says. "The people doing the work will continue to have direct contact with the most important people in the entire operation—our clients."

ADI's four divisions handle projects from conceptual designs through construction inspection and commissioning. The divisions include buildings, for institutional, commercial, and industrial applications; environmental engineering, including municipal services and wastewater treatment; power and process, providing energy and instrumentation expertise to industry; and public works, incorporating a wide range of services from bridge and highway designs to feasibility studies and geotechnical engineering services.

ADI has branches in Saint John and Moncton, New Brunswick; Ottawa, Ontario; Charlottetown, Prince Edward Island; and Salem, New Hampshire. Services are currently provided throughout North America and to some parts of the Caribbean, Asia, and Europe. At present the firm has a total staff of 150, including engineers, management consultants, technologists, technicians, and supporting staff.

Dean sees ADI Limited's future as a growth company at the leading edge of technology with increased employee participation and share ownership. Growth will involve expansion of service lines to provide a more comprehensive range and depth of expertise for clients as well as expansion of the company's international business.

LOCK-WOOD LTD.

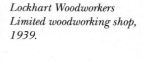

Although the company was incorporated in 1952, the history of Lock-Wood Ltd. goes much further back than that, explains chairman Leonard H. Lockhart. "In truth it goes back to 1900, when my grandfather, B.W. Lockhart—he was known as "Ben," but his name was Bent Weatherhead Lockhart—came to Notre Dame, just 25 kilometres north of Moncton, to set up two sawmills with his brother, C.E. Lockhart."

Ben moved to Moncton in 1917 and operated a sawmill with W.D. Gunter. In 1922 Ben purchased Paul Lea Lumber Company Limited on Westmorland Street, where the Lockharts Beaver Lumber store is today. In 1935 Leonard's father (Ben's eldest son, Leonard) bought the business from Ben and renamed it Lockhart Woodworkers Limited. Then, in 1952, encouraged by the postwar building boom, the millwork department separated to become Lock-Wood Manufacturers Ltd. and took on a life of its own—a life that developed into an industry that now employs 400 people in its 250,000-square-foot plant, another 25 workers in Ontario, and is planning a 50,000-square-foot plant expansion.

"We manufactured a wide range of products made from wood, including all the lockers for Camp Gagetown," Lockhart says. "Then, in the 1960s, we reduced our product line and concentrated on commercial and residential windows in standard sizes. In 1968 we moved out to Scoudouc, a wartime Air Force base.

"We hired our first industrial engineer in 1970; he is now president of the company, and in 1971 we hired our current vice-president/sales and marketing, along with two of his staff. We discontinued production of commercial widows in 1971 and decided to specialize in exterior residential millwork products. In 1972, when the company name was shortened to Lock-Wood Ltd., sales jumped by 270 percent. We had to double the plant and equipment in order to meet the increased demand."

Anticipating the decline of housing construction in the late 1970s and early 1980s, Lock-Wood began to market its products in Western Canada, Ontario, and, more recently, the United States.

"Our prime focus today is the expansion of our markets outside the Atlantic region. Forty-five percent of our business is done here in Atlantic Canada and 40 percent in Ontario through our distribution branch in Newmarket. Our western distributors account for 10 percent of our business, with 5 percent coming from the United States.

"We are one of two or three Canadian window companies distributing on a national basis. In 1985 the firm was presented with an Export Achievement Award from the Province of New Brunswick."

It was typical at one time for a carpenter to come to Lock-Wood with his own measurements. Today, while Lock-Wood still does custom work, it is done on a computer system that allows the company to convert one of its nine standard windows to meet the need of the contractor.

In addition to windows, basically manufactured from wood, Lock-Wood Ltd. makes a patio door and a complete entry system. Says Lockhart, "We are proud of our product-development department, which continually presents new product designs and improvements."

Lockhart Woodworkers Limited woodworking shop, 1939.

Lock-Wood Planning Centre, in a dealer's showroom, 1989.

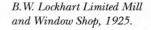

B.W. Lockhart Limited Mill and Window Shop, 1925.

MMH PREFAB LTD.

Within a few hours of delivery new owners can move into their Cape Cod cedar home by MMH Prefab.

In 1973 mobile homes represented a growing lifestyle in the Maritime Provinces—a lifestyle and a business potential recognized by John de Winter and his partners in MMH Prefab Ltd. of Sussex, New Brunswick.

De Winter, president and general manager, and partner Terence Gulliver were both working in the mobile home business: de Winter in management and Gulliver in sales and marketing. A third partner, Benoit Gagnon, was part owner of a related business endeavor with de Winter that provided framing and other products to the industry. "With my 17 years' experience in the business and Terry's three years in sales, we had some ideas of our own," de Winter says.

MMH's idea was prefabrication, and it was the first Maritimes company to go into the business of building mobile homes by assembling all the parts in advance.

"We bought 16 acres of land in the industrial park from the town of Sussex," de Winter says. "We built our first plant—a building 520 feet by 100 feet. We had about 50 employees to start with, and a lot of them are still with us. We have been very lucky with our labor force; we could not have grown as we have without their dedication."

The first MMH mobile home came off the production line in April 1974. The product was well received, and it was not long before the firm was producing more than 200 units per year. Today that figure is more than doubled, along with the work force (now around 100 employees), and expanded plant space and acreage.

Changes in the mobile home industry, much of it initiated through the creativity of MMH, are reflected in the company's product.

De Winter explains, "When we started, the product was called a mobile home because it was on wheels, but generally it didn't go anywhere—except to the lot where the owners intended to live. Traditionally the chassis or undercarriage was built as part of the entire structure. Our idea was to build the home separately, because that way you can be sure everything is square and even, and it has more stability. Then we put it on the undercarriage for transportation. When it arrives at the site the wheels and chassis can be removed, and the home is placed on a foundation if the owner wants that. It was a very successful move for us."

The Williamsburg design is one of the most popular of the MMH Prefab selections.

In 1978 MMH came up with the idea of making its mobile homes more like a traditional home. The firm took off the galvanized roof and put on a pitched roof with asphalt shingles. The company went from aluminum siding to vinyl or wood siding. House-type windows were introduced just like the ones used in regular home construction. Then MMH changed the interior from the traditional plywood panelling to prefinished sheetrock that gave its customers a half-dozen different patterns and colors from which to choose. They were called mini-homes.

"Unfortunately we couldn't copyright the name, so it's now used throughout the Maritimes by anyone in the business of building mini-homes. But we know we did it first," states de Winter.

It was around 1981 that MMH made more changes in its mini-homes by increasing the width to 16 feet. "It gives people a larger home, and within that extra space you can enhance the interior a great deal more by enlarging the bathroom, for example, or putting in two bathrooms instead of one.

"They have been very successful, and, although they look even more like a traditional

John B. de Winter, president of MMH Prefab (right), with partner Benoit Gagnon.

house, they are still within a modest price range. Today's mini-home buyer can be completely moved into their home within six hours of delivery. Everything is installed: Kitchens are complete with all the utilities, including dishwashers. All people have to do is hook up the plumbing and move in their furniture."

While MMH's mobile home industry was forging ahead, the company was developing a parallel industry. In 1977 it bought another four acres of land and built a second plant for production of modular housing. The firm had been importing modular units from Quebec for its dealers, but when delivery became too slow MMH decided to produce the units on its own. The first modular unit came off the line in September 1977. In the beginning the company did modular houses in a semifinished condition; the partitions would be built, but the carpets, trim, and crack filling all had to be done after the house had been placed on the foundation. In 1981 the organization started doing complete modular homes that were as complete as mini-homes and ready to occupy once the utilities were hooked up.

The modular home industry has been a phe-

nomenal success for MMH, particularly in the American market where it began selling in 1985. Three years later the company won the New Brunswick Department of Commerce and Technology Export Achievement Award for its U.S. sales, which represented 20 percent of the annual sales that year. Along with a strong U.S. market, the firm has developed products that meet housing needs around the world. Its homes have been shipped to West Germany and Iraq as well.

"Exporting has resulted in a completely redesigned modular home industry for us," de Winter says. "We picked up a lot of new technology, and we are selling not just the very popular Cape Cod-style home but condominiums and duplexes as well."

De Winter says MMH can produce a modular home and have it ready to place on its foundation in less than two weeks. Modular design and construction is without bounds at MMH, which now includes modular office buildings, such as the CBC and Air Nova complexes in Nova Scotia, as well as classrooms and even jails.

Among its latest endeavors is the Garden Suite or Granny Flat that the firm has done for Canada Mortgage and Housing Corporation. The concept is a simple one; it provides independent living for aging parents on the same property as their children's homes.

Growth at MMH Prefab Ltd. shows no signs of slowing, and the plants now produce up to 450 units per year for the company's dealers throughout the Maritime Provinces, Quebec, and in the United States.

Terence Gulliver, one of the founding partners, was actively involved in the business until his untimely death in July 1989.

SHERATON HALIFAX

Her Excellency Governor General Jeanne Sauve at the Sheraton Halifax during a visit to Nova Scotia, with hotel manager Hugh Harper.

Located on the bustling water-front adjacent to Historic Properties, the Sheraton Halifax overlooks the tallship Bluenose II, *in the fore-ground, setting out for a harbor cruise.*

Even before the Sheraton Halifax opened on June 1, 1985, there were clear signals of the marked impact it would have. That April, for three hectic days, about 3,500 people applied for jobs at the Sheraton. "We had the interviews up at the World Trade and Convention Centre," recalls gereral manager Hugh Harper. "They literally lined up around the block."

The $46-million waterfront hotel with 356 guest rooms meant more than jobs. It introduced a hotel of international calibre. "With its arrival, the level of accommodation and food changed dramatically in this city," says Harper. "Haligonians wanted a high-quality building where they would feel proud to bring in royalty, celebrities, and high-ranking government officials and associations."

Already the Sheraton has an impressive guest list. Included are dignitaries such as Prime Minister Brian Mulroney, Governor General Jeanne Sauve, Prince Andrew and Prince Edward, Iceland's President Vigdis Finnbogadottir, and NATO's Secretary General Lord Carrington. Entertainers have included Kris Kristofferson, Tony Bennett, Phyllis Diller, Kenny Rogers, and the Beach Boys.

The Sheraton was built on property declared a national historic site in 1971 that served as an ordnance yard for military supplies during the 1800s. The Sheraton's design is in the scale and character of the nearby restored and renovated historic properties. The six-storey stone Sheraton has a reproduction of a 150-year-old clock tower, pitched copper roof, dormer windows, and a rooftop courtyard.

Three special Sheraton suites commemorate the sea-going achievements of Nova Scotians. They are named after Sir Samuel Cunard, founder of the first transatlantic steamship ser-

vice; Captain Angus Walters, master of the original schooner *Bluenose*, whose sailing replica berths near the Sheraton's boardwalk; and Captain Joshua Slocum, the first to sail solo around the world. Throughout its lobby, guest rooms, and restaurant the Sheraton has commissioned many works from Maritime artists.

It has consistently won the Canadian Automobile Association/American Automobile Association's Four-Diamond Award and Mobil's Four-Star Award. The Recreation Council on Disability in Nova Scotia honored the hotel for extensive provisions for the handicapped in 19 specially equipped and outfitted rooms.

The Sheraton, also winner of the Canadian Architect Design of Excellence Award, was designed by Halifax architects Lydon Lynch Associates Ltd. and built by Newfoundland-based Lundrigans Construction Ltd. The hotel employs more than 350 people at peak season. The Sheraton is a limited partnership owned by more than 700 Canadian shareholders and managed by Sheraton Corporation.

Responsive to guests' needs, the Sheraton has set high standards of culinary excellence by establishing The Grand Banker Restaurant as one of the finest seafood restaurants in Canada. In 1988 the hotel added the services of a fully equipped Business Centre and added a take-out deli as an alternative to restaurant dining. State-of-the-art computerized systems service guests with VingCard guestroom keys that offer each guest a personalized code. Guests can also conveniently check out of their rooms or order room service via remote control through their televisions.

The Sheraton Halifax' management and employees are active with community organizations such as Junior Achievement, the United Way, and Cystic Fibrosis. Harper is an executive member of the Tourism Industry Association of Nova Scotia and assisted Mount Saint Vincent University start its tourism and hospitality management program.

G.E. BARBOUR INC.

Filled with merchandise from days long past, the centennial project for G.E. Barbour Inc., Barbour's Old Country Store, is located on the spot where the Loyalists landed in Saint John in 1783.

G.E. Barbour Inc. can trace its roots back to Canada's birth as a nation in 1867, when the Barbour brothers, George L. and William, left their jobs as clerks to set up as commission merchants at South Market Wharf in Saint John, New Brunswick. They were in the business of selling fish, butter, eggs, poultry, and molasses.

Although the Great Saint John Fire of 1877 destroyed the Barbour premises, the founders salvaged what they could and moved across Market Slip (where the Loyalists landed less than 100 years earlier) to North Market Wharf, where the company continued in business for the next 90 years.

In the course of those years the business grew and expanded, particularly after 1895, when George E. Barbour took over. He named the firm the G.E. Barbour Company and began acquiring numerous complementary businesses, thus widening the organization's horizons.

On the death of George E. Barbour in 1955, the company was purchased by Ralph B. Brenan, Sr., a widely experienced businessman. Today all four members of the third generation of the Brenan family are involved in the G.E. Barbour Inc. interests, with Grant Brenan serving as president.

In 1967, to mark its 100th year in business and Canada's 100th anniversary, the company established Barbour's Old Country Store, now situated at Market Slip in Saint John. Thoroughly researched and authentically stocked, the award-winning tourist attraction building is, itself, authentic. It was floated by barge down the Saint John River from its location in Sheffield in Sunbury County and restored to its original charm.

Also in 1967 G.E. Barbour Inc. built a modern manufacturing plant in Sussex, New Brunswick, and moved its head office to this agricultural centre.

Barbour's major product is King Cole tea. The label was the trade name of Dickeson and Armstrong, a Saint John company taken over in 1911 by George E. Barbour, who retained the King Cole brand name.

Barbour continues to maintain a full staff of tea tasters at its plant, ensuring that its century-old reputation for quality is maintained. In fact, quite by accident, the company has found itself in the mail-order business in a small way. Americans in particular, from as far away as Texas and California, discovered King Cole Tea in their travels and wrote to the firm asking if they could order by mail. The result has been a steadily growing, unsolicited business.

In addition to King Cole tea, products bearing the Barbour trademark include spices, extracts, peanut butter, mustard, and cake decorations. In addition, G.E. Barbour Inc. produces Acadia baking powder, McCready pickles, and, since 1974, Barbour Sussex cheddar cheese.

Today G.E. Barbour Inc. is supplying the needs of the grocery trade in all of Atlantic Canada and Quebec. Like the industry it has served over the past 123 years, the company and its products continue to evolve and keep pace with society while maintaining its historic tradition of quality.

A favorite in the Maritimes for more than 100 years, King Cole tea is the famous forerunner of Barbour's product line.

TRIANGLE KITCHEN

Roger Fournier, owner of Triangle Kitchen in Dieppe, New Brunswick, was in many ways a typical Acadian growing up after World War II. He was born in Pointe-Verte, a small village in northern New Brunswick. He did what many of his generation sought to do—he went off to university, earned a master's degree, and then went to work for the government.

But then Fournier did something different. He left the security of a federal government job and went into business for himself.

There had always been something pulling at him to have his own business. Going to university and then securing a job were things he did because that is what his society expected of him. Still, he found it peculiar that he enjoyed his summer jobs in the construction industry far better than poring over books or working in government offices.

Roger Fournier, owner of Triangle Kitchen.

In 1975 Fournier decided to throw caution to the wind. He bought a small kitchen retail business. Before too long he enjoyed a great deal of success, and the business expanded considerably.

However, Fournier saw opportunities for more potential. He aquired Triangle Kitchen, a manufacturer producing traditional frame kitchens. He quickly began producing European-style kitchens along with frame kitchens, and the product began to sell at a tremendous clip, out-performing even his own high expectations. When he purchased Triangle in January 1984, the firm employed 12 people. It now employs 50. In addition, by 1989 the production capacity had grown to eight times what it was when Fournier bought the firm.

The U.S.-Canada Trade Agreement (FTA) looms large for the future of the kitchen and cabinetmaking industry. Indeed, the Canadian Kitchen Cabinets Association voted unanimously against the agreement at a recent meeting. The reason is simple: The pre-FTA sectoral arrangements favored Canadian manufacturers.

While others may sit back and ponder what the future holds, Triangle has decided to take the offensive. It currently is expanding its production capacity. With the expansion the total production capacity will exceed 30,000 square feet.

Roger Fournier has also moved aggressively on other fronts. He has turned to the most modern equipment and new technology available to put Triangle on a firm footing to compete in the global economy. He purchased a European paint system, one of only two in Canada. This sprayer is part of a fully automated system that includes a sanding and drying room that is controlled electronically, painting only designated surfaces.

The firm has also moved ahead on the marketing front by looking to new markets in New England, the Middle East, Europe, and the Caribbean. Triangle has already met success in some of these areas. In short, the company is looking to Atlantic Canada, where it has laid down firm roots, as a springboard to new opportunities in the international marketplace.

What are the keys to Triangle's success? According to Fournier: "One is to have top-notch employees—in fact, I firmly believe that a company is only as good as its employees." He quickly adds that once you have been able to get top-notch employees you must ensure that in return you do something for them. It is why, he explains, that "Triangle has excellent pension and health benefits and why the firm is always trying to improve individual employees' conditions."

The second key, he says, is that a firm must "always deliver the best-possible product at the best-possible price." He adds, "Honesty pays in business. Quite apart from any moral issue, honesty is the best business policy. There is simply no better way to get clients to come back."

Triangle Kitchen now manufactures both conventional "face-frame" and European-style "frameless" kitchen cabinets of solid wood seven-eighths of an inch thick, in oak (the most popular), maple, pine, and cherry. The firm also makes just about anything one can see in a modern kitchen, including china cabinets and bookshelves.

ANTHONY INSURANCE INCORPORATED

The firm owes its origins to Rex' father, Robert C. Anthony, an entrepreneur with insurance experience who established his own business in 1953. With one employee, he began operating out of premises on Water Street. In 1957 the company was incorporated as R.C. Anthony (Insurance) Limited. Three years later, with eight other shareholders, Anthony founded the Insurance Corporation of Newfoundland (ICON), a property and casualty insurance underwriting company.

"The idea was to assemble a group of Newfoundlanders who would form their own company to keep some of the profits at home," says Anthony, adding that ICON employs 25 people who might otherwise be working out of mainland offices.

Robert C. Anthony (left) established his insurance business in 1953. Today his son, Rex (seated), is president and major shareholder of the Anthony Group of Companies. Photo by Lane Photographics Limited

It is not unusual to find mainland Canadian businesses with branches in Newfoundland, but it is a little different to discover Newfoundland companies with interests in other provinces.

Anthony Insurance Incorporated, a St. John's based firm, has also been serving the Maritimes since 1979, when it established an office in Halifax. Three years later the company became a partner in Lloyd, Sadd, and Anthony Insurance Ltd., the largest independently owned broker in Alberta, which does business in the four western provinces.

The decision to expand into mainland markets was a factor of the size of the local market, says company president Rex Anthony. "Newfoundland has 550,000 souls. You can only get so far, and then you start running into yourself. To expand in other parts of Canada seemed reasonable."

At home, the company has not forgotten that its particular strength in the early days was in rural Newfoundland. Anthony Insurance Incorporated has 13 branches on the island and a network of representatives called sub-brokers in "most other nooks and crannies in Newfoundland and Labrador," says Anthony.

Today ICON is part of the Anthony Group of Companies, a parent corporation for the family's holdings. Robert Anthony, who retired in 1977, is honorary chairman, but the business is owned by Rex, the major shareholder, and his younger brother, David, president of ICON. The Anthony Group of Companies, which operates out of the ICON Building at 187 Kenmount Road, includes Anthony Insurance Incorporated, ICON, Claims Management Ltd., and Triton Data Systems, as well as the mainland interests.

The Anthony Group employs about 150 people in Atlantic Canada and 50 more out west. One of Anthony Insurance Incorporated's strengths is that its employees tend to stay with the firm.

"At a recent company appreciation night, I added up the number of years of service of Newfoundland employees who have been with the firm more than three years. It came to well over 1,000 years," Anthony says. "We encourage social interaction—keeping in mind that business is business. The rest is hard work."

HOTEL NEWFOUNDLAND

When people take a taxicab in St. John's and say, "the hotel," they will find themselves in front of Hotel Newfoundland, even though there are more than a dozen other hotels/motels in the city. It has always been that way, ever since the original Newfoundland Hotel—as it was then called—was built in the 1920s.

Hotel Newfoundland is situated in the east end of the city, within easy walking distance of Signal Hill, the harbour, and the downtown business centre. A few hundred yards away is Government House, home of the Lieutenant-Governor. A short walk along Duckworth Street will take one past the National War Memorial, built when Newfoundland was still a self-governing colony of the British Empire.

Outside the door of the hotel is a range of stone Victorian houses that survived the Great St. John's Fire of 1892. Nearby in one direction are the traditional wooden row houses, a distinguishing feature of St. John's, and along another route are the Victorian mansions of the merchant class.

The hotel stands on the site of Fort William, where British troops were stationed from the early seventeenth century. A national historic marker on a retaining wall in Cavendish Square, where the hotel is located, tells of the battles that were fought there.

History has often been made at or near the hotel site. In the 1880s, when the trans-insular railroad was begun, the station was situated on the site adjacent to what is now the hotel. The island's first train left from that spot. A modern hotel was later planned for the site, and in 1901 a cornerstone and foundation were laid for the Avalon Hotel. However, a fire in the adjacent railway yard brought construction to a halt.

In the 1920s the plan to build a great hotel in the city was revived, and construction was begun

The new Hotel Newfoundland opened its doors for business on December 5, 1982.

on July 24, 1925, by T.E. Rosseau Limited of Quebec. More than 50 tonnes of equipment to be used in the hotel construction arrived by ship. During excavation, remnants of the old fort, such as powder horns, were found. When the cellar was being dug out, two tunnels were discovered, one of which supposedly connected to Signal Hill. These tunnels were undoubtedly important during the French invasions.

On June 1, 1926, the new hotel opened its doors for business. The management boasted that the hotel was fireproof, modern and comfortable, and had unexcelled cuisine. The hotel was operated by Newfoundland Hotel Facilities Limited, with principals Honorable Sydney D. Blandford and Mr. E.B. Stafford. It had 150 rooms, 24 suites, and a ballroom.

From its opening, the hotel was always more than a hotel. It became the centre of social activity and began to figure prominently in many important events in the island's history. In the early 1930s, as Newfoundland hurtled toward bankruptcy, the British government established a commission headed by Lord Amulree to look into the colony's affairs. The Amulree Commission took up quarters in the then-government-owned hotel.

Upon the commission's recommendation, self-government was suspended, and Newfoundland was placed under the rule of an appointed commission. In February 1934, when the new Commission of Government was sworn in, the historic event took place in the hotel ballroom. During the period of the commission

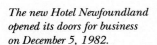

The elegant Cabot Club offers a true dining experience and a spectacular view of St. John's Harbour, the Narrows, and Signal Hill.

One of the main attractions of the hotel is the Court Garden, where guests can enjoy fine piano playing or just relax amidst the greenery.

(1934-1949), the hotel came under the jurisdiction of the Department of Public Utilities and, later, the Department of Finance. The government radio station, VONF (later CBC), made its home at the hotel from September 1934 until Confederation.

When the proposal to join Canada was introduced in Newfoundland, the hotel continued as an important meeting place. The Newfoundland Confederate Association, Joey Smallwood's umbrella organization, was launched at a meeting in the hotel ballroom on February 21, 1948, with Smallwood becoming general secretary. He was already a familiar sight around the hotel as the "Barrelman," an im-

mensely popular storyteller who broadcasted on VONF radio.

The hotel has never lost its role as a venue for important historic events. Both the Atlantic Accord (1984) and the Hibernia Statement of Principles (1988) were signed there with Prime Minister Brian Mulroney and Premier Brian Peckford present on both occasions. Mulroney was not the first prime minister to stay at the hotel. John Diefenbaker, Lester Pearson, Pierre Trudeau, Joe Clark, and John Turner have also been guests.

In fact, the hotel guest list includes many prominent persons, such as Frank Sinatra, Chicago gangster "Legs" Diamond, the writers

The Admiral's Suite, the most prestigious suite in the hotel, overlooks the Narrows.

Zane Grey and John LeCarre, Robert Ripley (of *Ripley's Believe It or Not*), Charlie McCarthy and Edgar Bergen, the Beach Boys, Corey Hart, Tina Turner, Anne Murray, Ken Taylor, Kenny Rogers, Rod Stewart, and numerous others. Victor Mature is said to have come by one day for a bath when he was stationed in St. John's during World War II. Those were the days when a passerby could come to the hotel and have a bath and fresh towels for one dollar. Mature is also said to have carried on a telephone romance with Rita Hayward from the hotel.

When Newfoundland joined Confederation, the hotel was turned over to CN Hotels, part of the Canadian National Railway, for the sum of one dollar. In the 1980s, when a decision was made to construct a new hotel on the same site, new partners were needed for the project, and a joint venture was formed. When the new hotel opened on December 5, 1982, Mutual Life of Canada held 50-percent interest, Baine Johnston and Co. Limited held 25 percent, and CN held 25 percent. On April 1, 1988, the hotel became part of the Canadian Pacific Hotels and Resorts chain.

The old hotel had been a landmark in the city, and, when its contents were put on auction, much interest was generated. Many people bought furnishings for homes and summer cabins. A 100-year-old house in Bonavista Bay boasts a fine hardwood floor salvaged from the old ballroom. Some furnishings from the old hotel were donated to the Rotary Club to help furnish a hostel for parents of children who are patients at the local children's hospital.

The new Hotel Newfoundland—a federal government Bilingualism Act in the 1960s necessitated the name change—was built at a cost of $28 million; the old hotel was built for slightly more than one million dollars. Again the architectural firm was from Quebec, Burman Bouchard of Montreal, and its Newfoundland associate, Dove, Whitten, and Associates Ltd. The interior designer was IDEE Design, also of Montreal, a specialist in hotel design.

The new hotel has 302 guest rooms, including a variety of one- and two-bedroom suites and a presidential suite. Its 12 meeting rooms contain more than 12,000 square feet of space; its convention facilities can accommodate from 20 to 1,000 people. Conventions are not new to the hotel—the old hotel was barely open when it held its first convention, the Newfoundland Medical Convention, in July 1926.

The Hotel Newfoundland, rated a four-diamond hotel, has an indoor swimming pool, saunas, and squash courts. This idea is not new either—the old hotel featured tennis courts that converted into a skating rink during the winter. The elegant hotel lobby leads to and overlooks a spacious atrium (Court Garden) filled with a wide variety of trees and plants. A waterfall flows from the entrance of the Narrows quiet bar to the atrium below. Guests can sip a drink and enjoy the piano playing of many fine local pianists in the Court Garden, or they can listen from above. Just as in an earlier era, afternoon tea is served in the British tradition with scones, crumpets, and pastries.

Bruce Turner is general manager of the hotel. He came to Newfoundland and assumed the position in 1983, although Turner had been an accountant with the old hotel from 1958-1959.

The new hotel is very different looking, but the traditions remain the same. "Today the hotel carries on the early traditions and still has as its

thereof. In 1988 the invitation was printed on a scroll and placed inside a miniature treasure chest, handmade for the occasion by Vera Industries and hand delivered by men in pirate costumes. Entertainment throughout the evening is provided by Newfoundland artists— 1988's event featured an eight-year-old ballerina and an 80-year-old fiddler. In the 24 hours prior to the event, the entire ballroom is converted into a replica of a ship from the John Cabot era, surrounded by scenery that suggests actually

The hotel offers guests a quiet elegance.

aim to be a home away from home for all travellers," says Turner. "The hotel continues to place great importance on Newfoundland tradition and culture."

The names of the various outlets in the hotel all have relative significance to Newfoundland. The Outport is a restaurant and coffee shop. The Cabot Club is an elegant dining room offering a spectacular view of the Narrows and Signal Hill.

Newfoundland history and culture are the central theme at the annual Cabot Club Dinner, an exclusive evening held each October. "When I first came here I wanted to create an event that would be singled out as the event of the year in St. John's," Turner says, describing the event as an evening of good food, good fun, and good fellowship.

It is a unique invitation-only evening, with a portion of the proceeds going to the Salvation Army. Special attention is placed on the invitations and delivery

sailing in Newfoundland waters. The theme of the evening is always in keeping with the hotel's commitment to Newfoundland heritage.

The brass mailbox in the lobby of Hotel Newfoundland is inscribed "Royal Mail" and was retained from the old hotel. It is installed in the new lobby as a reminder of the old hotel and provides a link between the traditions of both.

"The old hotel played an important role in the development of St. John's and Newfoundland as a whole, as a host to visitors," says Turner. "We feel that with the opening of the new hotel this tradition has continued and will carry on into the 1990s and beyond."

Guests can enjoy an indoor swimming pool, saunas, and squash courts, even in the most inclement weather.

NUPORT HOLDINGS LIMITED

Cyril Morgan, president and chief executive officer.

When the St. George's Court apartments opened in St. John's in 1970, owner Cyril Morgan was pioneering a new concept in apartment living in St. John's. The 74-unit complex was designed specifically for senior citizens. The idea proved a popular one, and one year later Morgan opened a second complex, called Kelly's Brook. The waiting list for the first building ensured that the new complex would fill quickly.

Morgan was working as a civil servant when he decided to launch his own construction business. He had built his own home and sold it, and he had also constructed a four-unit apartment building before he ventured into bigger projects. After his success with senior-citizens' complexes, his company, Nuport Construction Limited, expanded in the construction industry. Morgan records now that he has built thousands of dwelling units in various areas of St. John's.

Nuport also became involved in construction of major office buildings. Some of these structures, such as the Bally Rou Building, were sold to mainland interests before construction was finished. This led Morgan into a facet of the industry that he likes most—property management. Morgan manages several other structures in St. John's that he built, such as the Prince Charles Building on Torbay Road, as well as apartment and office buildings owned by others.

Morgan has not lost touch with his original projects. His office is housed at Kelly's Brook apartments, where he is planning major renovations. "We find it best to be right on site," he says. "My operation is totally hands on. I'm here every day."

During the 1970s and 1980s Morgan, a member of the local Rotary Club and board of trade, became more active in the construction industry. In the early 1970s he was president of the Newfoundland and Labrador Homebuilders Association and a representative on the national Canadian Homebuilders Association. In 1982 he became president of the 6,000-member national organization. His tenure was an active one. With Jean Chretien, then-Minister of Energy, Mines, and Resouces, he signed an agreement that the government and the association would work together to pursue energy-efficient-designed homes. Nuport built an R-2000 energy-efficient home in St. John's in 1985.

"I felt it was very beneficial for me to participate in the association. There was knowledge to be gained, contacts to be made, and things to be accomplished," Morgan says.

Now, as president and chief executive officer of the Nuport Group of Companies, his major area of interest is property management. "Right now we are extremely well set up to increase our level of property management," Morgan says. "We have a completely modern computer system, and our size is limited only by the business we can obtain."

M&M MANUFACTURING LIMITED PARTNERSHIP

Dartmouth-based metal-fabricating firm M&M Manufacturing Limited Partnership has shown resilience since it was founded in 1980. The company, started by Melvin Mattie in Monastery, Nova Scotia, has already weathered business ups and downs and has positioned itself to get through future market setbacks.

A highly skilled welder, well connected in industrial construction circles, Mattie moved operations to Dartmouth in 1982 during the offshore oil exploration boom to service the oil rigs. The firm thrived, and offshore projects accounted for 95 percent of the company's revenues. However, by 1985, the offshore activity evaporated, and the timing was opportune when M&M joined with Montreal-based industrial conglomerate, The MIL Group, to form M&M Manufacturing Limited Partnership.

M&M had established itself as a firm known for carrying out projects to the exacting certified specifications and demanding schedules of the oil-rig operators. Partner MIL offered worldwide marketing support, financial strength, and managerial and technical backup that M&M needed to keep growing.

"We've had a pretty tremendous growth rate in recent years [25 percent annually through the late 1980s]" says John McStay, vice-president and general manager. "We intend to keep growing, but are always careful not to overextend ourselves."

David Hynes, vice-president/business development, says, "We target international clients and marketplaces as well as Canadian projects. This approach has been very successful, and our location in Halifax/Dartmouth, with its excellent communications and access to trade routes, has been instrumental in the growth of the company."

Aggressive marketing efforts and the ability to produce high-quality products to stringent schedules are "hallmarks" of the company. These have been translated into licensed products, innovative production methods, and a wide range of capabilities in ventures new to Atlantic Canada.

For example, one project involved the contouring of 42-inch-diameter piping through a unique process of heat line bending, a system not previously used on such large diameters. Under licence from Fuchs Systems Inc., M&M built the main components of the high-technology, new electric arc furnace selected by Sysco for its major plant modernization in Cape Breton. M&M has devel-

oped and manufactured, in conjunction with Hunting of Britain, a marine helicopter refueling system that is approved by, and in operation with, the Canadian Coast Guard. As prime contractor, M&M is refitting Canada's M113A1 armored personnel carriers, a project that, like many others, has not previously been performed in Atlantic Canada.

Internationally, M&M has won contracts for projects in Europe, Central and South America, North Africa, Asia, and the United States. Today M&M serves key clients in the industrial, defence, and offshore market sectors from its three plants in Dartmouth, Nova Scotia. These facilities are located on 20 acres of land and provide more than 80,000 square feet of covered fabrication, storage, and office facilities, which include direct access to the Woodside dock and from there to the open sea and Atlantic shipping lanes.

M&M constructed mammoth ceramic-coated lead kettles for New Brunswick Mining and Smelting.

Crystallizer for a potash mine in New Brunswick—the largest load to move on Maritime roads.

N.C. HUTTON LTD.

Noel C. Hutton, president of N.C.H. Holdings Ltd. and East Coast Converters Ltd.

Noel Hutton combined two significant events with his trip to Toronto to visit the Canadian National Exhibition in September 1953. The 12-hour, DC-3 flight, with repeated stops, was his first outside Newfoundland. It also later led to laying the groundwork for N.C. Hutton Ltd., when he spent a week in Toronto approaching dozens of Canadian manufacturers trying to become their Newfoundland sales agent.

"I just had an itching to start something with the advent of Confederation," recalls Mr. Hutton, who was then a brash 22 year old. "Anybody who was not down in Newfoundland was looking for a representative for the new territory."

Noel Hutton did not come away empty handed. He was designated as the Newfoundland agent for a Winnipeg flour miller, a Toronto candy maker, and a Montreal pickle and olive supplier. The following years saw Hutton transform N.C. Hutton Ltd. from distributing foodstuffs and other items to specializing in packaging materials for Newfoundland processors and producers, with an emphasis on fish packers.

Incorporated in July 1956, N.C. Hutton Ltd. is based in St. John's, Newfoundland, and represents manufacturers of corrugated containers, folding cartons, polyethylene packaging, glass containers, as well as crowns and closures. The firm directly employs 11 sales and support staff and has gross annual sales of about $25 million. It indirectly employs another 180 people in three plants producing the packaging materials for which N.C. Hutton Ltd. is the exclusive marketing agency in the province.

Before his pivotal trip to Toronto, Noel had already had a few years sales experience. After

he graduated from St. Bonaventure's College in 1949, he worked for C.R. Bell Ltd. and A.H. Murray & Co. Ltd., distributor and agent firms that sold foodstuffs, provisions, and cosmetics. Noel covered his territory, organized store displays, and gave away food samples. He reminisces, "It's a good way to get your feet wet in the selling game."

In addition to St. John's, Noel sold foodstuffs and hardware throughout the Bonavista and Avalon peninsulas. Each month he spent one week travelling and calling on the main merchants in his district. He had a company car and was earning $300 per month plus commission. He was moving large volumes of merchandise and developed a knack for hunting down items that his accounts were having problems bringing in.

In the early years in his travels as an agent he saw there was a need for packaging supplies of various kinds. Fish processors, breweries, biscuit, margarine, dairy, and meat factories needed all types of packaging, and, because of the remoteness of Newfoundland, all had to carry large inventories of each item used. By the mid-1950s Noel zeroed in on packaging as a product line. Displaying the same sort of initiative as he did at Toronto's Canadian National Exhibition, he assembled his own stable of manufacturers of packaging materials in Boston, Philadelphia, and Menasha, Wisconsin. When one of his key U.S. suppliers bought a Canadian operation, he switched and gradually converted all his packaging needs to Canadian manufacturers.

Noel concentrated initially on fish processors who were, for the most part, packaging their fish for export to the Boston area. The majority of fish plants were inaccessible by road and brought in their supplies by boat—so he received orders for all their yearly requirements and split shipped them in coordinated amounts. Sales broadened out to other Newfoundland manufacturers, getting orders from "anybody who used a package, big or small," he says.

Business went well, with N.C. Hutton Ltd. earning a profit of $7,000 the first year. Sales volumes increased to the point where his sales success and in-depth knowledge of the market made him instrumental in having his suppliers set up Newfoundland operations. Corrugated containers were bulky and costly to ship, and dictated massive inventories to be on hand so his customers could respond quickly to market demands. A corrugating plant, now called Canadian Pacific Forest Products Ltd., was set up in St. John's in October 1959, with N.C. Hutton Ltd. as the sole sales representative.

Noel was yet again the mover for another packaging material factory. June 1976 brought the formation of East Coast Converters Ltd., with N.C. Hutton as president, making all kinds of polyethylene products. His eldest son, Christopher, coordinated the package, installed all the machinery, and manages that operation.

In August 1987, after 17 years of promoting, a folding-carton plant was opened by Somerville Packaging, occupying 60,000 square feet of N.C. Hutton's main building in Donovan's Industrial Park.

Noel was none the less strategic in getting around Newfoundland to service his accounts.

He bought his own aircraft to fly to the less accessible Newfoundland fish plant clients as well as fish industry accounts in Nova Scotia, New Brunswick, and Prince Edward Island. He qualified for flying licences for fixed-wing aircraft and helicopters, moving from a Cessna 180 in 1959 to an Amphybian Cessna 185 in 1975 and a Bell Jet Ranger helicopter in 1979. He was well travelled and well known. "I did not own a business card. I do not need one in Newfoundland," Noel says, which points to the relative success he has had.

His name was known in the early days because of his association with sports, especially hockey. The Hutton name is synonymous with music, dating back to the late 1800s. His grandfather was knighted by the King and the Pope for his musical contribution to Newfoundland.

During the early 1960s, to help with the distribution and supply of his packaging material, Noel rented several warehouses in various locations in St. John's. He consolidated all storage in 1972, building a centralized warehouse in Donovan's Industrial Park. He was the park's first tenant. Warehouses were also built in Burin and Grand Bank to service fish plants on the Burin Peninsula and the south coast of Newfoundland.

In 1986 a holding company, N.C.H. Holdings Ltd., was set up with N.C. Hutton Ltd. remaining as the operating company. In February 1989 sales staff was hired to cover the Maritime Provinces, particularly for the fish-packaging potential there. Says Noel, "It is my hope to re-establish N.C. Hutton Ltd. in the Maritimes, offering the same services and know-how as we do here in Newfoundland."

The head office and warehouse of N.C. Hutton Ltd. in St. John's, Newfoundland.

Christopher Hutton manages East Coast Converters Ltd., located in Donovan's Industrial Park. A variety of customized polyethylene products are manufactured at this facility.

OCEANS LTD.

One of the firm's current projects is the development of an OCEANOMETER to monitor sampling by bongo nets. Shown here are bongo nets used for plankton sampling.

RIGHT: OCEANS Ltd. is housed in a unique row of stone houses that slope down to St. John's Harbour. Company president Judith Bobbitt conveniently lives two doors away.

Judith Bobbitt, physical oceanographer and president of OCEANS Ltd., is involved in both administration and scientific work.

Judith Bobbitt grew up in a small fishing village on the lower north shore of Quebec. She learned to read and write there, but it wasn't until she moved to Montreal at the age of 14 that formal schooling was possible. Her maritime background shaped her academic career and led her to the field of physical oceanography.

Today Bobbitt sits as president of her own company in St. John's. She was working in Newfoundland as a consultant when she decided to become independent. In 1981 she took her last paycheck and established OCEANS Ltd. to carry out applied research.

"The biggest hurdle at the beginning was getting clients to take me seriously," Bobbitt recalls. But as the company grew, clients came—all by word of mouth.

Clients now include Petro Canada, the Department of Fisheries and Oceans, and local firms. OCEANS Ltd. has developed a vertical plankton sampler system with multiple nets for the federal government.

"What makes us unique is our combination of expertise," explains Bobbitt. There are physical oceanographers, marine meteorologists, electrical engineers, fish biologists, and electri-

cal technologists among the staff of 12. This means the company can combine scientific, engineering, and technical capabilities for the development of innovative products and services.

"The staff has to be adaptable and willing to learn. There's a lot of in-house training. Sometimes it's three years before they are productive," says Bobbitt.

There are three fields of activity at OCEANS Ltd. As a physical oceanographer the firm is involved in researching and understanding the dynamics of the ocean. In the area of instrumentation it is developing new products

for data collection—the company is presently constructing an OCEANOMETER, a new underwater instrument for monitoring and data acquisition in marine research applications. The toxicology sector of the company is looking at the effects of contaminants on fish.

OCEANS Ltd. is housed at 31 Temperance Street, part of an historic row on one of the steepest streets in downtown St. John's. The four stone houses stand out in a city built almost completely from wood. Bobbitt resides two doors away at number 35, a few hundred yards from the harbor.

"I bought the house in 1983. Two years later I was suffering from a spinal injury and couldn't get around," Bobbitt explains. "So the company had to be moved to me." OCEANS Ltd. now owns a second house in the row.

Bobbitt's ambition? The next step is the establishment of a commercial laboratory for monitoring the health of commercial species around Newfoundland. Then OCEANS Ltd. wants to become more involved with acoustic research. "There's lots of water around," Bobbitt says, "and plenty of work to be done."

MEMORIAL UNIVERSITY OF NEWFOUNDLAND

The ocean at my door: That's how one local writer captured the essence of Newfoundland.

The ocean is indeed at the door, and Memorial University of Newfoundland is paying close attention to it.

"The destiny of Memorial University is clearly tied to the Atlantic Ocean, and indeed to the world oceans," says Memorial's president, Dr. Leslie Harris. "The way in which the oceans affect our lives, the interrelationships of ocean resources with the present and past activities of man, and the means by which they can best be managed are all very poorly understood."

Recently Memorial established an Ocean Studies Task Force to explore ways of building on the university's strength in ocean studies. An impressive International Advisory Council of 27 experts has been set up to ensure that ocean studies in Newfoundland maintain world-class standards, and set new ones. The task force will consult on the multidisciplinary approach to marine education and research that has been adopted by Memorial.

One of the offshoots of the task force is Oceans 2000, a bold new initiative designed to

position Memorial and Newfoundland as world leaders in ocean studies and enterprise by the year 2000. Under the banner of Oceans 2000 an aquaculture laboratory is proposed for construction at Memorial's Ocean Sciences Centre at Logy Bay. A state-of-the-art cold ocean university research vessel is under consideration by government, and there are plans for the creation of a National Centre for Ocean Studies with headquarters at Memorial.

Concern with the ocean is not new to the university. Within a year of the institution's establishment in 1925 as Memorial University College, a faculty member travelled to Nova Scotia to study techniques of fish flesh preservation. When Memorial was granted full university status in 1949—one of the first acts of the new government after Confederation—the commitment was made to provide facilities for "the application of science to the study of fisheries."

The broadly based university now has 17,000 full- and part-time students studying in six faculties and eight schools. But an awareness of the importance of Newfoundland's maritime environment is found throughout the campus in many ocean-related fields of study. These include ocean engineering, aquaculture, earth sciences, maritime history, sub-marine archaeology, and folklore.

"The university," Dr. Harris says, "looked at rocks, at ice, at the sea, at the cold ocean, and at isolation and what that does to culture. And in doing that we have concentrated to a considerable extent upon the oceans."

Memorial University's motto, *Provehito in Altumis* means "launch forth into the deep." That's just what Memorial is doing as it charts its way as a centre of excellence in marine research and development.

The 238-acre Ocean Sciences Centre (formerly the Marine Sciences Research Laboratory) at Logy Bay was established by Memorial University in 1967.

Memorial University stands at the doorstep of the Atlantic Ocean, as this aerial view of the south campus shows. The St. John's harbor is in the background.

AE SERVICES LTD. ARCHITECTS/ENGINEERS

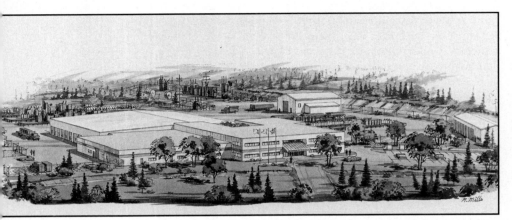

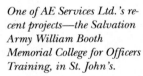

The St. John's regional facility of Newfoundland Light & Power Co. Limited, located in the O'Leary Avenue Industrial Park in St. John's, is another major AE Services Ltd. project.

One of AE Services Ltd.'s recent projects—the Salvation Army William Booth Memorial College for Officers Training, in St. John's.

AE Services Ltd. is a sound and respected consulting firm offering design and management services in architecture and structural and civil/municipal engineering. The firm was incorporated in 1980 by five professionals who had worked together previously. They became working shareholders, and, although some of the shareholders have changed, the policy of active principals has been maintained.

"We've built our reputation on personal service, and we've assured this by having at least one principal involved in every project we do," says company president W. Robert Osmond, P. Eng.

The staff of AE Services Ltd. includes 20 architects, engineers, technicians, and administrative personnel. The company undertakes small-scale to multimillion-dollar projects in Newfoundland, Labrador, and, occasionally, in mainland Canada and the United States.

"We're not small, and we're not really large either," Osmond says. "In the Newfoundland context we're a medium-size firm, and that helps us respond to any project from the small-est to the most demanding."

When the company was first established, the major portion of business dealt with educational facilities. Now the firm's clients include rural and metropolitan municipalities, school boards, universities and technical institutions, provincial and federal governments, and crown corporations. In the private sector, clients come from industry, manufacturing, residential, commercial, public utilities, and land-development sectors.

One of the company's most recent projects is the provincial government's new Motor Vehicle Registration Building at Mount Pearl. Part of the facility is a driver test track for preliminary testing of new drivers before the public road test—only a few other provinces have this.

Two other recent major projects are the Newfoundland Light & Power Co. Limited St. John's Regional Facility in the O'Leary Avenue Industrial Park and the Salvation Army William Booth Memorial College for Officer Training in St. John's, the latter being one of only two in Canada.

While the company is relatively young as a corporate body, the principals and staff have extensive experience in the field. The four other principals are Peter F. Hennebury, P. Eng.; Glenn D. Barnes, B.E.D.S., B. Arch., MRAIC; Wallace Earle, C.E.T.; and Murray Kearley, C.E.T.

AE Services Ltd. has not been pursuing offshore work directly, but is ready to respond if and when the offshore market moves. Says Osmond, "We still want to maintain our medium-size type of business so that we don't lose the personal touch with our employees and clients."

NEWFOUNDLAND LIGHT & POWER CO. LIMITED

The present Newfoundland Light & Power Co. Limited is an amalgamation of five companies: the Union Electric Light and Power Company, United Towns Electric Company Limited, the Public Service Electric Company Limited, the West Coast Power Company Limited, and the old Newfoundland Light and Power Company Limited. Since these companies joined in 1966, the new entity has been responsible for the transmission and sale of all electricity for the island of Newfoundland, except for those areas where Newfoundland & Labrador Hydro (formerly the Newfoundland Power Commission) has its own system. The firm operates 31 generating plants and maintains more than 8,000 kilometres of distribution and transmission lines.

Newfoundland Light & Power Co. Limited serves 189,000 customers, which represents

about 85 percent of the total retail market in the province. More than 160,000 of these customers are in the domestic sector, and about 50 percent of these use electricity for home heating, which is one of the highest percentages of electric heat use in Canada. For a number of years the demand for electricity was double the national average growth rate for Canadian utilities because of a rural electrification program and a rapid growth in electric heat use. In 1989 sales were about 4 billion kilowatt hours. The annual growth rate is expected to be about 5 percent during the next few years.

Since December 1, 1968, a uniform schedule of rates for both urban and rural customers has been in place, ensuring that all customers receiv-

ing the same type of service pay the same rate.

The company has spent more than $500 million on capital works since its incorporation in 1966. Its net fixed assets at the end of 1989 were $407 million. In 1990 the expenditure on capital works will be $68.5 million, and it is expected to remain at this level or higher for the next few years.

Throughout the years the firm has been a major employer of local technical and construction personnel. Its permanent work force is approximately 1,000 people. These employees work from 10 regional and area offices across the island, as well as from the head office in St. John's, where centralized functions such as accounting, engineering, and administration are carried out.

On November 24, 1987, the shareholders of Newfoundland Light & Power Co. Limited approved an arrangement under which a parent company, Fortis Inc., was formed, and common shares in the utility were exchanged for those of Fortis on a one-for-one basis. About one-third of the 8,000 Fortis shareholders are residents of Newfoundland. Newfoundland Light & Power continues as a public company, with its 3.3 million first preference shares widely held throughout Canada.

The original turbine and generators at the Petty Harbour hydroelectric station, 1900.

The original powerhouse, penstock, and flume at Petty Harbour, 1900. This station was entered into the Canadian Engineering Record in 1978 and has been declared a Registered Historic Site by the provincial government.

NBTEL

Recognized as a creative and innovative company since its founding in 1888, NBTel's prime focus has been on building a digital switching network and expanding its fibre-optics transmission system throughout New Brunswick.

Athletic telephone repairmen show off for the camera from the top of a 70-foot-high pole in 1897 in Saint John.

Before the 1880s telephone companies in New Brunswick didn't exist. There were some telephones, most of them bought from Alexander Graham Bell's father, but they were little more than intercoms strung between houses.

Lewis McFarlane tried to line up subscribers in Saint John for Bell's new invention, but he only sold one and didn't sign them up because they wouldn't have anyone to talk to!

Numerous small telephone companies eventually did spring up around the province during the 1880s. Subscribers were few, and there was concern that none would get proper service unless there was a single company co-ordinating it. Thus was born The New Brunswick Telephone Company, Limited, by an Act of Assembly of the Province of New Brunswick on April 6, 1888. The firm began with 75 subscribers in Fredericton.

Progress was slow and understanding of how the system worked was limited. A St. Andrews subscriber called the telephone company office to inform them her family would be away on holiday for two weeks in July and suggested they let "her" operator go for that period, under the impression that every subscriber had a personal operator.

While understanding was often marginal, dedication to the telephone company by its employees was without bounds: A fire at the Bathurst office in the home of Reginald Boss failed to stop services to his subscribers. The Boss family lost all their possessions, but they managed to save the switchboard, plugging it in down the street at a neighbor's home.

During the 1930s telephones were still considered a luxury by many, but the industry took a quantum leap during World War II. NBTel found itself facing increasing demands for service while at the same time experiencing severe shortages of manpower and materials. In 1945 the firm posted a record volume of telephone calls—nearly 100 million local and more than 2 million long-distance calls.

Telephone poles replaced the wires that were initially strung across rooftops, and long-distance service became an everyday affair—unless a bad storm toppled all the poles like tenpins for miles around.

In 1945 the company had 44,268 telephones in service in the province and employed 879 people. Today The New Brunswick Telephone Company, Limited (NBTel), with 2,500 employees, provides more than 280,000 customers with a wide range of integrated voice, data, and mobile telecommunications services. Its equipment and facilities represent an $800-million investment in the province.

Today's technology—fibre optics, the burgeoning cellular telephone business, and digital switching—virtually assures continuous service around the world on land, sea, or in the air.

NBTel is a wholly owned subsidiary of Bruncor Inc., a New Brunswick-based management holding corporation with primary interests in telecommunications, real estate, and financial services. Head office for NBTel is located at One Brunswick Square in Saint John. Company president is Lino J. Celeste.

NEILL AND GUNTER LIMITED

Neill and Gunter Limited officially began operations when Bob Neill went to work in his basement on October 2, 1964. The business began as a partnership with Harold C. Gunter.

The goal of the designing and consulting engineering company was to tackle engineering projects for a broad range of clients with expertise and cost efficiency—with emphasis on industrial projects.

By mid-October of that year Roderick C. Nolan, the company's first employee, had joined Neill in the basement. They sat at the same desk and worked hard to make the operation grow. In December they rented space in the basement of an established engineering company. They were joined by Harold Gunter on a full-time basis in January 1965. The firm was incorporated later that year, and in 1966 it opened a branch office in Halifax.

The forte of Neill and Gunter's present staff of more than 240 engineers and technical staff is engineering for industrial clients, especially in renewable resources and energy. The first company airplane, purchased in 1969, helped the Neill and Gunter staff provide service quickly to clients in isolated locations.

When the firm suffered during a general economic recession in 1970, management realized that greater geographical diversification was necessary. In 1975 the firm set up a subsidiary in Portland, Maine, as Neill and Gunter Incorporated. Now about 40 percent of the company's assets, and 40 percent of its business, are in the United States.

The firm's expertise in the areas of renewable resources and energy-based industries has earned it a world-class reputation and allowed it to complete projects as far afield as the Soviet Union and the Philippines. It became a multinational corporation by giving clients full attention and providing unique solutions to difficult problems.

Neill and Gunter often conducts a feasibility study for a client, designs the factory, supervises construction, works on the start up, trains the staff, and leaves engineers on site to cope with any problems that come up once the factory is in operation. It's also not unusual for them to invest in a worthwhile venture if the potential gains offset the risks.

Neill is enthusiastic about the future prospects of the company. "We have good people, and we are going to continue to grow. The forest products industry was, and will continue to be, a niche we are pleased to fill; the future is in high-technology engineering applications for industry. I see a big potential in the utility industry."

Neill is chairman of the board and chief executive officer and Rod Nolan is president of the main holding company, Neill and Gunter Limited. Doug Skinner is president of Neill and Gunter (Nova Scotia) Limited, and Waldo Preble is president of Neill and Gunter Incorporated.

Roderick C. Nolan, president (left), and Robert D. Neill, chief executive officer, worked out of Neill's basement when Neill and Gunter began in the engineering consulting business in 1964. Today the multinational corporation has its headquarters in a modern office building on Prospect Street, Fredericton.

Neill and Gunter Limited's computer facilities help the firm to complete projects for its broad client base.

ST. ANNE-NACKAWIC PULP COMPANY LTD.

The town of Nackawic, overlooking the Mactaquac headpond, was conceived as a model community—the perfect location for those displaced when the Mactaquac hydro-electric dam on the St. John River flooded the upper-river valley in the mid-1960s, drastically altering the landscape and the lives of those who had lived along the original river banks. Most of the displaced population built their new homes above the high-water mark, close to their original properties.

Although Nackawic (based on a Maliseet word, "Nelgwaweegek," meaning straight stream) was the location of the first post house above Saint Anne, when the land was first settled it was a place without people.

Clifford and Ernest Corey of Southampton Contractors Ltd. thought Nackawic was a perfect spot for a small pulp and paper mill. They went looking for partners and found Parsons and Whittemore, owned by the Landegger family of New York.

Parsons and Whittemore bought out Southampton Contractors, and instead of the small mill envisioned by Southampton they built a big one. The St. Anne-Nackawic Pulp Company Ltd. started producing corrugating medium in April 1970; pulp production started in June of the same year. Today it is one of the two leading mills in North America for quality hardwood pulp.

Under the same ownership, Valley Forest Products Limited was set up to take charge of the mill's timber supply from the provincially licensed crown land, as well as from surrounding private lands. Southampton Saw Mill Ltd. was then created to make use of the valuable softwood saw logs harvested at the same time as the hardwood for pulp.

St. Anne Chemical Company Limited came on line in 1979, made economically viable by the development of potash mining in the southern part of the province. The salt fields associated with potash mining provided the raw material to manufacture caustic soda, sodium chlorate, and chlorine, all used in the pulp mill. It reduced the mill's dependency on multinational chemical companies and reduced the necessity to transport these dangerous chemicals.

Although the mill started by producing corrugating medium, a severe downturn in that sector shut down the operation in June 1971. It was never restarted. The mill has been exclusively a kraft hardwood pulp mill ever since.

Market downturns in 1972 and 1977 saw the mill turn to specialty pulp markets in an effort to survive. Now between 60 and 70 percent of the mill's volume is specialty pulp for the production of photographic tissue, writing, and computer paper. Even high-quality paper plates are manufactured from the mill's low-dirt, high-brightness pulp. Photo buffs will appreciate that the Kodak Paper Good Look starts in Nackawic. The mill just received its fourth consecutive Kodak Gold Quality First Award.

The future of the mill is seen in developing more specialty markets, but the company is keeping the door open for integration, and a paper mill is possible. Shipping logistics and costs have made it prohibitive to send paper to Canadian or American markets in the past, but free trade may make the Boston market accessible.

It cost $60 million to build the St. Anne Nackawic Pulp Company Ltd. in the late 1960s; since then more than $100 million has been spent on improvements. But Parsons and

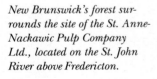

New Brunswick's forest surrounds the site of the St. Anne-Nackawic Pulp Company Ltd., located on the St. John River above Fredericton.

Whittemore built more than a mill—they built a town.

"The firm is very supportive of the community and the area in general," says engineer Byron Meredith, one of the first dozen people on the mill staff in 1969, even before the mill opened.

The firm helps the community financially with support for non-profit organizations, such as its New Brunswick Bicentennial gift of a top-notch double tennis court and its sponsorship of some sports teams.

"The company also supports the community with people, even during working hours," says Meredith. Mill employees are encouraged to get involved in community politics, projects, and the school board. Meredith was elected mayor in 1970; the town's present mayor is Steven Hawks of Valley Forest Products. Volunteers on Nackawic's fire department are free to leave work when they are needed—the town's fire calls actually come through the mill's security office. Many mill employees are volunteers on the ambulance brigade.

The most famous contribution of the mill to the community is the preschool. Carl C. Landegger, eldest son of K.F. Landegger, founder of the corporation, has a very strong commitment and concern for company workers and their families. He decided the town needed a good preschool.

A special facility was built, and Gail Silverman from New York City (associated with the Children's Television Network, producer of TV's "Sesame Street") was hired to set up the facility. Lynda Homer was hired as director (a position she still holds) and was trained under Silverman. The school gained national and international publicity for the small town and has provided quality early-childhood education to children of mill workers as well as members of the community at large.

The Landegger family, with current Parsons and Whittemore president George Landegger, still maintain an active interest in the mill, frequently meeting with Barry Stephen, mill vice-president and general manager. George Landegger also plays softball at the annual tournament during Family Days, a company-sponsored summer festival featuring everything from hot dogs to helicopter rides.

The first laborers hired at the St. Anne-Nackawic Pulp Company Ltd. in 1970 were paid $2.25 per hour. On August 1, 1989, that hourly wage went to $15.37. With more than 600 hourly and staff positions the mill and its associated companies mean prosperity for Nackawic and all the surrounding communities in the picturesque upper Saint John River Valley.

Louis J. Robichaud, premier of New Brunswick (left), and K.F. Landegger, owner of Parsons and Whittemore, "turned the sod" to begin construction of the St. Anne-Nackawic Pulp Company Ltd. in Nackawic, New Brunswick, in 1968.

THE NEW BRUNSWICK ELECTRIC POWER COMMISSION

NB Power's Dock Street plant in Saint John was built circa 1889 and continued in service until 1976. Although modernized over the years some of the original equipment was still being used.

January 15, 1988, was a bitterly cold day in New Brunswick with the temperature dropping to minus 26 degrees Celsius. NB Power customers demanded a record 2.3 million kilowatts of electricity, nearly 11 percent higher than the previous record and almost 5 percent more than predicted. Surplus energy, normally bought from Quebec, was not available because of similar peak demands in that system.

January 15, 1988—a bitterly cold day—but New Brunswick homes stayed warm, and industry stayed productive. NB Power's oil, coal, and diesel-fuelled thermal generating stations and the Point Lepreau nuclear generating station all operated at full output, meeting both the record in-province demand and the commission's firm export commitments.

New Brunswick has come a long way from the first power plant in the province, built in 1884 by the Saint John Electric Light Company on Paradise Row in Saint John. It could supply 2,000, 16-candle-power lights with electricity—the equivalent of six, 100-watt light bulbs.

By 1918 there were about 20 organizations, both public and private, engaged in producing and distributing electricity in the province, most of them thermal plants (burning fossil fuel to produce energy). A few were hydro stations (water powered), but each supplied power only to specific industries and/or principal populated areas. What power was available was expensive and unreliable; not only were rates high, they varied from location to location. Public demand called for electric power distributed to all parts of the province.

The New Brunswick Electric Power Commission, now referred to simply as NB

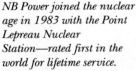

NB Power joined the nuclear age in 1983 with the Point Lepreau Nuclear Station—rated first in the world for lifetime service.

Power, was established by an act of the New Brunswick legislature on April 24, 1920, with a mandate to generate and distribute power to all areas of the province.

The commission's first generating station was the Musquash hydroelectric plant 15 miles west of Saint John. It served Saint John and the small communities such as Fairville, Hampton, Norton, Petitcodiac, and Shediac.

In 1931 the commission's first thermal plant was built at Grand Lake. It supplied the cotton mill at Marysville and Fredericton. This plant was expanded later in the decade and again in the 1940s.

By 1949 the Saint John head office was badly overcrowded, and the commission moved to a modern, four-storey building on King Street in Fredericton. Not only did the impressive brass front doors and the black-and-white marble lobby reflect the growth and prosperity of the commission, the new location brought it closer to the provincial government offices with which it worked so closely.

In its early years NB Power was concerned mainly with the supply of power to domestic and light-industry customers. By 1952 nearly every community in the province had access to electric power. In 1954 it was estimated between 90 and 95 percent of homes had electricity available, and the commission expected the number

of new customers joining the system each year to level off.

Heavy industry, such as pulp and paper mills, for the most part generated their own power. In 1956, with increased generating capacity and a transmission and distribution system extending to most populated areas of the province, NB Power went after those big users. The Beechwood Hydro Project on the Saint John River came on line at the time, but the commission knew that large and efficient thermal units integrated with hydroelectric generation and possibly even nuclear power would be necessary if it was to meet the demands of growing industries.

In 1960, for the first time in its history, NB Power's annual production surpassed one billion kilowatt hours—77 percent generated by hydro and 23 percent by thermal power.

In 1964 the firm decided to proceed with a major hydroelectric development at Mactaquac. This six-unit generating station on the Saint John River is still the largest hydro station in the region.

Until the early 1960s thermal generation depended largely on New Brunswick coal, but as inexpensive imported oil became available utility planners made use of the cheaper, cleaner-burning, and more easily transported fuel. In the late 1960s and early 1970s new generating stations built at Dalhousie and Coleson Cove were fuelled by oil.

The energy crisis of 1973 sent oil prices skyrocketing. NB Power embarked on a program to diversify its sources of electric generation and to decrease the use of imported oil. Part of that plan was nuclear power, and in 1983 the Point Lepreau nuclear generating system came on line.

In the fall of 1983 the head office of NB Power was moved to a nine-storey modern building connected to the four-storey facility opened in 1950. The commission now occupies both structures. The move consolidated head office staff under one roof with resultant improvements in productivity and communication.

That's communication of the human kind. Communication of the power kind takes place at the heart of NB Power's system, in the Energy Control Centre, Fredericton North.

In 1989 NB Power generated electricity from 14 thermal, hydro, and nuclear facilities. It serves more than 300,000 customers through the efforts of 2,500 regular and temporary employees.

A 450-megawatt coal-fired plant in Belledune is scheduled to be in full-power operation by late 1993. It will burn low-sulphur imported coal. But NB Power is also continuing with research on controlling the sulphur-dioxide emissions caused by burning New Brunswick-mined coal so this important local resource can be used safely.

Orimulsion, an emulsified bitumen fuel from Venezuela that could eventually replace bunker-C oil, is being tested at Dalhousie; engineering and environmental work continues at Colson Cove to confirm the viability of converting one oil-fired unit to an alternative fuel; and a 150- to 200-megawatt coal-fired unit is proposed for Grand Lake by 1994-1995.

As the history of electricity moves into its second century, the New Brunswick Electric Power Commission moves into the twenty-first century, searching for answers to the power needs of its customers that are both economically and ecologically sound. Additional nuclear units, power from natural gas, the Bay of Fundy's tides, the sun and wind, as well as from peat moss and waste wood are all possibilities.

NORTHUMBERLAND CO-OPERATIVE LTD.

Northumberland Co-Operative Ltd. of Newcastle, New Brunswick, started with an idea that took 40 years to germinate, came close to being ploughed under because of management problems, and then finally blossomed under William Vickers.

In 1933 G.P. Burchill, later to become Senator Burchill of Nelson, was impressed with the work of agriculture councils in Ontario and organized one in Northumberland County. The group planned routes for collecting cream from area farmers that was shipped to Moncton.

An attempt was made to establish a farmers' creamery in 1939, but it wasn't until 1942 that a private creamery was taken over, a charter was obtained, and a small pasteurizing plant serving the Air Base at Chatham was purchased. In May

on every farm with as many as 1,200 farmers producing milk for the co-op in the course of one year. Today all the milk required for the co-op's wide-ranging operation comes from only 70 farms in the area," Vickers says.

Throughout the 1950s and 1960s members supplied money for new buildings and the purchase of land. The feed business was started, milk storage space was enlarged, other dairies were purchased on a regular basis, and a railway spur was brought in to serve this fast-growing industry.

In the mid-1970s the co-op was using a truck trailer and refrigerated 10-wheeler, 4 tankers, 26 delivery trucks, plus 15 other trucks operated by vendors. The Dairy Plant, destroyed by fire in 1975, was rebuilt and became one of the most

Employee Paul Preston, shown here in a 1971 photograph, still works in the Northumberland Co-operative Ltd. plant in Newcastle, New Brunswick.

1943 work by the newly formed co-operative got under way, but the struggle was just beginning.

Many capable people endeavored to manage the unyielding enterprise—over a four-year period six managers gave it a try. The last manager told the board he could see no hope for success but recommended William Vickers be made manager.

Vickers, a follower and student of Dr. Moses Coady, started work at the creamery in August 1943 and was trained as a grader. After he took over in 1947 the deficit of four years dramatically changed to a surplus.

"At that time there was an average of six cows

modern facilities in the Maritime Provinces.

Northumberland Co-operative Ltd. started as a creamery. Now it has six divisions, runs its own garage to service 50 vehicles and other equipment, distributes frozen foods and ice cream, and runs its own co-op building and home supply store and picks up milk between Moncton and Bathurst selling as far north as Campbellton and as far east as Moncton.

Jack Christie, who replaced Vickers as manager following his retirement in November 1988, says, "We are now looking at growth in Moncton and are at the early growth stage of our branch in Fredericton."

CONNORS BROS., LIMITED

Two Irish boys, born of a farm family, succumbed to the call of the sea in the 1880s. They bought an open vessel, built a small fish house and a wharf, and set up weirs in Blacks Harbour, New Brunswick. Their names were Lewis and Patrick O'Connor, and the business they established was to grow to become the largest processor of sardines in North America.

In 1889 the O'Connor brothers built their first canning factory. They packed blueberries in the fall, clams in the spring, scallops, and eventually sardines. They installed wooden flakes on which to dry the fish and built a long brick fireplace where they fried the small, silvery herring in cottonseed oil.

Incorporated in 1893, Connors Bros., Limited, by 1917 was one of the most important businesses operating in the Maritime Provinces. Its Brunswick brand label, introduced in 1889, is still used. It continues to dominate the Canadian sardine market and has a significant share of the American market as well as other overseas markets.

In 1923 a conflict between the families of Patrick and Lewis led to the sale of the business to a Saint John group led by A. Neil McLean and his brother, Allan M.A. McLean. The new company was incorporated October 23, 1923, and the two men held the positions of president and treasurer, respectively, from then until its sale to George Weston Limited in 1967.

By 1971 Connors Bros., Limited, was not only the largest producer of sardines in North America, but also the only remaining sardine company in Canada. Connors Bros. is also a major processor of groundfish, crab, and other fish products. By 1989 more than 1.6 million cases of sardines and canned herring were produced and sold to more than 50 countries.

Today the company employs as many as 5,000 people in the Atlantic Provinces and operates a dozen factories in the area.

The success of Connors Bros. is attributed to its geographic location, adjacent to the only commercial source of small herring (sardines) on the East Coast; its ability to produce large volumes of canned fish products at reasonable costs, in containers it has manufactured for more than 100 years; and the reprocessing of fish waste into salable products, such as fish food for today's burgeoning aquaculture industry.

Connors Bros. has recently entered the salmon aquaculture industry with a hatchery producing more than 800,000 salmon smolt per year from its own breeding stock, and the firm markets one million full-grown salmon per year. Aquaculture, the company believes, will be the most significant seafood industry of the future and one in which it expects to play a major role.

Aquaculture may soon go beyond today's salmon into a wide variety of species farmed in the waters of the Bay of Fundy, which, for more than 100 years, have continued to supply a quality product for Connors Bros., Limited, to distribute worldwide.

Connors Bros., Limited, in Blacks Harbour, New Brunswick, is North America's largest sardine factory.

Connors Bros., Limited, has always claimed the annual sardine-packing prize.

ATLANTIC WHOLESALERS LTD.

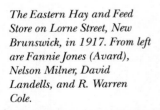

J. Leaman Dixon, founder of Sackville Hay and Feed Company.

J. Leaman Dixon of Sackville, New Brunswick, founded the Sackville Hay and Feed Company Limited in 1903. At first the company exported hay and feed grains to the United States and then gradually expanded into the wholesale grocery field.

Dixon's business philosophy was based on the principle that the day-in and day-out operations of the company exist solely for the benefit of those it serves.

A.F. Rose, president of Atlantic Wholesalers Ltd., the multimillion-dollar grocery company that grew out of J.L. Dixon's ambitions and philosophy, agrees. "This philosophy has served the company well over the years and is a prime reason for the success we have achieved," he says.

During the first 10 years Dixon kept increasing the number of grocery items the Sackville Hay and Feed Company handled. The firm also experimented with retail outlets in Sackville and opened retail stores in Sackville and Albert, New Brunswick, and Amherst, Nova Scotia.

After 10 years of successful business the company was reorganized in 1913, a new charter obtained, and the name changed to Eastern Hay and Feed Company Limited. In 1919 Eastern opened its first branch warehouse in Moncton, and the number of branch openings and acquisitions that followed carried the company successfully through the Depression and World War II.

A major move was the acquisition of the Jones-Schofield Hatheway Company of Saint John in 1944, which provided a manufacturing plant for the production and packaging of tea, coffee, spices, and molasses, and added wholesale outlets at Bathurst and Campbellton, New Brunswick. Following this acquisition Atlantic Wholesalers Limited was formed as a holding company for Jones-Schofield Hatheway Limited and Eastern Hay and Feed Company. J.L. Dixon was named president of the new company, and his two sons, Edgar and Carman, were named general manager and treasurer, respectively.

This move was followed by the first step into the franchising business, when, in 1946, the firm acquired the Red & White franchise for New Brunswick, Prince Edward Island, and mainland Nova Scotia; the purchase of wholesale companies in Digby, Nova Scotia, and Chatham and Grand Falls, New Brunswick; and the opening, in 1947, of the first fruit and produce division at Saint John, New Brunswick.

The year 1947 also saw the death of J.L. Dixon, at which time Dixon's son, Edgar, took over as president of the company.

The present head office at 4 Charlotte Street in Sackville opened in 1948 as the firm continued to grow and expand its borders. Despite a downturn in the economy beginning in 1948 and the destruction of its Saint John plant by fire in the early 1950s, Atlantic Wholesalers maintained its position and succeeded in continuing to return a profit to shareholders.

In the early 1950s Atlantic Wholesalers started introducing fresh produce departments in its supermarkets, an innovation that was to become an integral part of all supermarkets.

By 1954 the company was on the move again—this time into the Nova Scotia market, acquiring branches in New Glasgow, Pictou, and Truro through the acquisition of R. McGregor and Sons Limited and MacKenzie, Irish and MacDonald Ltd. Two years later the firm made its first big move into the retail end of the business with the purchase of two St. George Foods Ltd. supermarkets in Moncton, New Brunswick.

With the purchase in 1958 of Kitchen Bros. Limited of Fredericton and Woodstock, Atlantic Wholesalers had a solid wholesale position in western and central New Brunswick.

Edgar Dixon, forced to retire in 1959 due to ill health, was succeeded as president by his brother, Carman. That same year, backed by a strong retail division and vigorous advertising and promotion, further store development boomed at both the Red & White and Lucky

The Eastern Hay and Feed Store on Lorne Street, New Brunswick, in 1917. From left are Fannie Jones (Avard), Nelson Milner, David Landells, and R. Warren Cole.

The first Real Atlantic Superstore, opened in Moncton in August 1986, was an immediate success.

Dollar stores. In June of that year the first voluntary franchise Save-Easy store opened in Lewisville on the outskirts of Moncton.

The introduction of the company-owned Save-Easy franchise was another major turning point in the history of Atlantic Wholesalers Ltd. "By 1962 it was evident that a success story was in the making," says Rose. Atlantic Wholesalers had 23 more Save-Easy stores by the end of the year, in addition to one Red & White Foodmaster store, 35 Red & White stores, and 74 Lucky Dollar stores.

"Nowadays," Rose says, "franchise systems are solidly entrenched in the marketplace, selling everything from hamburgers to drugs and hardware, but in the late 1950s the concept was still something of an innovation, particularly in grocery retailing."

On the death of Carman F. Dixon in 1962, D.J. Hamm took over as president of Atlantic Wholesalers. The company's rapid growth and expansion continued unabated. By the end of 1968 there were 47 Save-Easy stores, 13 Red & White Foodmaster stores, 47 Red & White

stores, 78 Lucky Dollars, 2 supermarkets operating as St. George Foods, and 3 Shamrock Stores.

In 1959 Loblaw Companies Limited acquired all outstanding shares of Atlantic Wholesale Ltd. "A principal characteristic of this relationship has been the high degree of freedom that Atlantic retains to run its own operations," states Rose, who succeeded Hamm as president of the firm in 1983. He stresses that Loblaws recognizes that each company, operating in its own market area, has its own management style and must be able to respond to the specific needs of the people it serves.

In August 1986 Atlantic took yet another innovative step in Atlantic Canada with the opening of its first Real Atlantic Superstore in Moncton. The immediate success of the first Superstore, which offers one-stop shopping for both food and general merchandise, resulted in the addition of four more Superstores in quick succession. They are located in Lower Sackville, Dartmouth, and Halifax, Nova Scotia, and in Saint John, New Brunswick.

In 1989 the company had a total of 396 stores under the Superstore, Save-Easy, Foodmaster, Red & White, No Frills, Capitol/Valu-Fair, Quik Mart, and Valu-Mart banners, and also served 3,000 other accounts comprised of independent food stores, drugstores, service stations, and institutions. In addition, Atlantic Wholesalers operates five computerized distribution centres and five Cash and Carry outlets in the Maritime Provinces, all of which are strategically located. The firm also operates its own advertising and printing department in Sackville, New Brunswick.

The company employs a total of 194 people in Sackville and more than 3,200 retail and wholesale workers throughout the Maritime Provinces. Atlantic Wholesalers Ltd. is Atlantic Canada's largest food-distribution business.

A.F. Rose, president of Atlantic Wholesalers Ltd. Located in Sackville, the company is Atlantic Canada's largest food-distribution business.

HOYT'S MOVING AND STORAGE LTD.

When Leonard Hoyt began moving household goods in 1940, he had two small trucks and a 2,000-square-foot warehouse/garage in the north end of Halifax. Today his son Clifford controls the largest locally owned and managed transportation and storage organization, specializing primarily in household goods and family relocations, in Atlantic Canada. Although Clifford Hoyt is understandably proud of the firm's success, he takes greater satisfaction in pointing out that Hoyt's Moving and Storage Ltd. is still a family-owned and -operated business that spans three generations and 50 years of service to the Atlantic region.

Leonard Hoyt was only 11 years old and his brother, Russell, 13 years old in 1924, when they helped to move the family's farm furniture, cattle, and machinery 25 miles from Minas Basin to Truro. Six years later his brother, Russell, formed Hoyt's Transfer, the first highway truck-

Leonard Hoyt, founder.

by his company. By 1949, when he incorporated as Hoyt's Moving and Storage Ltd., Leonard had a fleet of eight highway transport trucks and an assortment of smaller vehicles for local jobs.

Moving a customer from the Atlantic to the

The Hoyt Fleet in 1953 in front of the Halifax Armouries. This was just prior to the United Van Line affiliation.

ing company in Nova Scotia. The operation was based in their hometown of Truro and carried goods to Halifax, Sydney, and Moncton, New Brunswick. Leonard soon moved to Halifax as local manager, where, in addition to handling the firm's regular freight shipments, he began using the trucks to move household furniture in the area.

In 1940 the Hoyt brothers ended their partnership. Leonard stayed in Halifax to run his own moving business while his brother continued the highway transport company from Truro. Unable to join the armed forces because he was blind in one eye as a result of a childhood accident, Leonard, under the firm's original name of Leonard Hoyt the Mover, transported goods and supplies to the docks and military camps during the years of intense military activity in Halifax. The warehouse on Young Street expanded to keep up with the demand for packing, storage, crating, and moving done

Pacific Coast a few years later was another landmark in Hoyt's history. Using a combination of Canadian and northern U.S. roads, driver Lloyd Stewart piloted a Hoyt's truck on a 10,000-mile trek from Halifax to Victoria, British Columbia, and back to become the first moving-van driver in Canada to complete a sea-to-sea round trip.

Founder Leonard Hoyt continued to direct the activities of the company and build its reputation for quality and service until his death in 1961. He was succeeded by his eldest son Clifford.

During the 1960s Hoyt's remained primarily a Halifax-Dartmouth operation. But the moving industry was beginning a period of radical change. Families no longer lived their whole lives in one area. Long-distance national and international moves were becoming commonplace. Hoyt's expanded its part of the trend to long-distance highway moves through its affiliation with United Van Lines, a national organization owned by independent moving companies throughout Canada. United functions like a co-operative that allows its member companies to provide personal attention at the local level while having the benefits of nationwide purchasing, co-ordination, and advertising.

Leonard Hoyt was one of five founding members who purchased United Van Lines Canada Limited from the U.S. parent United Inc. Clifford Hoyt served for seven years as president or vice-president of United and has been on the board of directors for more than 18 years. Hoyt's continues to be one of United's largest owners and shareholders, with 25 membership locations in Atlantic Canada. Hoyt says that being part of United gives the customer the benefits of being part of the largest nationwide mov-

Halifax-Dartmouth base. It opened or acquired branch offices in Fredericton, Saint John, and Newcastle, New Brunswick. Another son of the founder, Barry Hoyt, is a vice-president and manages all New Brunswick operations. An office in Middleton, Nova Scotia, to serve the western end of the province, followed in 1978. In each of these locations Hoyt's intensified its commitment to Atlantic Canada by investing in real estate, building new warehouses and offices, and hiring local drivers, packers, and warehouse people.

In 1978 Hoyt's, as part of United Van Lines, also pioneered the use of weatherized containers as an alternative to the traditional van for moving household goods in the region. The use of containers revolutionized the moving indus-

A modern Hoyt short-haul unit meets a Hoyt container unit at the entrance to Hoyt's Halifax terminal.

ing organization in Canada, plus all the advantages of dealing with hands-on, independent, and interested owners at all the local branch levels.

In 1971 Hoyt's began expanding from its

try. These large sanitized boxes eliminate the need for any further handling of household goods until they are delivered to their destination. If storage is required en route, the containers serve that purpose as well. Containers full of furnishings can be loaded from one vehicle to another easily and safely because no repacking is required.

Clifford Hoyt says that containers are also a boon for career drivers employed by the company. "It's now possible to schedule routes and vehicles so that drivers don't have to be away from home for weeks at a time. Instead of staying with one van all the way to a destination that may be across the country, the container can be transferred to another vehicle, and the driver can return with a different load in time to spend the weekend with the family."

Hoyt's concern for its employees and their families is reflected in the fact that the firm has never had a strike or lockout in its 50-year history. This concern is rewarded by the commit-

Clifford E. Hoyt, president.

ment and loyalty of the employees. Many, from managers to warehousemen and mechanics to drivers, have more than 25 years of service with Hoyt's.

With the increased use of containers and the expansion to locations outside the Halifax-Dartmouth area, Hoyt's soon outgrew its original Halifax site, which by then had grown to 60,000 square feet spread over six city lots. In 1981 the company moved its headquarters to a seven-acre property just outside the city limits of Halifax. Four major buildings were constructed on the site. Despite the size of the new location, the Young Street property is still needed as storage space for the fast-growing operations of the organization.

"Computers, containers, special packing material, and custom-designed vehicles are changes to the business that help to make moving safer

100 years. In keeping with its policy of integrating and retaining the employees of companies it has purchased and merged with, Hoyt's retained many of the longtime employees of LeDrew Transfer and installed Bob LeDrew as a vice-president and Newfoundland general manager.

In the same period Hoyt's also purchased and merged with another established Nova Scotia company and opened new centres in Truro and Sydney to serve the markets in eastern Nova Scotia and Cape Breton. These latest mergers and purchases have nearly doubled Hoyt's size and won it the position of the largest household moving firm in Atlantic Canada. "We made a long-term commitment in the transportation and storage industry of Atlantic Canada," says Hoyt, "and these purchases and mergers are continuing proof of that commitment. We stand by our policy begun many years

The company's first tractor-trailer. Note the lettering "Leonard Hoyt the Mover" on the trailer. This was the company's first name before incorporation.

and more efficient," says Hoyt. "But one thing hasn't changed. We're still a people business. We haven't developed robots to pack and load shipments. That's where the training and commitment of our employees makes the difference in our success." Hoyt's encourages and supports special training programs for its packers and drivers, and was one of the first to commit to United's Perfect Move Program.

Hoyt's truly became an Atlantic Canada firm in 1989, when it purchased and merged with LeDrew Express in Newfoundland. LeDrew, like Hoyt's, was a family firm with a history stretching back through six generations and almost

ago when we were the first mover ever to offer written guarantees of next-day delivery within the Maritimes. Many of our services are fully insured at no additional cost to our customers."

Hoyt's involvement in the region goes beyond the services it offers to its customers. The moving company has been a longtime supporter of minor-league sports teams in all of its branches. And its managers and employees have been active in service clubs and other local community activities. Members of the Hoyt family have relocated their families, too, and become active in the community affairs of Fredericton, St. John, and Sydney.

Now celebrating its golden anniversary, Hoyt's Moving and Storage Ltd. is still owned and operated by the founding family. The children and grandchildren of founder Leonard Hoyt, among the current staff of more than 200 permanent, part-time, and management employees, are proof of Hoyt's continuing commitment to the future of the Atlantic Provinces.

An aerial view of the original Halifax warehouse.

ROBINSON-BLACKMORE PRINTING AND PUBLISHING LIMITED

Robinson-Blackmore Printing and Publishing Limited is the largest printing and publishing house in Atlantic Canada. It has been a presence on the Newfoundland printing and publishing scene for nearly 100 years. From humble beginnings in St. John's and Grand Falls, the company has grown to its present status as a major newspaper and creative book publisher and commercial printer.

Robinson-Blackmore is housed in a new 38,000-square-foot building on Austin Street in St. John's. Here, and in modern facilities in Grand Falls, web offset presses operate seven days per week, 24 hours per day, to produce 14 community newspapers with a combined circulation of 85,000. These include metropolitan papers such as *The Sunday Express,* which serves St. John's and major centres across Newfoundland, *The Aurora* in Labrador City, as well as newspapers in remote districts of the island, such as *The Coaster* in the Harbour Breton area and *The Gulf News* in southwest Newfoundland.

Serving rural Newfoundland is a tradition with Robinson-Blackmore that dates back to its early days. Shortly after the company produced its first newspaper at St. John's in 1894, a second newspaper was founded to serve isolated communities. That first paper was *The Daily News,* the dream of a school principal named John Alexander Robinson, who printed the paper in a small plant on Duckworth Street. Six weeks later *The Weekly News,* designed to serve isolated communities around the island, rolled off the press.

A quarter-century later two teenage boys in Grand Falls decided to try their hand at printing. By 1923 the brothers, Michael and Walter Blackmore, were printing handbills, tickets, and stationery items on a small tabletop press. In 1936 they produced the first edition of the *Grand Falls Advertiser,* which is still in circulation. The Blackmore operation grew, and by 1968 Blackmore Printing Company was publishing three other community newspapers.

That year a consortium headed by the Crosbie Group of Companies bought Robinson Company. In 1969 a merger with the Grand Falls printers resulted in Robinson-Blackmore Printing and Publishing Limited. In 1982 the firm was sold to a group of its former directors, presided over by president Doyle Roberts. Three years later Newfoundland Capital Corporation, headed by industrialist Harry Steele, acquired the company. The current president is Lorne B. King, C.A.

In addition to its publishing aspect, Robinson-Blackmore Printing and Publishing Limited also prints brochures, advertising flyers, catalogues, magazines, business cards, corporate brochures, telephone directories, and commercial place mats. The firm's computerized typesetting services and its Heidelberg two-color presses enable it to meet the volume and variety of its printing demands.

Early premises of the Blackmore Printing Company on Mill Street in Grand Falls. From left are Cornelius Connors, Michael Blackmore, Jack Skinner, and Joe Ennis.

From its new head offices and plant at 36 Austin Street in St. John's, Robinson-Blackmore Printing and Publishing Limited produces 14 community newspapers with a combined circulation of 85,000.

ATLANTIC INDUSTRIES LIMITED

Ask any Maritimer "What's in Dorchester, New Brunswick?" and for many years the answer would have been a swift and sure, "Dorchester Penitentiary." These days people are beginning to realize that is no longer the only answer. It is Atlantic Industries Limited that has surfaced as the major industry in this small New Brunswick town.

It isn't high profile with a high fence around it, but it does have customers from all over the country. While convicts may be famous for making licence plates, AIL is famous for making corrugated steel pipe, structural plate pipe, and polyvinyl chloride (PVC) pipe as well as spiral seam duct. It also manufactures guardrails and operates a hot-dip galvanizing plant.

Until 1988 operations were confined to the Atlantic Region with plants in Eastern Passage, Nova Scotia; Deer Lake and Mount Pearl, Newfoundland; and the head office and major plant in Dorchester.

RIGHT: Corrugated steel pipe, emerging here from Pipe Mill Plant No. 2 at Dorchester Cape, is Atlantic Industries' major product. It is used for culverts (underground water channels).

ABOVE: This attractive facility houses the head office of Atlantic Industries Limited, the major industry in Dorchester.

In 1988 AIL bought Koppers International Canada, Ltd., with headquarters in Cambridge, Ontario, and plants in Quebec, Ontario, Alberta, and British Columbia. Key personnel from Cambridge will be transferred to the company's head office in Dorchester, a refreshing change from many businesses that have an Ontario head office and Maritimes branch offices.

With today's communications, computers, and facsimile machines, one can run a business from anywhere, says company founder, president, and chief executive officer John W. Wilson. Wilson makes no secret of the fact that he prefers the Maritime Provinces to anywhere else, including his native Ontario.

He fell in love with the region in September 1949, when, as a newly graduated mining engineer from the University of Toronto, he was sent to do a job near Fredericton. He promised himself if he ever had an opportunity to live in the Maritimes, he would take it.

Wilson got his chance in 1954 when he was offered the position of Maritime regional general manager for Armco Canada. He grabbed the opportunity, although he admits it was not the most generous offer, since the firm had no buildings or staff in the region. He was on his own to develop a market and build the company.

He built the first plant in Newfoundland and a second in Sackville, New Brunswick, where he and his wife settled. They bought a home and 11 acres of land overlooking the Cumberland Basin and raised five sons.

In 1965 Wilson decided it was time to do things his way. He left Armco Canada and started Atlantic Industries Limited. He was in direct competition with Armco and people he had hired and trained. It was an awkward position, but Wilson considers competition the spice of life.

He chose Dorchester as the site for his first plant because it was close to his home in Sackville, and a newly opened industrial park looked like a promising location. AIL started with a staff of 10 people. A staff of 200 now keeps the highly automated firm in production from coast to coast.

Corrugated steel pipe, used mostly in culverts (underground water channels), makes up the largest part of AIL's business with a 35-percent share of the Canadian market. Structural plate pipe up to 40 feet in diameter is used in small bridges, while PVC (plastic) pipe is used in sewers. Spiral seam ducts are used in air conditioning and ventilation.

The highway guardrails manufactured in AIL are galvanized (covered thickly with zinc). The Dorchester plant maintains a galvanizing tank filled with molten zinc at a temperature of 840 degrees Fahrenheit and offers custom galvanizing.

AIL has an aggressive marketing team. Armed with glossy brochures, they sell galvanized steel pipe for storm and sanitary sewers, highway construction, and forestry applications. The technical sales representatives can also provide on-site engineering evaluation and recommendations.

AIL representatives also have PVC pipes down pat and can advise on everything from fittings (the stock is complete and special cuttings can be provided) to color. (Hot, sunny climates need white PVC pipe, but Canadian projects that have to worry about excess heat and sunlight are few and far between.)

Sewer pipes and culverts may not be the most glamorous commodities in the world, but they are certainly among the most stable, Wilson says. Since the company was founded in 1965 the economic climate in Canada, and especially in the Maritimes, has been anything but consistent.

Inflation, recession, depression, and booms have all come and gone. When times are good the private sector builds and expands. AIL reaps the benefits. Even when times are bad the public sector spends money on public works. AIL comes out ahead again.

In 1985 AIL looked toward expanding into the United States, but the low value of the Canadian dollar made it economically unfeasible. The firm looked toward the rest of Canada, and in 1986 set up a distribution centre in Maple, Ontario. However, when Koppers International came on the market in 1988, AIL bought the company, providing the firm with a nationwide manufacturing and distribution network. Koppers and AIL are one of only two national corporations in the nation that manufacture corrugated steel pipe.

The end of a long, lonely, narrow shoreline road in a small New Brunswick community is not a likely spot to find the head office of a national company. But when Wilson sits in his large and well-appointed office in a new, modern building, he is master of all he surveys and more.

The new building has room for the staff that will be coming from Cambridge. That group includes Wilson's son Michael, who recently added president of Koppers to his other titles of executive vice-president and chief operating officer of AIL.

AIL will probably expand into the United States and is always looking for new products. It is a young, aggressive organization. The people who are doing the work and making the decisions in Atlantic Industries Limited are all in their late twenties and early thirties.

"With that kind of energy I predict we will be number one in Canada in another five years," says Wilson. "That's not just a reasonable expectation, it's a fearless forecast."

Galvanized and asphalt-coated structural plate pipe arch being lowered into a trench.

Structural plate pipe, usually used in small bridges, awaits shipment to the customer.

CANADIAN NATIONAL RAILWAYS

At CN's Moncton Intermodal Terminal, a Piggy Packer gently lifts trailers onto specially designed rail cars in preparation for departure on one of the company's intermodal trains.

On December 20, 1917, all government-owned railways in Canada were placed under the management of the Canadian Northern Railway Company, now known as Canadian National Railways. In Atlantic Canada, the Intercolonial Railway, the National Transcontinental Railway, the Prince Edward Island Railway, as well as a number of New Brunswick short lines were incorporated in the new CN. Although consolidation was completed by 1923, the network needed some fine tuning.

Many of the lines assembled under the Canadian National banner had been constructed along parallel routes and, in many areas, competed for the same traffic. As well, much of the track and roadbed belonging to smaller, poorer railways were not up to standard, and decisions had to be made as to which lines would be repaired and kept. This process continues even today as CN adapts its network and facilities to ever-changing market conditions.

Throughout Canadian National's early history there are many examples of innovations that later became separate major companies.

In 1923 the CNR Radio Department was formed when experiments proved radio reception was possible on moving trains. Early in 1925 the first radio program from Canada to Great Britain was broadcast from Moncton. In the 1930s the CNR Radio network became a separate company, the forerunner of today's Canadian Broadcasting Corporation.

After the Canada-West Indies Trade Agreement was signed in the mid-1920s, Canadian National was asked by the government of Canada to establish a fleet of passenger ships for service between Canada and the Caribbean. For the next few decades ships, operating under the company's marine pennant, sailed from Montreal, Halifax, and Saint John to the Caribbean until severe competition from the airlines forced the end of this service. In 1985

A SuperTherm trailer takes a load of potatoes from Prince Edward Island to CN's Intermodal Terminal in Moncton and from there, using a dedicated overnight train service, to the markets of Central Canada.

Canadian National's remaining marine interests of coastal service vessels and car ferries were transferred to Marine Atlantic.

In 1937 then-Federal Transportation Minister C.D. Howe entrusted the organization of a national airline to Canadian National. By 1939 Trans Canada Airlines, later to become Air Canada, had established a national service to Montreal, Toronto, and Vancouver. The airline became transcontinental when service was extended to Moncton in 1940.

Canadian National was involved during the war years in the urgent movement of tanks, guns, supplies, and troops from Central Canada to the East Coast for subsequent transport to the war effort in Europe. With the complexity and sheer volume of traffic being handled, a new method for controlling the movement of trains was required. As a result, Canada's first Centralized Traffic Control signal system was installed between Moncton and Halifax.

As Canada flourished in the postwar boom, railways were faced with a new challenge. There now was a network of highways that had been built to connect virtually every community across the country. With a significant increase in the number of automobiles, Canadians now had the freedom to travel whenever and wherever they pleased. In addition, airplanes became increasingly popular with time-conscious travellers. In order to better adapt to the changes taking place in passenger travel in Canada, the passenger service divisions of both Canadian National and Canadian Pacific were entrusted to a new Crown corporation, VIA Rail, in 1977.

Prior to World War II, the train was the only choice for both passengers and freight shippers.

The completion of the Trans-Canada Highway saw a significant increase in the movement of freight traffic by trucks, which could offer a more flexible door-to-door service. This increased competition, which in Atlantic Canada included water movement, meant that Canadian National had to offer services that were tailored to customer needs if it was to remain a major player in the transportation marketplace. New technology and equipment were introduced to make rail service faster and more affordable. The late 1950s saw powerful diesel locomotives replace steam, new freight cars carry heavier payloads, and improved track and roadbed designed and maintained to meet the increasing tonnage.

The introduction of computer technology brought a new dimension in efficiency to railway operations as well as a significant increase in safety. Since the early 1960s CN has adapted and developed computer systems that keep track of every locomotive, freight car, and customer load throughout Canada and the United States. Computers operate switches and signals safely, and are employed to test track and roadbeds, in addition to handling the everyday business of running one of Canada's largest corporations.

CN has consistently evolved with the times, realizing that anything affecting the nation's economy affected the railway. With the recession of the early 1980s, manufacturers quickly realized the importance of transportation in the cost of producing goods. Just-in-time systems of inventory control provided industry with large productivity gains that enhanced their competitiveness in the emerging global marketplace. This meant the railway had to change once

again and offer not only more flexible rail transportation but also innovative distribution services.

The introduction of containerization, particularly in import-export activities, revolutionized international freight handling. With the development of large containers terminals served by dependable daily train service and connected to a network of strategically located inland terminals, the Port of Halifax has emerged as an important port-of-call for steamship lines calling on North America.

By "piggybacking" or loading highway trailers onto railway flat cars, CN's Intermodal service combines the door-to-door flexibility of truck delivery with the efficiency of low-cost rail movement. This innovation, first introduced by CN in the mid-1950s, has allowed the company to recapture markets that were being lost to truck competition. Similarly, other intermodal services such as distribution centres and break-bulk facilities have enabled CN to expand its services to shippers in areas that are not served by rail.

In some areas the rail network no longer generates the level of traffic needed to remain viable and, as CN responds to increased market demands for lower-cost transportation and distribution services, it has embarked on a program of becoming a more efficient operation. The corporation is actively working to reduce the number of high-cost, low-traffic-volume branch lines that no longer satisfy customer demands for increased transportation flexibility.

As a rail-based transportation and distribution company charged with the safe, effective, and affordable movement of goods, Canadian National Railways, a crown corporation operating on a strictly commercial basis, continues to play a vital role in Atlantic Canada's economy.

ABOVE: CN connects direct ship-to-rail service for import/export traffic moving through Halterm Ltd. at Halifax to strategically located inland terminals in Canada and the United States.

BELOW: Like a giant conveyor belt operating between mine site and port, a CN unit train pulls up to 60 rail cars of gypsum to Halifax for export to the international marketplace.

NEWFOUNDLAND AND LABRADOR CREDIT UNION

Since 1978 the Newfoundland and Labrador Credit Union headquarters has been housed in its own building at 341 Freshwater Road in St. John's.

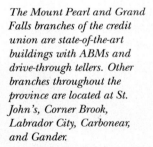

The Mount Pearl and Grand Falls branches of the credit union are state-of-the-art buildings with ABMs and drive-through tellers. Other branches throughout the province are located at St. John's, Corner Brook, Labrador City, Carbonear, and Gander.

On March 2, 1957, a teacher named Margaret Doyle entered the offices of the Newfoundland Teachers' Association (NTA) and opened an account with its newly formed credit union. Her $10 deposit marked the beginning of what is known today as the Newfoundland and Labrador Credit Union, the largest credit union in Atlantic Canada.

The credit union was initiated by the NTA as a means for helping teachers help each other with their financial affairs. It remained a wholly owned and controlled subsidiary of the NTA until 1974, when it was granted autonomy. By this time membership had expanded to include spouses and children of teachers, but eventually the organization exhausted its growth within the teacher population. Since 1981 membership has been open to anyone who lives or does business in Newfoundland.

Because of its association with teachers, the population base has always been spread province-wide. The credit union offers mail and phone services—it has a toll-free telephone number—but since 1974, when it opened a branch in Corner Brook, it has attempted to provide counter service to as many clients as

possible. A staff of 57 full-time and 12 part-time employees operates out of seven branches in Newfoundland and Labrador. The Mount Pearl and Grand Falls branches boast state-of-the-art buildings with drive-through tellers, automated banking machines (ABMs), and play areas.

The Newfoundland and Labrador Credit Union today is a community credit union, unique in Canada in that it is province-wide. It has 14,500 members, about half of whom are teachers and their families, with total assets of more than $90 million.

"The family is our focus today," says Michael W. Boland, who is serving his third term as president of the credit union. "We provide cradle to grave financing. The philosophy of the credit union is to provide a homespun alternative to banks," states Boland, who has served on the board for 25 years. The volunteer board consists of 12 members of the credit union who are elected by the general membership.

The Newfoundland and Labrador Credit Union is owned and controlled by Newfoundlanders, and its ever-increasing multi-million-dollar budget remains in the local economy. The credit union provides traditional banking services—approximately $55 million in loans was granted in 1989—and offers its clients a MasterCard payment card that gives them access to funds and credit at more than 80,000 international financial institutions. Affiliation with the Interac & Plus system allows members access to ABMs internationally. Other services offered by the credit union include travel insurance, disability insurance on mortgage loans, and witnessing of documents.

In 1978 the Newfoundland and Labrador Credit Union purchased the building on 341 Freshwater Road, which remains its headquarters today.

STORA FOREST INDUSTRIES LIMITED

Stora Forest Industries Limited's pulp and newsprint mill on the shores of the Strait of Canso in Cape Breton.

Stora Forest Industries Limited is a youngster compared to its 102-year-old parent company, STORA Kopparbergs Bergslags AB of Falun, Sweden. But it has been a vital part of the life and economy of eastern Nova Scotia since 1962.

Some 1,000 employees work at its Point Tupper mill and woodlands offices, producing 340,000 tonnes (375,000 short tons) of market pulp and newsprint annually. Another 1,300 people work for contractors in silvicultural operations and harvesting and trucking of wood to the mill.

Nova Scotia Pulp Limited, the original name of the company, was STORA's first manufacturing operation outside of Europe. Construction of the bleached sulphite market pulp mill began in 1959 and was completed two years later at a cost of $40 million.

More than 400 much-needed local jobs were provided to run the mill, and another 800 full-time jobs were created in the forests of eastern Nova Scotia during these early years. A unique feature of the plant was an 18-storey recovery building, which was taller than any structure in Nova Scotia at that time.

In the late 1960s the company decided to expand its pulp operation from nearly 120,000 tonnes (130,000 short tons) annually to its present capacity of 160,000 tonnes (176,000 short tons). In 1971 it completed a second mill to produce newsprint and became known as Nova Scotia Forest Industries. The company again changed its name to Stora Forest Industries in 1985 to better reflect the relationship with its Swedish parent corporation and the STORA group of companies.

Stora's woodlands operation manages 600,000 hectares of Crown land, while 30,000 hectares are company-owned lands. To help meet worldwide demand for pulp and newsprint, the mill requires 600,000 cords of wood each year. That number of cords, if stacked end to end, could make a road almost 2.5 metres (eight feet) wide and more than one-half metre (two feet) thick, stretching over 1,450 kilometres (900 miles).

Recognizing that its continued existence requires a constant supply of wood, Stora's operations are carefully planned to ensure long-term sustainable harvests and increased forest productivity, while at the same time safeguarding wildlife, water, and recreational aspects of the woodlands. Professionally trained foresters and technicians collect data prior to harvesting, prepare management plans using computerized analysis and mapping systems, and supervise operations to strict standards.

Stora Forest Industries is widely recognized for its large-scale silvicultural program. In its relatively short history in Nova Scotia, the company has planted more than 83 million trees between 1962 and 1989, and expects to plant its 100-millionth seedling in the early part of the 1990s. By the end of the 1980s Stora was replanting annually as many hectares of land as it was harvesting.

The commitment by Stora Forest Industries Limited to the future of Nova Scotia is not only reflected in its efforts to improve the quality of the province's forests. Local sports teams, arts and culture, charities, and scholarship funds receive support from the company in a substantial way. The well-being of its workers is also of paramount concern at Stora, as shown by the company policy that states, "The health and safety of employees takes precedence over all other responsibilities and activities of the company."

Newsprint comes off the wrapping line.

MIRAMICHI PULP & PAPER INC.

The Boise Cascade Kraft Mill before the Repap purchase in the early 1980s.

The economy is booming in Miramichi country. People are enjoying the good things in life: the unique beauty of New Brunswick's Miramichi River, the support of a caring community, a rich cultural heritage, as well as modern remote-control televisions and videocassette recorders.

These luxuries are not significant only because they symbolize modern convenience and the presence of a reasonable purchasing power, but because George Petty had the vision to see what such technological advances would do to the advertising world.

Petty is chairman of the board and chief executive officer of Repap. Repap is paper turned around—not spelled backward, says Petty, but turned around. And that is just what Petty did with the pulp and paper industry on the Miramichi River. He turned it around through Repap Miramichi.

He realized that videocassette recorders and remote-control televisions made it possible for people to avoid watching television commercials either by fast forwarding through them on recorded programs, or by instantly switching to another channel when the commercials interrupted the shows they were watching. Petty figured it as a pretty sure bet that advertisers worldwide would be reverting to print advertising in glossy catalogues and newspaper inserts, all made from lightweight-coated paper.

In 1974 he purchased a sawmill and ground wood pulp mill in Nelson-Miramichi from Acadia Forest Products Ltd. This mill grinds logs to make a short-fibre ground wood pulp.

The Groundwood Pulp Mill in Nelson-Miramichi began as a sawmill. This view was taken in 1970 before the Repap purchase.

Across the Miramichi River in Newcastle there was a kraft-pulp mill, owned by Boise Cascade. Kraft pulp is made from a cooking process that separates fibres and makes a stronger pulp. On May 21, 1985, Petty bought the kraft mill, and the economy of the entire region turned around.

Ground wood and kraft pulp with a white clay from Georgia make lightweight (for cheaper mailing and distribution costs) coated (for high-quality color photography reproduction with a minimum of ink) paper. It is the most popular paper used in print advertising. Importing the clay from Georgia poses no problem for Repap; it has the Miramichi deepwater port on its doorstep.

On the same day that Petty bought the kraft mill, the sod was turned for an A-1 paper mill to be built on the kraft mill site. In only 14 months it was complete—ahead of schedule and under budget. It is the world's widest, fastest, lightweight coated papermaking machine, christened Miramichi Belle.

The completion of the paper maker meant that instead of selling all the pulp on the open market, half the ground-wood mill pulp production and one-third of the kraft-mill production were used within the company, and the value-added paper product went to market. The fortunes of both mills and of the region were significantly turned around.

To celebrate the completion of this exciting project, Petty invited politicians, paper makers, industrialists, and VIPs from all over the world to the official opening on October 16, 1986. The mill site was spruced up with asphalt parking areas and sodded lawns. Tents and awnings protected magnificent buffets and exciting entertainers. The firm chartered five planes to bring guests, including Prime Minister Brian Mulroney, to the grand celebration. By the end of the day the world knew that Newcastle, New Brunswick, had a world-class paper mill.

It was a dream come true in a community with a rich history of working in the woods and on the river. Repap Miramichi made a video called "A Dream Come True." It tells the story of a woodsman in the 1940s lamenting about the Depression and the failure of the pulp and sawmills on the river. He dreams of modern pulp and paper facilities and a better life for the community. On awakening he finds his dream has come true with viable pulp mills and the new A-1 paper machine.

That is the end of the video, but it is by no means the end of the Repap story on the Miramichi.

Some enterprising research chemists have recently perfected the technology necessary to recover the by-products and alcohol in a revolutionary process for making hardwood pulp. This new process, known as the Alcell® process, cooks pulp in alcohol rather than sulphides. In contrast to traditional technologies, valuable by-products including sulphur-free lignin are recovered and sold to a diverse range of industries.

The chemists were looking for someone to build the first commercial-size hardwood pulp mill. Petty did, having first acquired the rights to the new chemical process. There has been no shortage of offers from companies interested in building the second mill, once someone else has proved that the process works on a large scale.

On May 6, 1988, only 1.5 years after the gala opening of the A-1 paper plant, again came the tents, the food, and the VIPs for a sod turning for three more major projects: the Alcell® commercially sized research and development facility for making hardwood pulp, a second paper machine to meet the ever-increasing demand for lightweight coated paper, and a recovery boiler project to significantly reduce the odor in recovering the cooking liquor used in the kraft mill process. It represented a billion-dollar in-

The Repap Kraft Mill in Newcastle started as the Edward Sinclair Mill in the early 1860s. Shown here are the employees in 1890.

vestment in the Miramichi area over the five-year period.

The Alcell® mill produced the first batch of hardwood pulp on March 6, 1989, and its quality exceeded targets based on kraft pulp—from a process that greatly reduces pollution. Repap plans to license the technology worldwide and expects to sell 105 mills before the year 2000.

The second paper machine and recovery-boiler project is still under construction. When it is complete the second paper machine will mean the mills use nearly all of the groundwood pulp produced at Nelson Miramichi and two-thirds of the kraft pulp produced in Newcastle.

A satellite project of the recovery boiler is a new clarifier system to help clean up the environment—a project important to the company. Repap and the people of the region are identifying area environmental concerns, especially those relating to the river and the air.

The needs of the two pulp mills are assured by 1.8 million acres of timberland under licence to Repap until the year 2007, with renewal provisions built in. Repap's woodlands planning and

RIGHT, ABOVE and BELOW: Men and machinery at work in the Repap Paper Mill in the Miramichi area of New Brunswick.

silviculture activities have involved them in a 25-year forest management plan with the Province of New Brunswick. The firm has identified all the cutting areas necessary for the next 25 years, as well as all the areas that will need planting and thinning.

Buffer zones around communities, lakes, and rivers are automatically built in to harvesting plans in order to protect the aesthetics and quality of life of the area, as well as to protect the resource. Even recreation areas such as lakes and streams for hunting and fishing are protected, and lands have been set aside for animal refuge. Repap reviews the plan

with the province yearly.

Petty came to the Miramichi to help the economy—so people could enjoy their own unique way of life. He saw in them the spirit of their pioneer ancestors who "spat upon their hands and pushed the forests back," as sung by Miramichi balladeer Hedley Parker. Today approximately 1,500 people are employed in the Repap Miramichi complex, and another 1,000 to 1,500 work in the woodlands division.

Since William Davidson arrived on the Miramichi River in 1765 and started supplying the Royal Navy with schooner masts from the tall trees that abounded in the area, the forest has been a way of life there. Davidson also employed men in a salmon fishery. He decided they needed work in winter, so he sent them to the woods to cut timber. Water-powered sawmills were built on the northwest Miramichi as a result.

The Repap ground wood mill had its

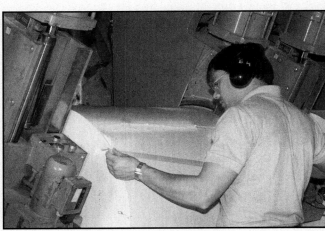

beginnings at the turn of the century as a sawmill owned by Thomas W. Flett. It was purchased by William M. Sullivan in 1914 and became a large-scale sawmill. The South Nelson Lumber Company bought the mill in 1937, and J. Leonard O'Brien bought the land and its proprietary rights in 1943. He added a Plaswood mill to manufacture four-by-eight-foot panels out of mixture of dust, shavings, and chips, held together by resins.

In 1957 the Plaswood mill and sawmills burned. Four years later O'Brien sold the property to a group of Italian investors who built the ground wood pulp mill and rebuilt the sawmill.

In 1966 Atlantic Sugar Refineries Company Ltd. of Saint John decided to diversify. It bought the mill, which became known as Acadia Pulp and Paper Limited. The mill gained a reputation as one of the world's largest ground woodpulp producers and brought much needed employment to the Miramichi region. In 1974 Petty bought the mill and made some major changes in order to keep the mill competitive in the world market.

The Repap kraft mill also began as a sawmill built by Edward Sinclair in the early 1860s. It was owned briefly by John McKane in the early part of this century, but in 1909 Sinclair's sons William and Hubert bought it and ran it until 1921, when it ceased operations.

Fraser Companies bought the mill and its land in 1924 and operated it on and off well into the 1940s. In 1949 Fraser Companies announced it would build a new sulphate pulp mill on the site, finally bringing a market to the lumbermen and pulp makers of the region, who

had been denied such a facility for more than 25 years.

In 1970 Fraser Companies sold the kraft mill to Boise Cascade Canada Ltd. in partnership with several European owners. The mill operated under the name Miramichi Timber Resources Ltd. until 1978, when Boise Cascade Canada Ltd. became sole owner. The name was changed briefly to Ontario-Minnesota Pulp and Paper Company, but was changed again in 1979 to Boise Cascade Canada Ltd., Newcastle Division.

Petty bought the mill in May 1985. When he decided to invest in the Miramichi region it was not solely because there was money to be made from the natural resources; it was because he saw people willing and able to do the work. No one in the area had any papermaking experience before the paper machine was built, but they were willing to learn, and they did learn. To Petty the resource is nothing without the people, and the people of the Miramichi are a unique people with a lifestyle and attitude he respects.

Repap has brought an economic prosperity and stability to the region that it has never known before. It lets the people of the Miramichi enjoy their way of life to the fullest. Petty's plans for the area are not yet complete, but certainly Repap is on the Miramichi River to stay, and the community appears glad of it. November 19, 1988, was George Petty Appreciation Day in Newcastle. He and his family were wined, dined, and entertained. It was the community's way of demonstrating how much he is appreciated—every day of the year.

Today's tools of the trade are far different from those a century ago. Here employees operate state-of-the-art equipment that produces lightweight, coated paper for the advertising sector.

METRO FUEL CO. LTD.

Service is the theme of Metro Fuel Co. Ltd.

Alonzo Landry owned three lobster fishing boats by the time he was 30 years old. In the village of Robichaud, New Brunswick, there were no gasoline pumps at the docks, so Landry and the other fishermen carried gasoline in five-gallon cans. Although this was the custom it did not seem to him very practical, so Landry bought a truck and out-fitted it with a 200-gallon skid tank. This made a lot more sense to him and apparently to his fellow fishermen, too. It was not long before he was fuelling their boats as well.

When the fishing season ended, Landry decided he would begin hauling his own stove oil

Metro Fuel Co. Ltd., and he took that name for his burgeoning organization.

By the early 1980s Metro Fuel had expanded from a 10-million-litre per year operation to a

Metro Fuel Co. Ltd.'s head office employees.

from Moncton. His friends came to him and asked him to haul their stove oil, too.

That was in 1956, and before he knew it, Alonzo Landry was not only a lobster fisherman but in the oil and gasoline trucking business as well. In 1960 his business was incorporated under the name of Landry Fuel Ltd., handling domestic heating oils and gasoline in the Shediac to Cap-Pele area.

He began to develop gasoline outlets and industries related to farming, lumbering, trucking, and fishing. In 1968 he acquired a heating-oil business operating under the name

100-million-litre per year industry. In 1986 Metro became affiliated with Imperial Oil Ltd., providing Metro with security of supply and capital to maintain existing operations and expand into the marketplace beyond New Brunswick into Nova Scotia and Quebec.

Victor Landry, a Moncton/Shediac-area native with a background of more than 20 years in the petroleum industry and marketing, is the current president.

The company realized that it had to "grow or die" and began a carefully orchestrated growth move with Metro's capable team. Its major

Maintaining tradition is important to Metro Fuel. The company began by supplying fuel to fishing boats.

market in the past was in the French-speaking areas of New Brunswick, but Metro is rapidly moving into a wider marketplace. "We are not only a complete Atlantic company, but a bilingual one as well," Landry says.

"We stress service, in fact we have practically no self-service outlets," he says. "We can compete with the big names in the industry by having easy-to-see locations and competitive prices, but we believe we can beat them on service. Our philosophy is that if a motorist gets good, friendly service and his windshield cleaned, chances are he or she will go back to that outlet."

The philosophy is obviously succeeding. In 1988 Metro had sales in excess of $30 million per year and a network of 100 automotive outlets throughout New Brunswick, Nova Scotia, and Quebec—including eight wharf facilities in the Northumberland Strait and Miramichi areas, providing full boat service. "We will never forget out roots," states Landry.

In addition to fuels, the firm sells petroleum products to homes and businesses. Metro Fuel Co. Ltd., with head offices in Dieppe, has 40 employees and 300 associates and their employees.

The head office of Metro Fuel Co. Ltd. in Dieppe, New Brunswick.

COADY-AC ENTERPRISES LTD.

Dave Coady got hooked on the hospitality industry at an early age when, as a teenager of 15 on Prince Edward Island, he helped a neighbor with a commercial barbecuing business.

"This neighbor organized a barbecuing catering business. We set up massive barbecues in portable pits that could barbecue as many as 480 chicken halves or steaks at a time. I just loved doing it and may just get into it again," says Coady.

All Ponderosa Restaurants in Atlantic Canada are getting new facelifts under the guidance of owner Dave Coady.

work. My family backed me 100 percent, and on May 2, 1986, Coady-AC Enterprises Ltd. (it's a play on the historic Codiac Indian name after which the Peticodiac River is named) became the owner of the Atlantic Canada Ponderosa restaurants."

Since then Coady has fine-honed the management of the franchises and begun remodelling. He originated an education and training program for the staff, stressing management,

He actually started as a bus boy at Gentleman Jim's in Charlottetown, Prince Edward Island, and worked his way up to management by the time he was 19. "Then I joined the Army. Three years later the owner of Gentleman Jim's asked me if I would manage a restaurant and night club here in Moncton for him, and I jumped at the chance. I managed the Railhead Cabaret and Lounge for several years before joining Dexleigh Inc., owner of the Ponderosa Restaurants franchise business, in 1979."

Coady was offered the position of vice-president/operations for Canada, based in Toronto, but refused to leave Atlantic Canada. Shortly thereafter General Mills of the United States purchased 36 of the Ponderosa Restaurants in Ontario and Quebec. It was at this time Coady was offered the opportunity to buy the Atlantic Provinces franchise from Dexleigh Inc.

"When you are 35 years old, and everything you have done has been in the restaurant business, you have the confidence you need to take on something like that. You know that you have skills—you can sell to someone else if it doesn't

quality of product, and cleanliness. One of his first moves was to begin buying Maritime products, including local beef. "It's Maritime people who support us so we should buy everything here we can—and we actually save money and get better service.

"We also made a major shift in the menu, adding items such as halibut steak, chicken breasts, and an enlarged salad bar. We added soup to the salad bar recently, and we're waiting to see how people like it."

In 1989 Coady spent a quarter-million dollars for renovations to the Moncton Ponderosa, putting in oak, brass, smoked glass, bright colors, and carpets in order to make it more upscale, brighter, and more modern than the original ranch-style Ponderosa. Saint John is next, and two more Ponderosas will be added to the chain, one in Halifax and a second in St. John's, Newfoundland. Other Ponderosas are located in Fredericton, New Brunswick, and Bedford and Truro, Nova Scotia.

"The restaurant business: You either love it or hate it with its constant changes and its long hours," says Coady. "I happen to love it."

G.M. ARMOUR & SON LTD.

Although incorporated in 1966, the G.M. Armour & Son Ltd. trucking business really began with a 1936 Ford truck.

Gordon Armour kept animals on his farm in Taylor Village, near Moncton, in the 1930s. He also owned a hay press, and, with the purchase of a 1936 Ford, he began travelling from farm to farm, pressing hay and transporting it to lumber camps or Moncton warehouses and then further afield to Nova Scotia. His instincts told him he should have a load going both ways so he returned with apples, soap, and chocolates to fill his truck space.

When the hay business dwindled in direct ratio with the increase of horsepower in trucks and cars in the 1950s, Gordon Armour bought a flatbottom truck and began trucking Christmas trees into the United States and transporting gravel in warm weather.

A 1955 contract to deliver Kraft Food products throughout New Brunswick was a big step up, and Armour's reputation as a reliable carrier grew. With his wife, Iris, as office help and dispatcher, Armour was still operating from his Taylor Village farm where his fleet was maintained by a neighbor, Fred Landry, who still works in the Armour maintenance garage.

Gordon's son, Wesley, exposed throughout his growing years to his father's trucks and philosophy, naturally turned to trucking, but Armour insisted his son continue his education with a two-year business administration course at the New Brunswick Institute of Technology in Saint John. He then joined his father as an employee in 1966 at the firm's new location in Dieppe.

The 1960s were a difficult time both for G.M. Armour & Son Ltd. and the trucking industry in the Maritimes. At his father's request Wesley climbed out of the cab of a truck and into the president's chair, at least symbolically, but in actuality he had exchanged the responsibility of a driver for that of a manager. After working all day he would spend evenings loading trucks, then making up the bills, falling asleep at his desk until the next driver woke him up to make up another bill.

"Finally our accounts began to balance, and we began to grow," says Wesley. "But we never would have made it without a dedicated staff.

Some of them are still working for us today."

In 1971 Armour moved to a three-acre lot in Moncton Industrial Development, where offices, a connecting warehouse, and garage were built. Contract hauling increased and so did specialized hauling. Facilities have been expanded on seven occasions, with today's operation occupying 18 acres.

"Last year (1989) was the greatest in our history," says Wesley Armour, past president of the Canadian Trucking Association. The company's success is shared with his 650 employees through numerous pension, health, and savings benefits, including a deferred profit-sharing plan.

Armour Transportation Systems now operates more than 950 tractors, trailers, and other vehicles, and has terminals in 16 Maritime locations.

This 1954 GMC was the type of truck driven by Gordon Armour and was one of the first trucks owned by G.M. Armour & Son Ltd. Its new value would be approximately $3,200 and it could gross weight up to 12,000 pounds.

Today the company employs tractor-trailer units such as this 1989 GMC Volvo hauling a 48-foot 1989 Roussy Trailer. This rig's approximate value is $150,000 and it can gross weight up to 112,000 pounds.

CIL INC. DALHOUSIE WORKS

New Brunswick premier Louis J. Robichaud closed the switch to symbolize the start up of the Canadian Industries Limited chlorine and caustic soda plant in Dalhousie, New Brunswick, in 1963.

Operators-to-be receive on-the-job training from production superintendent R.M. Burrell, (pointing) at the CIL Dalhousie Works in 1963.

CIL Inc. Dalhousie Works in Dalhousie, New Brunswick, is a far cry from the Hamilton Powder Company, manufacturer of the famous black powder explosive of the nineteenth century. But the Hamilton Powder Company was destined to become CIL Inc. and parent of the Dalhousie Works.

Throughout its history of new directions and diversification, CIL developments have ranged from explosives and ammunition to nylon, terylene polyester, coated fabrics for the automobile industry, paints and plastics, and the production of chemicals for the mining, metal refining, agriculture, and forest industries. It is the latter industry, forestry, in which the New Brunswick plant plays a major role.

Built in 1963, the Dalhousie Works operates a chloralkali plant that annually produces 33,000 tons of caustic soda, 30,000 tons of chlorine, and 1,000 tons of hydrochloric acid, primarily supplying the pulp and paper industry of the province.

"As long as there is a need for white paper there will be a need for our product," says John W.D. Johnson, assistant works manager. Johnson says CIL Dalhousie is proud of its long safety record and its continually increasing role in environmental protection in Atlantic Canada. The company's 17-member emergency response team handles chemical emergencies and acts as the response centre for the Maritime Provinces and the Gaspe Peninsula for the transport emergency assistance plan in the case of chemical emergency. The firm is also a member of the Chlorine Institute, responsible for answering chlorine emergencies in New Brunswick, the Gaspe, and Newfoundland.

The firm's only major accident may have been the plant's salvation. Beginning in the 1970s Dalhousie felt constantly threatened with possible closure, and the employees were concerned for their future.

In 1983 a hydrogen explosion destroyed a space 75 feet wide by 150 feet in length containing 38 cells, each of which contained 120 anodes that would have to be individually removed and examined before the cells could be reactivated. "It was a half-million-dollar mess," Johnson says.

The prognosis was not good. There were murmurs that the company would not think it worthwhile to repair the damage.

By some miracle the explosion occurred during a shift change. Only one man was walking through the area at the time, but none of the huge chunks of pipe or the minute splinters of plastic touched him.

The men at the plant decided to begin the cleanup on their own. Head office had predicted that restoration would take a minimum of six weeks. But in 12 days CIL Dalhousie was back in operation.

"We have good talent here," says Johnson. "They prove it over and over again, whether it is on the plant floor or in creating new equipment for the emergency team. We're a successful operation because of them."

CIL Inc. Dalhousie Works started out with 41 employees; today it has 55 full-time workers, and, according to Johnson, the majority of the increase in staff is due to environmental considerations taken by the company.

MICHELIN TIRES (CANADA) LTD.

Michelin has been making quality tires since it was founded in France by Edouard and André Michelin. Still managed by the same family today, the company has emerged from humble beginnings with 11 workers in 1889 to become an international corporation employing more than 120,000 people at 59 facilities in Europe, Africa, Asia, and North and South America.

Michelin came to Atlantic Canada in 1969. The first plant, erected by the firm in the rolling, rural countryside at Granton in Pictou County, produced its first tire in October 1971. A second facility, overlooking the LaHave River at Bridgewater in Lunenburg County, manufactures tires and fabricated wire for the steel-belted radial tires. Eleven years later, at the third plant at Waterville, the first off-road heavy-duty tire rolled off the line in March 1982.

In the summer of 1988 Michelin announced a major expansion of its Nova Scotia operations, representing an investment of nearly a half-billion dollars in new equipment and modernization.

Even before the recent expansion Michelin had become the largest private employer in the province of Nova Scotia. People from throughout the Atlantic region make up Michelin's complement of 4,000-plus employees in the three plants. By providing above-average wages, by maintaining a no-layoff policy for its work force, and by its commitment to promoting people from within the organization, Michelin has developed a solid core of loyal, committed employees, many of whom have remained with the firm since it came to the province.

Recognizing that the well-being of its employees is an important element to remain a quality leader in a highly competitive market, Michelin Tires (Canada) Ltd. has introduced a wide array of programs to promote health and safety for employees and their families. The range of topics, including drug and alcohol abuse, CPR courses, first-aid training, and on-the-job safety, are designed to provide the best in occupational health and safety training and awareness.

Michelin has a long list of notable achievements in the tire industry. It was responsible for the first heavy-duty truck tire to combine rubber with steel wire, the first radial tire, and the first radial tire for jet airplanes.

While maintaining its competitive position as one of the largest tire manufacturers in the world, Michelin is also deeply involved in service to the communities where its plants are located. In Nova Scotia, Michelin is the sole sponsor of the Special Olympics Summer Games. The company provides the financial support, graphics, banners, posters, and programmes. The symbolic torch run, involving hundreds of employee volunteers, from the three Michelin plants to the games site in Halifax provides a dramatic example of the firm's commitment to service in the community.

Michelin came to Atlantic Canada in 1969 and produced its first tire at the Granton plant in Pictou County in 1971.

Michelin founders Edouard and André Michelin.

VILLE DE DIEPPE

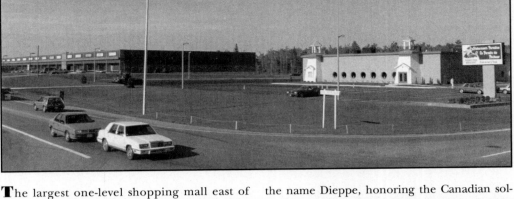

More than 1,400 people work at Dieppe's 450-acre industrial park near the Moncton airport.

The largest one-level shopping mall east of Montreal is not in Atlantic Canada's largest city. In fact it isn't in a city at all; it is in Ville de Dieppe, New Brunswick. Given that, one might be forgiven in believing this large shopping centre located in a small New Brunswick town is the only claim to fame that small town enjoys. The truth of the matter is that the Town of Dieppe has just about everything imaginable and probably a few things never even dreamed of—including a Sultan's tent.

The town's boundary starts at the eastern border of Moncton. Its rich history begins with Acadian settlers who came from Annapolis Royal in 1732 to farm the rich marshes. The population of 11,000 people is still 80 percent Francophone; the town boasts the only French-speaking high school in the region. It also has a French campus on the New Brunswick Community College campus.

Of the town's five elementary schools, one is English speaking; the other four are French. A new French junior high school is on the drawing board, and town officials are hoping the community will become involved in the project and convince the school board to incorporate a swimming pool in the plans. A municipal pool is one of the few recreation facilities the town does not have.

Originally known as French Village, the community was named Léger Corner in 1910. In 1946 it was incorporated as a village and adopted

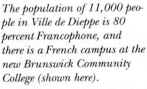

The population of 11,000 people in Ville de Dieppe is 80 percent Francophone, and there is a French campus at the new Brunswick Community College (shown here).

the name Dieppe, honoring the Canadian soldiers who fought and died in the Dieppe raid of World War II. In 1948 the village purchased 200 wartime houses in nearby Lakeburn and annexed that area into the village.

On January 1, 1952, Dieppe was incorporated as a town, and in 1973 the incorporated villages of St. Anselme and Chartersville and the local service district of Fox Creek-Dover were amalgamated. The town's population almost doubled, going from 4,500 to 7,500 people.

Development was well under way in the community, when, in 1971, Dieppe's industrial park was started on a 450-acre site near the Moncton airport, which is within Dieppe's boundary. Today more than 1,400 people work in the industrial park, and the town owns another 1,000 acres ready for development.

Certainly the proximity of the airport, which handles more air cargo tonnage than the combined traffic of all Maritime airports, has added to the success of the industrial park. The innovative pilot novel Incubator Mall has also been a major contributing factor. Entrepreneurs can rent space at just $4.50 per square foot (1989) for two years. This period of low overhead gives a fledgling business an opportunity to develop a market. Over the years plumbers, land surveyors, construction contractors, and communication businesses, to name a few, have taken advantage of the programme. At the end of the two-year period, the successful companies are

expected to be able to operate on their own and encouraged to locate in the Dieppe Industrial Park.

Dieppe's industrial sector accounts for 20 percent of the land in the town. Another 15 percent is commercial.

While crossing the border from Moncton to Dieppe, the intensity and prosperity of the town's commercial area is immediately apparent. The star of the show is Champlain Place Mall. It all began with a Sears department store in 1970. The mall was constructed and attached in 1975 and became a mecca for enthusiastic shoppers from all over New Brunswick, Prince Edward Island, and parts of Nova Scotia. Around the mall, fast-food chains, retail stores, hotels, restaurants, and car dealerships mushroomed.

Champlain Place Mall expanded in 1987 and now boasts 153 stores and services attracting more than 5 million shoppers every year. That number will grow with the addition of the Crystal Palace that opened in February 1990. A scaled-down version of the West Edmonton Mall, the Crystal Palace is an indoor amusement park covered by a spectacular glass dome. It will turn the area into a tourist attraction as well as a shopping centre.

This is also home to the Sultan's Tent, the Desert Island, and the Rock-and-Roll Room—just three of the 12 Fantasy Suites to be found in the Crystal Palace Hotel, a reasonably priced, 120-room hotel with a swimming pool.

Four Cineplex Odeon Cinemas, the Crystal Palace restaurants and Food Fair, a championship 18-hole mini golf course, a sports hall of fame, and a multilevel children's playground add hours of fun to any visit. A 3,500-square-foot community centre provides an elegant venue for special events. Across the street from the Crystal Palace Hotel, a 91-room hotel opened in 1986 with convention facilities, licensed dining, and swimming pool.

Dieppe's diverse and successful industrial and commercial sectors give the town a substantial tax base. This in turn keeps the tax rate very attractive for further industrial, commercial, and residential development.

The quality of life in Dieppe is exemplified by the elegant homes in its many charming neighborhoods. An auditorium, 2 arenas, soccer fields, community centres, day-care centres, municipal parks, 3 gymnasiums, 4 licensed kindergartens, 5 tennis courts, 9 ball fields, and 22 playgrounds, and one harness racing track ensure that the recreational needs of Dieppe residents are well met.

A 180-acre municipal park is in the development stage, and plans call for a walking/cycling corridor to connect Champlain Place to the new park, touching schools, residential areas, and other parks along the way.

The careful zoning of the town keeps the sectors operating in harmony. The town has already zoned the land around the airport as industrial so residential development will not occur in that area and lead to conflict.

Dieppe has the right mix of industrial, commercial, various single residential options, as well as the land and population base to seek incorporation as a city. Some local politicians have been promoting that option.

There are those who fear incorporation of Dieppe as a city might lead to amalgamation and the formation of a greater Moncton area, and if there is one thing Dieppe holds more dear than anything else it is its identity. Ville de Dieppe is a community with a rich past, an exciting present, and a promising future. It has small-town flavor, big-city sparkle, and a generous measure of *joie de vivre.*

NEWFOUNDLAND TELEPHONE COMPANY LIMITED

On March 20, 1878, some four years after Alexander Graham Bell's invention of the telephone, history was made in Newfoundland. That was the date of the first telephone call on the island, connecting the households of Postmaster General John Delaney and meteorologist John Higgins. However, it was not the weather that was the subject of this historic call—it was a simple rendition of the song "Annie Laurie." The *Royal Gazette* of the day reported: "'Annie Laurie,' plain as if the voice were at the ear, came borne along, but in a wee, small voice, silvery and sweet, conveying the idea of infinite distance."

That early telephone call was largely a homemade affair. Delaney had made his telephone by following instructions and illustrations in an edition of *Scientific American* magazine. At that time the telephone consisted of three boxes, mounted one above the other on a board

The equipment used by old-time telephone operators was onerous and weighty. The heavy mouthpiece had to be kept on throughout the shift. At work in Harbour Grace in September 1955 were Rita Cook (left) and Mrs. F. Morris.

attached to the wall. The uppermost box contained the magneto generator, which was cranked to signal the operator; the middle box contained the mouthpiece; and the lowest box housed the battery and transmitter.

By 1885 a proper telephone system was in place in St. John's. It was the Anglo-American Telegraph Company that introduced the first telephone system in the city. In 1919 J.J. Murphy, who had been a member of the House of Assembly, took over this system and incorporated the Avalon Telephone Company, which remained a family business until 1954, when the controlling interest was sold to a group of local and Montreal business people. In 1962 Bell Canada bought out the firm, and in 1970 the organization took on its present name, Newfoundland Telephone Company.

During the corporate change-overs, telephone service had made huge strides in Newfoundland. In 1921 the first long-distance line was installed between St. John's and Carbonear, Conception Bay. In 1939 the first off-the-island call was made to Montreal (considered an overseas call until Confederation with Canada in 1949). The first voice communication across the island was made in 1949, made possible by installation of a system at Port aux Basques on the western tip of the island.

Avalon Telephone expanded rapidly through the years as the instrument gained in popularity. World War II, in particular, was a period of great growth as the telephone became important as a social instrument. Young women wanting to contact the American servicemen stationed at the nearby bases would persuade their parents to have telephones installed.

In 1919 there were only 800 telephones in Newfoundland, but by 1950, 19,000 telephones were in service. Today there are more than 330,000 throughout the province.

Avalon Telephone's (and later Newfoundland Telephone's) greatest expansion came through the purchase of other phone systems on the island and in Labrador. In 1948 the firm purchased the Corner Brook telephone system from Bowaters—the pulp and paper company—and a few years later made a similar move, buying out the telephone system of the Anglo-Newfoundland Development Corporation in Grand Falls. In 1974 the Labrador telephone service was purchased from Bell Canada, and in 1979 the firm took over the Labrador City telephone system from the Iron Ore Company of Canada. The provincial network was completed in 1988, when the firm acquired Terra Nova Telecommunications.

As the telephone company expanded, a new building became necessary, and in 1980 the firm moved from its original headquarters at 343 Duckworth Street, St. John's, into the Fort William Building in the east end of the city. The deck off the cafeteria in the Fort William Building overlooks the commercial centre and downtown area of the city. From other points

Sleet storms, such as the March 1, 1958, and the April 13, 1984, storms, cause broken poles, damaged cables, and many weeks of repair and restoration efforts.

there are views of the harbor and the Narrows, Quidi Vidi Lake, and, of course, Signal Hill, where Guglielmo Marconi received the first transatlantic wireless signal in 1901.

"Communcations in a province like this is extremely important," says Newfoundland Telephone's corporate secretary, J.M. O'Keefe. "For a long time the only access to many places in the island was by boat. The development of telecommunications in this province has been hampered by geogaphy. What's simple now with a truck must have been horrendous with boats and horses and sleighs."

With all the advanced technology, it is still possible for nature to wreak havoc with the most sophisticated of systems. Newfoundland can still be swept by major sleet storms in March and April. These storms present challenges to technicians who work around the clock to restore service. "They are the unsung heroes of the company," O'Keefe says, adding that devastation can take days of steady work to repair. On March 1, 1958, for example, a savage sleet storm hit the island, and it took two weeks to repair the damage. Again in 1984 a similar sleet storm threw the system into disrepair until the firm's able corps of repair people restored service.

Newfoundland Telephone Company Limited is heavily involved in community projects in areas such as the arts, culture, recreation, and charitable organizations. The directors of the firm are high-profile members of the corporate community. Many of them have had family connections with earlier boards. The current directors are A.A. Brait, J.L. Carson, A.E. Hickman, H.L. Lake, A.R. Lundrigan, D.R. Newman, F.J. O'Leary, P.N. Outerbridge, and C.W.M. Scott. The officers are A.A. Brait, chairman; V.G. Withers, president and chief executive officer; G.H. Erl, vice-president/finance; R.F. Davis, vice-president/marketing and planning; K.A.A. Marshall, senior vice-president/corporate; R.A. Newell, vice-president/administration; F.F. Fagan, vice-president/operations and engineering; W.H. Holden, treasurer; W.G. Hudson, comptroller; and J.M. O'Keefe, corporate secretary.

THE HALIFAX HERALD LIMITED

ABOVE: A line drawing of the Herald building, located at 1650 Argyle Street in Halifax.

RIGHT:Three generations of the Dennis family, dating back to 1907, have been publishers of The Chronicle-Herald *and* The Mail-Star, *the two highest circulation newspapers in Atlantic Canada.*

BELOW: Graham W. Dennis, publisher of The Chronicle-Herald *and* The Mail-Star.

A fresh snowfall set the mood for the launch of the *Morning Herald* on January 14, 1875. The first issue, with 800 copies, was published on Bedford Row and founded on the "continuance of the British connection" and the Conservative Party.

Among the initial 88 shareholders was William Dennis, an 18-year-old English immigrant and junior reporter for the paper. Dennis' mentor was *Herald* editor John James Stewart, who bought all the shares in 1883. Fourteen years later Stewart in turn sold 50 percent of his holdings to his protege. Dennis, described as an abstainer and hard worker, obtained control of the company in 1907. He was the first member of the Dennis family to become publisher and began the chain of succession that still continues today. William Dennis was appointed to the Canadian Senate five years later.

When the senator died in 1920, the majority interest passed to nephew William Henry Dennis, who had been hired in 1900 and worked on the paper in a wide range of jobs. William Henry Dennis also went on to serve as a senator. When he died in 1954, company control went to his son, Graham William Dennis, current publisher and chief executive officer of The Halifax Herald Limited.

The *Herald* and its sister evening publication, the *Mail* (established in October 1879), for decades waged a vigorous struggle with other Halifax dailies, chiefly the *Chronicle* and its evening companion, the *Star*. However, as 1948 drew to a close, the second Senator Dennis purchased his rivals from their owner, F.B. McCurdy, and on New Year's Day, 1949, produced the first *Chronicle-Herald*, the offspring of the once-hot, impulsive *Herald* and the more measured *Chronicle*. The first *Mail-Star* appeared two days later.

One newspaper historian noted that "between them they succeeded in the promotion of a hearty, if often heated, interest in public affairs, and in the dissemination of widely, and wildly, opposing points of view."

Dennis' achievement was the first newspaper company in Atlantic Canada to produce and sell

more than 100,000 copies per day. Today *The Chronicle-Herald's* circulation is the highest in the region; *The Mail-Star's* is in second place. Their combined circulation is about 150,000.

Newspaper competition during the 1980s with local and national dailies has spurred contemporary changes at The Halifax Herald Limited in content, layout, and editorial tone. The publisher introduced a variety of regular special sections for readers. Among the weekend supplements is the "Novascotian," named after the paper once owned by press-freedom champion Joseph Howe. Editorial staff increased by 60 percent since the 1960s, while newsroom and press computerization halved the number of required printing employees.

The Halifax Herald Limited has taken an active role in supporting community needs, starting with the first members of the Dennis family. Some, as a matter of policy, have never become part of the public record. Well-known endeavors, however, include the Rainbow Haven children's summer camp, the Goodfellows Club for the less fortunate at Christmas, and the Dalhousie University Medical Research Fund.

ISLAND CABLEVISION LTD.

In the 15 years since its founding in 1975, Island Cablevision Ltd. of Charlottetown, Prince Edward Island, has achieved both growth of service to its customers and awards for its community programming.

Founded by Harry MacLauchlan, Dr. Lorne Bonnell, Howard Douglas, and Simon Compton, Island Cablevision Ltd. was granted a licence from the Canadian Radio and Television Commission (CRTC) in 1975. They cleared an area in the woods and erected a two-storey, 40-by 100-foot building and constructed a cable television system of 270 megahertz (MHz) to carry 30 television channels. The company now serves 16,000 households.

The route to providing wide-ranging service to the island was not without its obstacles. A major problem arose in 1984, when the firm received a licence from the CRTC to put cable service into communities with 100 homes or more.

to the building have resulted in an enlarged studio area, a new control room, and a new staff lunchroom.

Among the first employees brought on by Island Cablevision after its founding were community program director Wendell P. Ellis and technical director Bruce MacLean, who won the Omar Gerard Award for innovation in programming at the National Cable Television Association Convention in 1982.

The award was for a documentary on the abilities of disabled people. Similarly Island Cablevision set a world record for its non-stop, live television 244-hour fund-raising endeavor for the mentally handicapped people of Prince Edward Island. In all, more than $250,000 has been raised by the community channel for island charities.

Island Cablevision provides 20 hours per week of community programming involving

Island Cablevision Ltd. brought its wide-ranging service to Charlottetown, Prince Edward Island, and the surrounding area in 1975. Here the current staff was coaxed outdoors in the snow to pose for the annual Christmas card.

The utilities on the island demanded an increase on their pole rates, raising them from $6 to $9.40.

The nine-year-old company could not get an agreement for a lesser rate and was forced to return its licence to the CRTC while taking the matter to the Public Utilities Commission. However, in 1986, the situation was resolved, and Island Cablevision was granted a new licence for service to the smaller communities, 70 percent of whose residents are now connected to the system.

It was in 1986, too, that Island Cablevision decided the time had come to improve its plant, making the system capable of providing 60 channels (450 MHz). More recent renovations

sports, public affairs, the arts, and religion, as well as ongoing documentary coverage of special groups and interests.

Secretary/treasurer and general manager Simon Compton and plant manager Dale Murphy came to Prince Edward Island from Toronto in 1975. Compton says he is surprised at the amount of community involvement in a small city and has enthusiastically served as a member of numerous service, church, and business organizations. On a professional level Compton has served on the board of directors of the Canadian Cable Television Association and as vice-chairman representing Atlantic Canada for that association.

PATRONS

The following individuals, companies, and organizations have made a valuable commitment to the quality of this publication. Windsor Publications and the Atlantic Provinces Chamber of Commerce gratefully acknowledge their participation in *Atlantic Canada: At the Dawn of a New Nation.*

ADI Limited*
AE Services Ltd. Architects/
     Engineers*
Air Nova*
Allsco Building Supplies Ltd.*
Anthony Insurance Incorporated*
G.M. Armour & Son Ltd.*
Atlantic Industries Limited*
Atlantic Wholesalers Ltd.*
G.E. Barbour Inc.*
Bell Enterprises Ltd.
Ben's Ltd.*
Blunden Construction Limited*
Canadian National Railways*
Casino Taxi Ltd.*
Cherubini Metal Works Ltd.*
CIL Inc. Dalhousie Works*
Clark, Drummie & Company*
Coady-AC Enterprises Ltd.*
Connors Bros., Limited*
Dartmouth Cable TV Limited*
Dow Chemical Canada Inc.*
Farmers Co-operative Dairy
     Limited*

The Federal Business Development
     Bank*
Fundy Cable Ltd./Ltée*
The Halifax Herald Limited*
Hotel Newfoundland*
Hoyt's Moving and Storage Ltd.*
N.C. Hutton Ltd.*
Island Cablevision Ltd.*
Pat King Group Limited*
Lawton's Drug Stores Limited*
Lock-Wood Ltd.*
McInnes Cooper & Robertson*
M&M Manufacturing Limited
     Partnership*
Marine Atlantic Inc.*
Maritime Beverages Limited*
Memorial University of Newfound-
     land*
Metro Fuel Co. Ltd.*
Michelin Tires (Canada) Ltd.*
Miramichi Pulp & Paper Inc.*
MMH Prefab Ltd.*
Moosehead Breweries Limited*
NBTel*
Neill and Gunter Limited*
The New Brunswick Electric Power
     Commission*
Newfoundland and Labrador
     Credit Union*
Newfoundland Broadcasting Com-
     pany Limited*
Newfoundland Light & Power Co.
     Limited*
Newfoundland Telephone Com-

pany Limited*
Northumberland Co-Operative
     Ltd.*
N.S. Tractors & Equipment Ltd.*
Nuport Holdings Limited*
OCEANS Ltd.*
Port of Halifax*
Price Waterhouse*
Ramsen Engineering Associates
     Inc.*
Reinforced Plastic Systems Inc.*
Robinson-Blackmore Printing and
     Publishing Limited*
Royal Bank of Canada*
St. Anne-Nackawic Pulp Company
     Ltd.*
Sheraton Halifax*
Standard Paving Maritime
     Limited*
Stewart, McKelvey, Stirling, Scales*
Stora Forest Industries Limited*
Tractors & Equipment (1962)
     Ltd.*
Triangle Kitchen*
Ville de Dieppe*

*Partners in Progress of *Atlantic Canada: At the Dawn of a New Nation.* The histories of these companies and organizations appear in Chapter Five, beginning on page 175.

BIBLIOGRAPHY

CHAPTER 1: NEWFOUNDLAND

Alexander, David. *The Decay of Trade: An Economic History of the Newfoundland Saltfish Trade, 1935-1965.* St. John's: Institute of Social and Economic Research, Memorial University of Newfoundland, 1977.

The *Canadian Encyclopedia.*

Cell, Gillian. *English Enterprise in Newfoundland: 1577-1660.* Toronto: University Press, 1969.

————, ed. *Newfoundland Discovered: English Attempts at Colonization, 1610-1630.* London: The Hakluyt Society, 1982.

Chafe, Levi. *History of the Newfoundland Seal Fishery from the Earliest Available Records Down to and Including the Voyage of 1923.* 3rd ed. St. John's: Trade Printers and Publishers Limited, 1923.

Colonial Office General Correspondence. Series 194. Vol. 6. (CO 194: 6.)

Gunn, Gertrude. *The Political History of Newfoundland: 1832-1864.* Toronto: University Press, 1966.

Harris, Leslie. "The First Nine Years of Representative Government in Newfoundland." Unpublished M.A. Thesis, Memorial University of Newfoundland, 1959.

Head, C. Grant. *Eighteenth Century Newfoundland.* Toronto: McClelland and Stewart, 1976.

Inglis, Gordon. *More Than Just a Union: The Story of the NFFAWU.* St. John's: Jesperson Press, 1985.

Mannion, John J., ed. *The Peopling of Newfoundland: Essays in Historical Geography.* St. John's: Institute of Social and Economic Research, Memorial University of Newfoundland, 1977.

Matthews, Keith. "A History of the West of England-Newfoundland Fishery." Unpublished D. Phil. thesis, Oxford, 1968.

————. *Lectures on the History of Newfoundland: 1500-1830.* St. John's: Breakwater Books, 1988.

McDonald, Ian. *To Each His Own: William Coaker and the Fishermen's Protective Union in Newfoundland Politics, 1908-1925.* Edited by J.K. Hiller. St. John's: Institute of Social and Economic Research, Memorial University of Newfoundland, 1988.

Morison, Samuel E. *The Oxford History of the American People.* New York: Oxford University Press, 1965.

Neary, Peter. *Newfoundland in the North Atlantic World: 1929-1949.* Kingston: McGill-Queen's University Press, 1988.

————. *Politics in Newfoundland.* Toronto: University Press, 1971.

Pastore, Ralph T. "Fishermen, Furriers and Beothuks: The Economy of Extinction." *Man in the Northeast* No. 33, 1987.

Pope, Peter. "Clay Tobacco Pipes from Ferryland: Archaeological Analysis and Historical Interpretation." Unpublished Paper, Memorial University of Newfoundland, 1988.

Prowse, D.W. *A History of Newfoundland.* London: 1895. Mika Reprint, 1972.

Rowe, Frederick W. *Extinction: The Beothuks of Newfoundland.* Toronto: McGraw-Hill Ryerson, 1977.

————. *A History of Newfoundland and Labrador.* Toronto: McGraw-Hill Ryerson, 1980.

Ryan, Shannon. "Abstract of CO 194 Statistics." Unpublished Manuscript, Memorial University of Newfoundland, 1969.

————. *Fish out of Water: The Newfoundland Saltfish Trade, 1814-1914.* St. John's: Breakwater Books, 1986.

————. "Fishery to Colony: A Newfoundland Watershed, 1793-1815." *Acadiensis* Vol. XII, No. 2 (Spring 1983).

————. "The Newfoundland Cod Fishery in the Nineteenth Century." Unpublished M.A. Thesis, Memorial University of Newfoundland, 1972.

————, (assisted by Martha Drake). *Seals and Sealers: A Pictorial History of the Newfoundland Seal Fishery based on the Cater Andrews Collection.* St. John's: Breakwater Books, 1987.

Smallwood, Joseph R., ed. *Books of Newfoundland.* 6 vols. St. John's: Newfoundland Book Publishers, 1937-1975.

Story, G.M., ed. *Early European Settlement and Exploitation in Atlantic Canada: Selected Papers.* Memorial University of Newfoundland, 1982.

————, W.J. Kirwin, and J.D.A. Widdowson. *Dictionary of Newfoundland English.* Toronto: University Press, 1982.

Thompson, F.F. *The French Shore Problem in Newfoundland.* Toronto: University Press, 1961.

Tuck, James A. "Prehistoric Archaeology in Atlantic Canada." *Canadian Journal of Archaeology* No. 6, 1982.

Williams, Alan F. *Father Baudoin's War: D'Iberville's Campaigns in Acadia and Newfoundland, 1696-1697.* Edited by Alan Macpherson. Memorial University of Newfoundland, 1987.

CHAPTER 2: NOVA SCOTIA

Akins, Thomas Beamish. *History of Halifax City.* Belleville Ontario: Mika Publishing, 1973. (Original edition published Halifax: Nova Scotia Historical Society, 1895.)

Author, The. "Remarks on the Climate, Produce and Natural Advantages of Nova Scotia in a letter to the Right Hon. the Earl of Macclesfield." London: Printed for J. Debrett. n.d.

Bates, Jennifer L.E. *Gold in Nova Scotia*. Halifax: Department of Mines and Energy, 1987.

Blakeley, Phyllis R. *The Story of Nova Scotia*. Toronto: J.J. Dent & Sons (Canada) Limited, 1950.

Byers, R.B., ed. *Canadian Annual Review [1985] of Politics and Public Affairs*. Toronto: University of Toronto Press with support of York University, 1988.

Campbell, Duncan. *Nova Scotia in its Historical, Mercantile and Industrial Relations*. Montréal: James Lovell, 1873.

Clark, Andrew Hall. *Acadia—the Geography of Early Nova Scotia to 1760*. Madison, Wis.: The University of Wisconsin Press, 1968.

Dunphy, Clifford R. *The Geography of the Atlantic Provinces*. Toronto: W.J. Gage Ltd., 1961.

Elliott, Shirley B. *A History of Province House*. Halifax: Nova Scotia Government Publication, n.d.

Ferguson, Bruce, and William Pope. *Glimpses into Nova Scotia History*. Windsor, N.S.: Lancelot Press Ltd., 1974.

Gallant, Melvin, and Fernande Chouinard-Mclaughlin, Pierre Cormier, Rejean Ouellette, Jeannette Raiche. *Les Maritimes: trois provinces a decouvrir*. Moncton, N.B.: Les Editions d'Acadie, 1987.

Hamilton, William B. *The Nova Scotia Traveller, A Maritimer's Guide to His Home Province*. Toronto: Macmillan of Canada, A Division of Gage Publishing Limited, 1981.

Hill, Kay. *Joe Howe, the Man who was Nova Scotia*. Toronto: McClelland and Stewart, 1980.

Historic Nova Scotia. Halifax: Bureau of Information, Government of Nova Scotia, 1935.

Kerr, D.G.G. *An Historical Atlas of Canada*. Toronto: Thomas Nelson & Sons (Canada) Limited, 1959.

Lacey, Laurie. *Micmac Indian Medicine*. Antigonish: Formac Limited, 1977.

Mandale, Maurice. *Atlantic Canada Today*. Halifax: Formac Publishing Ltd., 1987.

Marsh, James H., Editor-in-Chief. *The Canadian Encyclopedia*. 4 vols. Edmonton: Hurtig Publishers, 1988.

Millward, Hugh A. *Regional Patterns of Ethnicity in Nova Scotia: A Geographical Study*. Halifax: International Education Centre, Saint Mary's University, 1981.

Moore, Christopher. "The Other Louisbourg: Trade and Merchant Enterprise in Ile Royale, 1713-1758." London, England *Social History* 12 (May 1979) 79-96.

Munroe, David, Alphonse-Marie Parent, Roger Guindon, and Bernard Poirier. *All Eyes Toward the Future*. Nova Scotia: Tribunal on Bilingual Higher Education in Nova Scotia.

Murdoch, Beamish. *A History of Nova Scotia or Acadie*. 3 vols. Halifax: Barnes, Printer and Publisher, 1867.

The Nova Scotia Legislature. Halifax: Nova Scotia Communications and Information Centre, 1979.

Parkman, Francis. *History of the Conspiracy of Pontiac*. 2 vols. 1851.

Payzant, Joan M. *Halifax: Cornerstone of Canada*. Burlington: Windsor Publications, Ltd., 1985.

Quinpool, John. (John Regan.) *First Things in Acadia, the Birthplace of a Continent*. Halifax: First Things Publishers Ltd., 1936.

Rawlyk, George A., and Ruth Hafter. *Acadian Education in Nova Scotia. An Historical Survey to 1965*. Ottawa: Information Canada, 1970.

Richardson, Jean M., and Diane J. Gregory. *Geology, Minerals and Mining in Nova Scotia*. Halifax: Nova Scotia Department of Mines, 1976.

Russell, Benjamin. *Nova Scotia Blue Book and Encyclopedia*. Toronto: Ryerson Press, 1932.

Whitehead, Ruth Holmes. *Elitekey: Micmac Material Culture from 1600 A.D. to the Present*. Halifax: The Nova Scotia Museum, 1980.

————, and Harold McGee. *The Micmac: How Their Ancestors Lived Five Hundred Years Ago*. Halifax: Nimbus, 1983.

Wilson, J. Donald, Robert M. Stamp, and Louis-Philippe Audet, eds. *Canadian Education: A History*. Scarborough: Prentice-Hall, 1970.

CHAPTER 3: NEW BRUNSWICK

Acheson, T.W. *Saint John: The Making of a Colonial Urban Community*. Toronto: University of Toronto Press, 1984.

Bailey, A.G. *The Conflict of European and Eastern Algonkian Cultures, 1504-1700: A Study in Canadian Civilization*. Toronto: University of Toronto Press, 1966.

Bell, D.G. *Early Loyalist Saint John: The Origins of New Brunswick Politics, 1783-1786*. Fredericton: New Ireland Press, 1983.

Condon, Ann Gorman. *The Envy of the American States: The Loyalist Dream for New Brunswick*. Fredericton: New Ireland Press, 1984.

Daigle, J., ed. *The Acadians of the Maritimes*. Moncton: Centre des études acadiennes, 1982.

Doyle, Arthur. *Front Benches and Backrooms*. Omega Publications, 1976.

Grant, B.J. *When Rum Was King. The Story of the Prohibition Era in New Brunswick.* Fredericton: Fiddlehead, 1984.

Hannay, James. *History of New Brunswick.* 2 vols. Saint John, 1909.

MacNutt, W.S. *New Brunswick: A History 1784-1867.* Toronto: MacMillan, 1963.

―――. *The Atlantic Provinces: The Emergence of Colonial Society, 1712-1857.* Toronto: McClelland and Stewart, 1965.

Raymond, W.O. *The River Saint John.* Saint John: John Bowes, 1910.

Reid, John. *Acadia, Maine and New Scotland: Marginal Colonies in the Seventeenth Century.* Toronto: University of Toronto Press, 1981.

Stanley, Della Margaret M. *Louis Robichaud: A Decade of Power.* Halifax: Nimbus Printing, 1984.

Starr, Richard. *Richard Hatfield: The Seventeen Year Saga.* Halifax: Formac, 1987.

Wright, E.C. *The Loyalists of New Brunswick.* Fredericton: Brunswick Press, 1955.

Wynn, Graeme. *Timber Colony: A Historical Geography of Early Nineteenth Century New Brunswick.* Toronto: UTP, 1981.

CHAPTER 4:
PRINCE EDWARD ISLAND

Bagster, C. Birch. *The Progress and Prospects of Prince Edward Island.* Charlottetown, 1861.

Beck, Boyde. "Hard To Get: Prince Edward Island and Confederation." *Horizon Canada* Vol. 5, No. 59.

―――. "The Image of Prince Edward Island in Some Descriptive Accounts, 1750-1860." Master's Thesis, Queen's University, 1984.

Bolger, F.W.P., ed. *Canada's Smallest Province.* Charlottetown: Prince Edward Island 1973 Centennial Commission, 1973.

―――. *Prince Edward Island and Confederation.* Toronto: University of Toronto Press, 1960.

Bremner, Ben. *An Island Scrapbook.* Charlottetown: Irwin Printing Co. Ltd., 1932.

Bumstead, J.M. *Land, Settlement and Politics on Eighteenth Century Prince Edward Island.* Kingston and Montréal: McGill-Queen's Press, 1987.

―――. *People of the Clearance.* Winnipeg and Edinburgh: University of Manitoba and University of Edinburgh, 1982.

Clark, Andrew Hill. *Three Centuries and the Island: A Historiographical Geography of Settlement and Agriculture on Prince Edward Island.* Toronto: University of Toronto Press, 1959.

Crosskill, W.H. *Prince Edward Island: Garden Province of Canada, With Information for Tourists.* Charlottetown, 1899.

The Earl of Selkirk. *The Present State of the Highlands of Scotland.* London, 1805.

The European Magazine. Autumn, 1819.

Fischer, Lewis R. "The Shipping History of Nineteenth Century Prince Edward Island." *The Island Magazine* No. 4 (Spring-Summer 1978).

Greenhill, Basil, and Ann Giffard. *Westcountrymen on Prince Edward's Isle: A Fragment of the Great Migration.* Toronto: University of Toronto Press, 1967.

Harvey, D.C. *The French Regime on Prince Edward Island.* New Haven: Yale University Press, 1926.

―――. *Journeys to the Island of St. John.* New Haven: Yale University Press, 1926.

―――. "Early Settlement on Prince Edward Island." *Dalhousie Review* 1931-1932.

Keenlyside, David L. "In Search of the Island's First People." *The Island Magazine* No. 13 (Spring-Summer 1983).

MacDonald, G. Edward. "External Factors and the Evolution of an Island Identity." Master's Thesis, Queen's University, 1980.

Stewart, John. *An Account of Prince Edward Island.* London, 1806.

A True Guide to Prince Edward Island. Liverpool, 1818.

"Understanding the Past." Archaeology Branch, Department of Historical and Cultural Resources, New Brunswick, n.d.

Vass, Elinor. "The Agricultural Societies of Prince Edward Island." *The Island Magazine* No. 7 (Fall-Winter 1979).

Weale, David. "The Gloomy Forest." *The Island Magazine* No. 13 (Spring-Summer 1983).

―――. "Prince Edward Island and the Confederation Era: A Question of Self or No Self." Master's Thesis, Queen's University, 1970.

Wells, Kennedy. *The Fishery of Prince Edward Island.* Charlottetown: Ragweed Press, 1986.

Wharburton, A.B. *A History of Prince Edward Island.* Saint John: Barnes and Co. Ltd., 1923.

INDEX

GENERAL INDEX

Italicized numbers indicate illustrations.

Legend: (N) - Newfoundland, (NS) - Nova Scotia, (NB) - New Brunswick, (PEI) - Prince Edward Island